# PROTESTANTS

Other Books by Steven Ozment

*The Reformation in Cities: The Appeal of Protestantism in Sixteenth Century Germany and Switzerland*

*The Age of Reform, 1225–1550: An Intellectual and Religious History of Late Medieval and Reformation Europe*

*When Fathers Ruled: Family Life in Reformation Europe*

*Magdelena and Balthasar: An Intimate Portrait of Life in Sixteenth Century Europe*

*Editor, Three Behaim Boys: Growing Up in Early Modern Germany: A Chronicle of Their Lives*

# PROTESTANTS

## The Birth of a Revolution

# STEVEN OZMENT

**DOUBLEDAY**

New York   London   Toronto   Sydney   Auckland

PUBLISHED BY DOUBLEDAY
a division of Bantam Doubleday Dell Publishing Group, Inc.
666 Fifth Avenue, New York, New York 10103

DOUBLEDAY and the portrayal of an anchor with a dolphin
are trademarks of Doubleday, a division of
Bantam Doubleday Dell Publishing Group, Inc.

*Library of Congress Cataloging-in-Publication Data*
Ozment, Steven E.
    Protestants : the birth of a revolution / by Steven Ozment.
        p.        cm.
    Includes bibliographical references.
    1. Reformation.    I. Title.
BR305.2.089    1992        91-27894
270.6—dc20                CIP
ISBN 0-385-42172-9

To

Donald Kagan

and

Frank M. Turner

Best of colleagues, best of friends

# Contents

# Preface

During the course of the sixteenth century, hundreds of thousands of people became Protestants. It was the most dramatic and important development of that distant century. New evangelical churches sprang up across northern Europe, leaving western Christendom permanently divided. The Reformation also drove the social and political history of the century in new and disturbing directions. It gave birth both to a new age of faith and to a century of unprecedented religious warfare.

When four hundred years later we look at the world the Reformation created, we confront a bewildering array of churches and sects. At one end of the spectrum stand the classic Protestant communions of Lutherans, Reformed (Calvinists), and Anglicans, who, despite declining numbers, still represent the defining core of Protestantism. Ironically, they are the Protestants most comfortable with modern culture and the most ecumenically minded as well, drifting today in large numbers back to the Roman Catholic church, which has remained the largest and most powerful Christian communion. At the other end of the Protestant spectrum, we find communities of Hutterites, Mennonites, and Amish, who trace their origins to sixteenth-century Swiss and German Anabaptists. These last rejected infant baptism as unbiblical (their name means "rebaptizers") and practiced only adult baptism upon confession of faith. Scorned and persecuted by the major Protestant confessions, they formed their own distinctive communities, separatist and pacifist. Today their modern counterparts still lead segregated "biblical" lives that suggest a world frozen in time for more than four hundred years.

Scattered between these two groups are the low-church evangelicals who separated from the national churches: the Baptists, Congregationalists, and Presbyterians of the seventeenth century; the Moravians, Methodists, and kindred pietists of the eighteenth century; and the many emotion-laden, individualistic sects sprung from the Evangelical Awakening in Britain and America during the nineteenth century. The majority of these churches have little direct connection with classic Protestantism, yet they more than any other modern Protestants have kept the original Protestant propaganda against Rome rhetorically alive in the modern world. The most combative of modern Protestants, they have given popular Catholicism its stiffest Protestant competition for the souls of ordinary people.

The division within Protestant ranks that is so striking to us today began almost immediately with the Reformation's initial success. Luther nailed his famous theses to the door of Castle Church in Wittenberg on 31 October 1517, and before a decade had passed he faced determined Anabaptist, Spiritualist, and Zwinglian competitors. Each took inspiration from his movement, while at the same time decrying its corruption and declaring independence from it. Here began the unending line of would-be reformers of the Reformation, who have ever since confronted the original and later versions of Protestantism with their own, allegedly truer interpretations of Holy Scripture. Since Luther's protest, hundreds of Protestant denominations and sects have sprung up in the modern world, and new ones continue to appear. The original, fundamental split with the Roman Catholic church only began the breakage; the divisions within the Protestant movement itself have proved to be just as fateful and permanent.

As the breach in Western Christendom widened, an ecumenical movement to repair it also appeared in the sixteenth century. It was nothing like the modern Second Vatican Council of the early 1960s or present-day Anglican and Lutheran initiatives. So small was its success that it left all of the participants demoralized and preparing for war by the early 1540s. Still, by century's end sizable numbers of Protestants had returned to the Catholic fold, albeit as often because of political coercion as by free acts of conscience.

Unlike the religious situation in the Western world today, conditions in the sixteenth century made it necessary for Protestants to maintain a clearer identity and gave them urgent reasons to unite. At that time they confronted a powerful and determined common enemy. The pope in Rome was as fearsome a prince of the world as he was keeper of the keys to heaven, as adept at giving (or taking) life, property, and wealth as he was at influencing the salvation (or damnation) of souls. Religious dissent proved particularly dangerous in such times, for people then had little concept of religious tolerance or of the separation of church and state. No one doubted that the presence of a Catholic ruler in a land meant the enforcement of Catholic religious practice there; the only public alternatives were voluntary exile or persecution. Where different confessions found themselves in close proximity to one another, areas of legitimate worship became strictly defined. A Catholic in Lutheran Nuremberg, for example, had to travel outside the city to hear Mass. A Protestant in Catholic Cologne had to do the same to hear a Calvinist preacher. The notion of a variety of religious confessions living side by side in harmony and mutual respect within the same community was alien not only to the Catholic and Protestant clergies, but to reigning political authority as well. The latter also found it incomprehensible that a loyal subject of a burgomaster or a king would not also share his religion.

Where rulers confronted a majority of citizens or subjects devoted to alien religious beliefs, they might elect a more prudent political course of action and convert to the religion of their subjects, recognizing that the use of force to maintain the status quo would only result in tumult and war. That, however, asked a lot of sixteenth-century rulers. As tolerance at this time lay only in conformity, most people found it desirable that the faith of rulers and ruled, by one route or another, reflect actual majority practice. In the mid-sixteenth century, the conflict between Catholics and Lutherans in the empire was managed by a pragmatic principle very close to the reality of the situation: the ruler of each land would determine its religion (*cuius regio, eius religio*). A near century of religious warfare followed before this principle could be successfully challenged and a degree of religious pluralism and tolerance legally recognized and practiced within a particular region or land.

There exists today in the modern Western world no internationally puissant religious authority comparable to that of the Renaissance popes, and religious pluralism and toleration are almost everywhere guaranteed by law. The boundary between church and state has long been secured, and vigilance is carefully maintained. The specter of an armed papal monarchy and fanatical religious persecution, which haunted nonconforming Christians in the sixteenth century, no longer exists. With them have gone also the fury and the risk of that age's religious dissent. The issues that arouse and unite most Protestants today are of a more general moral and social nature, and they are widely shared by conscientious citizens regardless of their religious upbringing, if any. They are such issues as the plight of the poor and the underclass, threats to the environment, war and peace, and the many problems that afflict family life, on whose behalf religious argument is only one among several and not always the most authoritative. It is rare today for religious belief alone to set major social policy and for coercive political power to radiate from clergy and churches, as still happened in the fifteenth and sixteenth centuries. Even in those rare instances of conflict in the modern world wherein religious banners are prominent, as in Northern Ireland, the issues that divide warring factions remain overwhelmingly political and social, not matters of faith and doctrine at all. A peaceful resolution could be achieved in such conflict without any alterations in the religious teaching and practice of either side.

Largely because of developments set in motion long ago by the Reformation, and often against the wishes of the Protestant clergy themselves, religion in the modern world has become confined to a strictly spiritual and moral sphere of influence. Today a pastor or a priest leads his life in most respects as any other citizen does, subject to the same civic responsibilities and under the jurisdiction of the secular courts. Before the Reformation, the clergy still had special immunity from secular courts and taxes, and the ideal Christian layperson, like the ideal Christian cleric, was one who approximated the otherworldly lifestyle, unquestioning obedience, and self-sacrifice of the religious. By contrast, in the modern world the clergy are more likely to approximate the lifestyles of the laity than the laity those of the clergy. Today in Protestant lands, the vast majority of clergy are married, most wear no distinctive clerical dress, and they find both their dearest friendships and their favorite pastimes among their congregations.

Ironically, but not surprisingly, the one group among whom the original issues of Protestantism continue to be debated in virtually the same terms and with the same passion as the sixteenth-century debates is among modern Roman Catholic clergy. Today prominent dissenting Catholic scholars and rank-and-file clergy and religious write and argue much as Luther and Zwingli did 450 years ago for the freedom to interpret Scripture without traditional restraints and papal veto, to marry and create families of their own, and to involve themselves in secular movements for economic and social justice as their consciences dictate.

What of the original Protestant movement may be said to have survived into the modern world and to be commonly shared by Protestants today? Where does one today find the heritage of the Reformation? Protestants of all persuasions have over the centuries come to share a spiritual "fix it," "get it right," "make it true" mentality. This is particularly the case in the moral management of their lives, where they have demonstrated little patience with church authority and traditional practice whenever these have proved to be impediments. Protestantism was born, after all, in reaction to failing spiritual leadership and church piety. In their place the reformers attempted to create a simple and effective alternative. Now, as then, Protestants are society's most spiritually defiant and venturesome citizens. When it comes to making their spiritual and moral lives whole, they have not hesitated to sacrifice institutions to conscience, unity to efficiency, and obedience to results. Whether it is an Episcopal congregation in a New England town plotting the removal of a weak pastor, stay-at-home fundamentalists refusing to send money to televangelists, or a cell of East German Lutheran pastors organizing resistance against a Communist government, modern Protestants do not bide their time, surrendering to tradition, any more than their sixteenth-century counterparts did. In the quest for a religious life that works, they unhesitatingly change churches and denominations, shedding the spiritual truths of yesterday as if they were just another bad investment or failed love-affair. No other modern religious communion is marked by such variety and mobility.

Such behavior is the surviving modern version of the original Protestant assault on traditional belief and practice in the sixteenth century. Of nothing were the first Protestants more shamefully convinced than that they had allowed themselves to be seduced and tormented by a contrived religious system. The experience engendered not only a readiness to take flight when spiritual pain replaced religion's promise of spiritual peace, but also a lasting suspicion of religious hierarchy, elitism, and spectacle. Ideally, the Protestants of the sixteenth century saw in their faith a workable lay religion with absolute safeguards against the bullying of conscience. Few suspected at the time that their own coercive measures might contradict and undermine that goal; the new faith by which Protestant hearts and minds were now to be bound was supposed to free them from the deceptions and tyranny of the past and preserve Christian freedom. During the Middle Ages, Catholicism had actually provided people a similar escape in territories in which the only possible alternative to royal or imperial autocracy was that of the pope and the church—a situation recently repeated in modern Poland, where a reigning Polish pope and grass-roots Catholic piety created a communal and spiritual alternative to Communist dictatorship.

This book has evolved over the past decade both as a critical response to new scholarship on the religious history of early modern Germany and as an effort to pull together my own conclusions about the nature and legacy of the Protestant Reformation. The focus, fittingly, is on the birth of Protestantism in sixteenth-century Germany, a story I have attempted to tell through sources that allow contemporary voices to speak loud and clear. My overriding goal has been to convey to the modern reader what it meant then to be a Protestant. Portions of several chapters have appeared at various stages of maturity in out-of-the-way journals and collections. But my intention has always been an original and seamless interpretation of the Protestant revolt that does justice to each of its stages and to all of its players: the intellectuals who invented and propagated it, the politicians who legislated it into law, and the ordinary laypeople into whose lives it came both by choice and by force. Together with the Italian Renaissance, the German Reformation has traditionally been viewed as the first of the great revolutions that created the modern world. I hope in the end to have made sense of the movement as a whole within its own time and of the role it has played in shaping the world in which we live today.

I am grateful to several friends and colleagues for their constructive criticism and comments: Mark U. Edwards, Jr., John W. O'Malley, Ian Siggins, and most especially James Hankins. Lynn Chu applied her pencil most sagaciously to the manuscript. And my wife, Andrea, as ever provided helpful editorial and technical assistance.

# Introduction

For people living today, the Protestant Reformation is three different stories, and each has an ending that would have saddened Martin Luther. It is, first of all, the story of the division of Western Christendom and the loss, probably forevermore, of its religious unity. When Luther nailed his famous theses to the door of Castle Church in Wittenberg in October 1517, it was not, as he might have hoped, the beginning of the reform of Christendom from the Mediterranean to the Baltic. At one point he even hoped for the mass conversion of the Jews, an ancient Christian dream he believed his new theology might realize at last. Ironically, many contemporary Jews also expected his Reformation to trigger a mass conversion, not of Jews to Christianity, but of Christians enlightened by Luther's criticism of Rome back to Judaism!

Luther instead started a process of spiritual fragmentation and competition that still goes on in Western Christendom today. In the end the Lutheran banner would fly only over selected regions in northern Europe and America, not over the whole of Western Christendom. In those regions, Protestant churches permanently established themselves and continue to this day to embody his ideals.

The second story the Protestant Reformation has to tell is the awakening of German nationalism and the shaping of German culture and character as we know them today. A long intellectual tradition, hostile to the Germans, traces everything that kept Germany backward and impeded its development as a modern nation to its "Protestantism." By this is meant something larger than Luther's movement, namely, Germany's claimed rejection of classical Greco-Roman and Judeo-Christian cultures in favor of its own pagan folk traditions. As the Russian novelist Fyodor Dostoevsky put it in the nineteenth century,

Germany's aim is her "Protestantism," not that single formula of Protestantism . . . conceived in Luther's time, but . . . her continual protest against the Roman world ever since [the German prince

Arminius defeated the Roman legions in A.D. 9]. Germans have never consented to assimilate their destiny and their principles to those of the outermost world. . . . They have been *protesting* against the latter throughout these 2,000 years.[1]

According to this harsh interpretation of German history, "Protestant-ism" suppressed both Roman and Christian concepts of natural law among the Germans, leaving them morally inferior to other Western people, who embraced the Greco-Roman and Judeo-Christian cultures and learned through them to recognize and act upon the dignity and unity of humankind.[2] This view of German history treats Luther's attack on the papacy as another expression of the ancient German protest against all things Roman. But for the many Germans who followed Luther in the sixteenth century, it was not a Teutonic tradition reaching back to Arminius, but the contrived teachings and practices of the Roman papacy that had kept Germany a backward and unchristian land for so many centuries. In the Roman traditions of the medieval church they found the political notions and unbiblical piety that had rendered Germany a subject and savage land. From the German point of view, Luther's movement, far from stripping Germans of a proper moral conscience, rather created the conditions for their challenge of the barbarism lamented by Dostoevsky.

The debate over Germany's historical place within the family of Western nations still continues unresolved. It is clear, however, that German resentment of Roman economic exploitation and Roman at-tempts to dominate Germany politically and culturally played as large a role in the birth of Protestantism as the religious ideals of Luther and his followers. The immense success of their protest gave German Catho-lics and Protestants alike a new sense of themselves as a people. In the sixteenth century as in the twentieth, the Germans rearranged heaven and earth in ways unforgettable and, for many, unforgivable as well. The results of their actions proved far more ambiguous in the sixteenth century than in the twentieth. If the Reformation taught Germans to take a new pride in themselves, it also tried to discipline their new identity and render it pleasing to God and man. The Protestant Reforma-tion was the first German national movement to warn Germans about themselves.

The birth of Protestantism is, finally, a story about modern historians and their audience. No other great event in Western history is more ignored by historians and the general public today than the Protestant Reformation. If given the option, most historians would prefer to write, and most people to read, a book on the American, the French, or the Russian revolution than one on the birth of Protestantism. Why are we more comfortable with the other revolutions that have shaped our world than we are with the great religious one? Unlike them, the Reformation was not so straightforward a contest for economic justice and political freedom. It forces us to think about history and human life in more varied and complex ways. We find in it not only a spiritual movement driving society and politics, but one that makes injustice and bondage within the inner life as portentous as those which afflict people's physical lives. For people living then, the struggle against sin, death, and the devil became as basic as that for bread, land, and self-determination.

The Reformation also occurred when domestic and political life were organized in ways many today deem unfair and autocratic. The hierarchy and strict discipline which then reigned in the family and in government seem to be misguided and irrelevant models for the modern home and modern politics. The Reformation confronts us with a far more primitive image of human nature and community than we are accustomed to facing in the modern world. It requires us to consider the rationale of a society in which order and security hold priority over equality and fairness.

Coming to terms with the age of Reformation has accordingly tested the agility of modern pundits and interested laypeople alike. Conventional historians who confront the Reformation find themselves having to search beneath the surface of changing laws and regimes to explain what has happened. Marxists and social historians, inclined to count and stratify, must cope with spiritual motives raising to the same level of causation as material ones. And what can modern intellectuals, who gasp when a modern president casts a horoscope, make of Tudor kings who join simple folk on pilgrimages to shrines, or an elector of Saxony who in 1519 Wittenberg, on the Reformation's eve, assembles northern Europe's largest relic collection? Ecumenically minded modern Protestants and Catholics discover in the Reformation confessional differences so fixed and inflexible that they must either ignore the facts of history or abandon the dream of a united Christendom. It is worse still for Jews who find themselves face to face with anti-Judaic sentiments so

provocative that they seem to set Germany irrevocably on the path to
the Holocaust. And who can blame feminists for averting their eyes? In
Protestant lands, the Reformation left in virtual ruins medieval woman's
apparently one true sphere of freedom from male domination, the
cloister, while enticing her into the seeming prison of the patriarchal
home.

Seemingly at odds with modern civilization at every turn, it is little
wonder that present-day historians diminish the Reformation. That was
not the case only a couple of generations ago. When in 1911 the great
historian of the German Reformation, Karl Holl, wrote a famous essay
on "The Cultural Significance of the Reformation," he glowingly cele-
brated its achievements.[3] He believed that nowhere could one find the
roots of modern German culture more wholesomely portrayed than in
the Reformation of the sixteenth century. Virtually all of the positive
achievements of modern German history, from religion and ethics,
culture and the arts, to education and politics, he traced back to the
German he admired above all others, Martin Luther.

Today we look at the Reformation from a perspective that Holl's
generation could not share. Living as we do in the wake of the Holocaust
and in the midst of present-day liberation movements, our inclination
has been instead to trace back to Luther and his reform what we deem
to be the negative achievements of modern German history, particularly
the totalitarian state. If the historians who lived at the turn of the
century tended to romanticize the past, we have become all too expert
at debunking it. It is not just a problem we have with the Reformation.
From the Italian Renaissance to the French Revolution and the American
West, leading scholars today chronicle movements they claim enlightened few people and set even fewer free; and, like modern-day Dioge-
neses, they search the past in vain for honest historians, presumably like
themselves, who neither idealize nor politicize the past.

The history and the historiography of the German Reformation,
like so much of modern German history itself, are filled with baffling
contradictions. A movement that succeeded in the name of "Christian
freedom," the Reformation soon became identified in the minds of its
critics, and not a few original converts, with a new level of bigotry and
intolerance. Its first Catholic detractors denounced it as anarchistic and
warned that Germany would become unrecognizable and ungovernable
to the extent that it succeeded; yet within their lifetimes in much of

Germany they saw Lutheranism become a pillar of the established order and its recognized moral spokesman. In the early 1520s, peasant rebels in the countryside embraced the Reformation as an ally in their struggle to escape serfdom, thinking it to be antagonistic to the mainstream of German ecclesiopolitical government. But by mid-decade Martin Luther denounced them all as "mad dogs" and urged the German princes to "strike, kill, and burn" them.

Even the achievements the reformers deemed their most progressive and unambiguous have become controversial. In their own time, they believed they had saved family life from the misogynistic and antimarriage sentiments of the medieval clergy. Yet today these same reformers are identified with the birth of an enslaving feminine mystique and with such pessimism about human nature's aptitude for reform that some even accuse them of encouraging child abuse. And the first generation of Protestant educators, who prided themselves on putting their schools on a more secure intellectual and moral foundation, would be shocked to read the scholars who today describe their work as mere brainwashing. Glorified by historians of Karl Holl's generation, the Reformation is damned by present-day historians who do not think that it has anything to contribute to their search for democratic traditions in the German past.

The Reformation deserves a more sympathetic study. Beneath its many contradictions, both real and imputed, both historical and historiographical, it was a struggle with many of the same problems that grip us today—and not just in modern Germany, but in modern Africa and the Soviet Union as well, indeed, wherever reform and revolution are contemplated or contested. How does one attain freedom without creating anarchy or occasioning new tyrannies? Once gained, how does one preserve freedom so that it cannot turn into mere license or be lost again? Can freedom be disciplined without being destroyed? To what extent are order and security necessary to ensure freedom?

But there is a more pressing reason for renewing our acquaintance with the birth of Protestantism. Every person has been inspired and carried away at least once in life by an idealistic fantasy, and it is an experience entire nations also know. Sometimes such fantasies are wholesome and enlightening. At other times they can prove to be purely seductive and even devastating. German Protestants in the sixteenth century claimed to be expert in knowing the difference between the two. They despised nothing so much as the illusions that robbed individuals and societies of their peace of mind and took a sizable toll on their substance as well. Whether one views the Reformation in terms of its literature, its laws, or the lives of the laity who embraced it, it portrays itself as the hand that interrupts unrealistic dreams and exposes false prophets. Protestant faith promised to save people above all from disabling credulity.

It is appropriate that such a movement should have begun as a protest against a cruel hoax: the selling of indulgences. These elaborately printed pieces of paper with the pope's seal affixed claimed to limit the time a deceased Christian would spend in purgatory for unrepented sins. The favorite target of the Protestant pamphleteers in the 1520s and 1530s was the so-called *Menschensatzungen* of Rome. By this opprobrious term they meant purely human pronouncements with little biblical basis, but which masqueraded nonetheless as God's very Word. Emotionally captivating for the laity, such contrived teachings also demanded from them their total belief and not a little self-sacrifice as well. The reformers scoffed also at the romantic social visions and utopian political schemes of the revolutionaries of the age, by whom the common man was so easily charmed. Protestant faith was supposed to save one from messianic social prophets as well as from false papal declarations.

The sobriety and industriousness that we today associate with German Protestants, and which lend them to easy caricature, are the result of a prior principled flight from people they believed had deceived and deluded them. The Protestant temperament finds nothing more painful than knowing it has believed in vain. It prefers being alone to being consumed. It would rather have a little than risk a lot. It will burden and afflict itself before it will allow others to carry it away. It defies custom and tradition not because it is intrinsically venturesome or wants to complicate its life, but because it needs simplicity and truth.

Such a posture contradicted another, more dominant side of human nature and destined its advocates to be always in the minority and swimming upstream. The reformers clearly recognized this problem. In a frank confession in 1532, Martin Luther of all people acknowledged his inability, after two decades of effort, to overcome the fantasy that he could save himself by his own works: "I myself have now been preaching and cultivating [justification by faith alone] for almost twenty years and still I feel the old clinging dirt of wanting to deal so with God that I may contribute something and He will have to give me His grace in exchange for my holiness."[4]

In the end the message of the German reformers may itself have been built on a fantasy—the belief that people wish to, can, or even should lead undeluded lives. Their teaching did not prove to instill the sobriety needed to save modern Germany from the outrageous *Menschensatzungen* of a captivating messianic social prophet who appeared in the 1930s. But there is something more here than just the ultimate "safe rather than sorry" philosophy. In a modern world that has seen so much chaos and still lives on its brink, a movement that succeeded in its own time by challenging harmful fantasy cries out to be rediscovered.

# I
# In Search of
# the Reformation

# 1. Turning the World Upside Down

R evolutions affect both the inner and the outer man; they alter attitudes, change laws, and bring about new social and political institutions. To understand a revolution it is necessary to take account of both body and soul and the many things that affect each.

A revolution is said to occur when there are broad, fundamental, and lasting changes in important aspects of a people's behavior and in major features of a society's institutions. Whether and to what extent the Protestant Reformation was such a revolution are questions that have generated much controversy.[1] If we are to understand its nature and explain its success, the first question we must answer is why so many Germans had become so mad at the church of Rome in the early sixteenth century. We will hear directly from Protestants themselves in subsequent chapters. But Protestants were not the only ones who were enraged. All Germans seem to have been at odds with the church of Rome at this time, and for understandable reasons. No other land in the history of Christendom had allowed itself to come more under the papal thumb than late medieval Germany. By the fifteenth century, Germany was a land of outrageous papal patronage and cronyism, with consequences as detrimental to its political and social life as to its religious and cultural life.

## GRIEVANCES

Consider the grievances against Rome presented to Emperor Charles V at the Diet of Worms in the spring of 1521 by the German estates (that is, the electors, princes, and imperial cities that made up the imperial diet), and transmitted two years later to the pope in Rome. Those present composed for the emperor a list of 102 "oppressive burdens and abuses imposed on and committed against the German empire by the Holy See of Rome."[2] They singled out virtually every species of Roman cleric for criticism: the pope; archbishops, bishops, and prelates; canons, prebendaries, and pastors; and high priests and ecclesiastical judges.

The authors were not Protestants, but powerful and pious patrons of the church they gathered in Worms to criticize. On 26 May 1521 the diet declared Martin Luther an outlaw within the empire (five months earlier Pope Leo X had formally condemned him as a heretic), so, the complaints had little direct basis in Protestantism. The diet's criticism rather reflects the anti-Roman sentiment that had become widespread in Germany by the turn of the century and from which Protestantism drew much of its initial strength.

One does not read far into these grievances before discovering a papal monarchy believed to be a mortal threat to Germany's very soul and substance. The Germans complain that the pope flaunts the German constitution; he transfers numerous lawsuits from German to Roman courts, allows German ecclesiastical princes to appoint their own diocesan judges, and forces laypeople to stand trial in church courts under the threat of excommunication. Then there was Rome's trafficking in church benefices or "livings" for the clergy. These handsome stipends are said to be awarded by Rome to the highest bidder, and as often as not to "unqualified, unlearned, and unfit" non-Germans. Many of these unfit people in turn hired even less qualified substitutes at a fraction of the money they received to perform the duties incumbent on their offices. In this way, Rome deprived the German people of proper spiritual care and counsel, "while a hoard of money flows yearly into Italy with no return to [Germans], least of all any gratitude."

The pope also sold German church offices to future occupants while others occupied those offices. A high church office was an attractive prize, and to gain one prospective candidates paid "reservation fees" of between two and three thousand gulden, a very sizable sum. (At the height of his career, Martin Luther made about four hundred gulden per annum.)

Another papal abuse was the taking of annates or the first year's income of a new church office. German kings and princes originally paid such fees freely to assist Rome in its defense of Christendom against the Turks. By the 1520s, such fees were mandatory and had greatly increased in number and amount. To obtain the pallium or symbol of episcopal authority in the great bishoprics of Mainz, Cologne, and Salzburg, officeholders paid Rome between 20,000 and 25,000 gulden, funds that eventually came from the pockets of the faithful.

The Germans saw no end to papal cunning when it came to taking money from German Christians. When a German cleric died in Rome or while en route there, the pope confiscated his benefice and office. Not only did the pope reserve many church offices and benefices for his own disposition; he reserved high sins and crimes as well, absolution for which could be obtained only in Rome and by payment in gold. "A poor German without money will not see his sin dispatched," the diet complains, "while a rich man . . . can for a sum obtain letters of papal indult that entitle him to priestly absolution for any sin he might commit . . . murder, for example, or perjury."

Foremost among Rome's predatory practices, according to the diet, was the sale of indulgences. By this practice simpleminded folk were being "misled and cheated out of their savings." An indulgence remitted punishment in purgatory for unrepented sins, and everyone, either from negligence or from the unpredictability of the moment of death, might expect to die with such sins. Indulgences sold for a small fraction of a person's annual income, never more than a week's wages at most, and theologically they were regarded more as an almsgiving than as a purchase.[3] But there was no limit on how much indulgence one might secure, as no one knew for sure how long one might have to suffer in purgatory for unrepented sins, despite confident clerical attempts to calculate it. The practice may be compared with a modern lottery, where a small, repeatable purchase relieves anxiety by giving people momentary hope for long-term future security—the lottery ticket being a chance at material security in an age that does not believe in purgatory, the indulgence a chance at spiritual security in a world that still did.

Close on the heels of the indulgence preachers came Rome's legions of mendicant friars, relic hawkers, and miracle workers, all of whom the Germans describe as "a riffraff going back and forth across our land, begging, collecting, offering indulgences, and extracting large sums of money from our people."

Still another clerical power said to be much abused in Germany at this time was excommunication. Originally a corrective spiritual censure of chronic immorality, it was now "flung at [Germans]," the diet complains, "for the most inconsequential debts . . . or for nonpayment of court or administrative costs ... sucking the life blood out of poor, untutored laity" who honestly fear it.

In these various ways, the pope was said to transfer church power and income from German to Roman hands, much to the detriment of the Germans and to the profit of Rome. The result: bad clergy and an inept cure of souls throughout Germany. Large numbers of German clergy are said to lead "reckless and dishonorable lives," morally indistinguishable from laymen. Some religious run gaming parlors on their properties and shamelessly claim the winnings as their own. And parish priests, despite their vow of celibacy, whore and live openly with women in an arrangement akin to marriage. Some priests even shame poor parishioners into buying Masses they cannot afford and collect a weekly tribute from local millers, innkeepers, bakers, shoemakers, smiths, tailors, shepherds, cowherds, and other craftsmen under threat of excommunication.

---

### FEEDING ON THE DEAD

*Protestants believed that there was nothing the living could do for the dead beyond entrusting them to the care of God. No teachings of the church were deemed to be more unbiblical and cynical than those alleging to minister to the dead and departed in purgatory. Protestants accordingly condemned popular church practices like indulgences and Masses for the dead, which they claimed only exploited people's fear of death and the afterlife and their love for their departed relatives, while at the same time undermining their faith and trust in the promises of Christ. Catholic belief that the world of the living could, by almsgiving and prayer, intrude on that of the dead was dismissed as "feeding on the dead" (Totenfresserei).*

*In this savage satire on indulgences, which probably appeared in the 1520s, a female devil sits on a large indulgence, an alms box extended in her right hand and her left foot planted in a chalice of holy water. A departed pope, key in hand, is brought with his monks and bishops to feast at a table prepared in the devil's mouth. The assembled clergy ostensibly feast on their lay counterparts, who are dismembered, aged, and cooked by demonic chefs: a spectacle of the devil feeding on the clergy, who in turn feed on the laity.*

Matthias Gerung, in *The German Single-Leaf Woodcut: 1550–1600: A Pictorial Catalogue*, vol. 1, ed. Walter L. Strauss (New York: Abaris Books, 1975), p. 259.

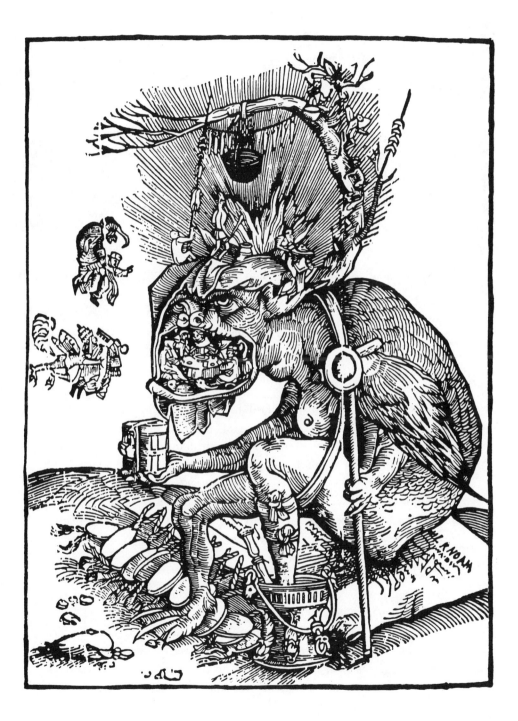

## A Monk Seduces a Maiden

*Late medieval clergy and religious were not universally celibate. This was well understood by the church, which arranged appropriate fines and punishments for clergy who visited prostitutes, seduced virgins, committed adultery (that is, had affairs with married women), or lived with concubines and had children of their own (a "cradle tax" was levied on each child). The laity resented such behavior on the clergy's part, but not in every case. There are many examples of laity accepting and even admiring local clerics who lived in monogamous relationships as responsible husbands and fathers.*

*Such popular sentiment helped make clerical marriage as prominent a part of the Reformation as changes in religious doctrine and practice. For the many clerics who turned Protestant, sexual freedom was as important as religious freedom, escape from celibacy as burning an issue as escape from false doctrine. The Swiss reformer Zwingli had cohabited with a widow, Anna Reinhart, before their marriage in 1524. Earlier, he almost lost the competition for the post of people's priest in Zurich because of an acknowledged affair; his chief competitor for the*

On the grounds of such allegations, some of which were exaggerated, but most of which had a firm basis in fact, the Germans petitioned the emperor to undertake "a general reformation [of the church and bring to an end] the despoiling of our nation."

The imperial diet was not the only occasion that such complaints were heard on the eve of the Reformation. In the cities and towns of Germany and Switzerland, grievances against the church appear in greater detail and with even greater indignation. In the far northern German cities of Wismar, Stralsund, and Rostock, for example, loud protestations to Duke Heinrich of Mecklenburg greeted the papal legate's request in 1517 for a three-month sale of indulgences in the region. Rostock's magistrates complained that indulgences were being sold too frequently, and declared their unwillingness to see still another shipment of city money to Rome. People also condemned the excessive numbers of clergy. Rostock, with a population of approximately 10,000 had 204 monastic and clerical offices (a quarter of these cloistered monks and nuns) with 182 working altars, each requiring its special financing. In addition to inflated clerical ranks and excessive indulgence traffic, people also complained about "church extravaganzas" on religious holidays, moral depravity within clerical ranks (rumors circulated of infanticide

---

*position lived openly in concubinage and was the father of six children. According to Wittenberg gossip and Catholic propaganda, Martin Luther had premarital relations with his wife to be, Katherine von Bora.*

*This illustration portrays lay anger at clandestine clerical womanizing. A monk, sitting at table, hands the father of a daughter he has seduced a coin, telling him, "Father, I will rent your daughter and right the situation." The daughter, whose hand the cleric holds, protests, "Father, I misunderstood the situation; otherwise, I would not have gone to the monk." The father, grasping his sword in obvious anger, declares, "Monk, you have deceived us and taken my daughter from me by lies." The tearful mother laments, "O, what great mockery must I suffer; I cry out to God for my child!" In the background on the far left, an honest cleric sighs, "I must be eternally silent about this affair, though it is against my will to do so."*

Leonhard Beck, in *Max Geisberg: The German Single-Leaf Woodcut: 1500–1550*, vol. 1, rev. and ed. by Walter L. Strauss (New York: Hacker Art Books, 1974), p. 120.

in cloisters as nuns disposed of unwanted offspring), and particularly the ever-growing fiscal dimension of religious services (people grouse that the price of a decent burial in Rostock approaches a hundred marks).[4]

In the cities and towns of fifteenth-century ducal Saxony, criticism focused on the church's traffic in benefices, its accumulation of land and property, and the idle and easy lives of the clergy. Anticlericalism in the region found a unique expression at Meissen in 1523. There laity staged a mock procession to ridicule a newly canonized local saint, Bishop Benno, an eleventh-century figure whose canonization had long been sought by Saxon princes desirous of a regional shrine. When the church decided to proceed with his canonization, silver shovels ceremonially disinterred the bishop's holy relics. In the mock version of the event, a horse's skull and animal bones became the bishop's relics; rags, the ceremonial flags; pitchforks, candles; and chessboards, songbooks in an irreverent procession that ended at the marketplace with a mock sermon, a sale of indulgences, and many unflattering words about the pope.[5]

In pre-Reformation Osnabrück in lower Saxony, lay distaste for clerical concubinage rivaled opposition to the clergy's privileges and immunities. In 1488, the city required priests' "wives" to dress plainly and to wear an identifying striped coat as a mark of opprobrium.[6]

Fifteenth-century Augsburg in Bavaria saw public demonstrations against both indulgences and mandatory fasting and in support of cloister reform. But throughout the century, reform-minded citizens preoccupied themselves most of all with containing the church's political and economic power and integrating the clergy into civic life.[7] In Augsburg, as elsewhere, a popular method of reforming religious life along the lines desired by the laity was the creation of well-endowed positions for model clergy. These posts, known as preacherships, came into being with government support. Designed to promote good preaching and a conscientious cure of souls, they attracted educated and devout clerics, with towns often grooming local youths for such positions. In such places as Augsburg, Nuremberg, Schwäbisch-Hall, Reutlingen, Konstanz, Lindau, and Strasbourg, preacherships became bases of operation for Protestant reforms.[8]

In these various ways, Germans still loyal to the church attempted to reform religion in the decades before the Reformation. But religious grievances were only one force disposing Germans to reform. Nonreligious forces also played a significant, if more indirect, role. The Reformation also had its origins in contemporary political and social experiences.

## POLITICS AND RELIGION

The German Reformation developed at a time of sharpest conflict between two ancient foes. On the one side were the emerging territorial states, some small and feeble, others already reaching their modern borders, and all bent on conformity and centralization within their respective realms. On the other side stood the self-governing small towns and villages that filled or bordered these politically awakening lands, where people had long been accustomed to running their own affairs. By the late fifteenth century townspeople and villagers in Germany and Switzerland had reason to fear for their traditional political rights and privileges.

Beginning as a protest against arbitrary, self-aggrandizing, hierarchical authority in the person of the pope, the Reformation came to be closely identified in the minds of contemporaries with what we today might call states' rights or local control. To many townspeople and villagers, Luther seemed a godsend for their struggle to remain politically free and independent; they embraced his Reformation as a conserving political force, even though they knew it threatened to undo traditional religious beliefs and practices.

The Reformation developed first in the free imperial cities of Germany and Switzerland. There were about sixty-five such cities, each in a certain sense sovereign. The great majority of these cities had Protestant movements during the sixteenth century, but with mixed success and duration. Some quickly turned Protestant and remained so; others were Protestant for a short period of time; and still others developed persisting mixed confessions only grudgingly tolerant of one another.

Cities at this time were not only engaged in what seemed to them to be a life-and-death struggle with higher princely or territorial authority; deep social and political divisions also existed within the cities themselves. Certain groups favored the Reformation more than others, and for reasons that had as much to do with money and power as with faith and piety. In a great many places guilds whose members were socially rising stood in the forefront of the Reformation. A prominent example is the printers' guild, whose members were literate, sophisticated, and in a rapid-growth industry. The printing industry, from inkers to owners, had an economic stake in fanning religious conflict by publishing Protestant propaganda, which a great many within the industry also devoutly believed.

Guilds with a history of opposition to reigning governmental authority also stand out among the first Protestant converts. In the city of Amiens in France—to take a striking non-German example—members of the weavers and woolcombers' guild, the city's largest, poorest, and least literate, became Protestant in disproportionate numbers.[9] The guild had long opposed controls that prevented wider marketing of their products and impeded the growth and prosperity of their industry, and its members also felt themselves to be overtaxed. The experience of arbitrary and unfair governmental restrictions on their business activity seems to have sensitized them to the sermons of Protestant preachers. The guild wanted greater freedom to manufacture and to market, and to this end had petitioned the city council for fewer holidays on which their businesses had to close. Local Protestant reformers also wrote and preached about freedom from arbitrary authority, albeit within a spiritual sphere; and they, too, demanded fewer religious holidays, while promising to get the hands of higher ecclesiastical authority out of people's pockets. Although the reformers were talking about a different kind of freedom, to aggrieved laity in Amiens and in many another European city with similar discontents, these were apples and oranges that seemed to fit nicely in the same basket.

There is plenty of evidence to suggest that people who felt pushed around and bullied by either local or distant authority—whether a struggling guild by an autocratic city council or a prosperous city or village by a powerful prince or lord—tended to see in the Protestant movement an ally. The parallels seemed obvious to contemporaries. When the citizens of a German town or a Swiss village, habituated to certain local customs and privileges, found themselves facing incorporation into the territory of a local prince and subject to his laws, Protestant sermonizing about the spiritual freedom and equality of Christians had an immediate, sympathetic ring and understandably gained captive audiences.[10] When Luther and his comrades wrote, preached, and sang about a priesthood of all believers, scorned the authority of ecclesiastical landlords, and ridiculed papal laws as pure fabrications, they could not help but touch political as well as religious nerves.

It was not just in the towns that Luther seemed to be a man with a political message. The peasants on the land also heard in the Protestant sermon a promise of political liberation and even a degree of social betterment.[11] Far more than the townspeople, German peasants found their traditional liberties, from fishing and hunting rights to that of representation at local diets, being progressively chipped away by the secular and ecclesiastical landlords whose fields they worked. They were a far easier prey than the townspeople, who, at least in the imperial cities, had the emperor as an overlord and a secure, if subordinate, place within the imperial diet. The peasants, by comparison, had few defenders in high places and even fewer ways to lobby their grievances effectively, short of threatening revolt.

The initial mass popularity of Protestantism in Germany and Switzerland probably lay as much in willful political misperception as it did in genuine spiritual attraction. The simple folk knew as well as their betters where their material interests lay. All sides, in fact, manipulated the Reformation to their own ends as best they could. Protestant pamphleteers cultivated support for their movement at the lowest as well as at the highest ends of the social spectrum. With Luther in the forefront, they enlisted the peasant farmer in the march on Rome, portraying poor Karsthans (the burly peasant with his hoe) as the ideal Christian, a man who worked with his hands as God intended all Christian men and women to do; nor, it was said, was he puffed up intellectually and obsessed with material things like the fallen clergy of Rome.

Long before Luther came on the scene, peasant leaders had proclaimed a biblical and divine justification for their traditional political rights.[12] Clever and worldly-wise, they knew well how to exploit a cognate theological argument for spiritual freedom when they heard it in Lutheran sermons. When, in 1523, Luther exhorted communities in Saxony to appoint their own clergy, peasant leaders claimed the great reformer's endorsement of local political control as well.[13] Luther had actually meant to say only the obvious about his own movement: that until traditional clergy were removed from their offices and new evangelical clergy put in their place, reform as he envisioned it would make little progress.

So there was mutual exploitation: the Lutherans by the peasants and the peasants by the Lutherans. Both sides came to regret it after 1525, when peasants revolted in central and southern Germany to the detriment of both the social and the religious revolutions.

The first reformers were themselves traditional clergy and quite a few, like Luther, renegade monks. But they also understood well the ways of the world. Those aware of the sexual escapades and military exploits of the Swiss reformer, Ulrich Zwingli, will know that the Protestant reformers were men of the sheets as well as of the cloth and as capable of tending harness and sword as they were an altar. Zwingli almost lost the competition for the post of people's priest in Zurich for impregnating a woman while serving as priest in Einsiedeln, and he accompanied the Zurich militia on campaigns at home and abroad. The sixteenth century knew little of the effete, pacifistic, moralizing cleric of modern caricature. Though politically weakened, the pope and his bishops remained true princes of the world, governing vast domains and commanding large armies. Occasionally, as in the example of Pope Julius II, they personally led troops into battle. The clergy of the later Middle Ages might as readily seduce one's wife or daughter, confiscate one's land, and imprison or kill one as pardon one's sins. The memorial to Zwingli in Zurich portrays a man with a sword in one hand and a Bible in the other—a fitting remembrance of a reformer who began his career in 1513 as a chaplain to mercenaries in Italy and died in 1531 fighting in the Swiss civil wars.

This means that the Protestant reformers knew from the start that theirs was a political as well as a spiritual contest. They also recognized the grave danger to their cause should it be perceived also as a revolt against legitimate political authority. It was one thing in this age for a religious reform movement to exploit popular discontent; it was quite another for it to be found openly encouraging social revolution. The latter path led only to summary execution or banishment, as Thomas Müntzer, a disenchanted early disciple of Luther who became a leader of the Peasants' Revolt, and other radical religious reformers quickly learned. From the start, the great reformers Luther, Zwingli, and Martin Bucer carefully distinguished the freedom and equality that characterized the spiritual lives of Christians from those relationships of dependency and subservience (with their attendant social and political inequality) that they believed had necessarily to prevail in society if there were to be any order and progress within it. The mainline Protestant traditions, both Lutheran and Reformed, were never socially and politically egalitarian, nor did they ever admire pacifism. Although in the Reformation's early years, contemporary politics and culture thrust upon it strong associations with political freedom and social equality, the reformers themselves did not battle for radical political and social change. Nor did such change come about in the Age of Reformation, which remained an age generally more fearful of anarchy than of tyranny and preoccupied far more with problems of continuity and order than with ways to bring about change.

The reformers understood as profoundly as any that winning in history meant getting society's reigning institutions on one's side. The object was not to overthrow existing magistrates and princes, but to convert, coerce, or coopt them into one's camp. Fortunately for the Reformation, a majority of magistrates and princes held the same point of view about religious reform movements. Only as the evangelical values that were elaborated in the new Protestant theologies found their way comfortably into city ordinances and territorial laws could the Reformation be deemed a success. Reform that existed only in pamphlets and sermons, and not also in law and institutions, would remain a private affair, confined to all intents and purposes within the minds of preachers and pamphleteers.

To the end, then, of making the Reformation a public event, all of the great reformers courted the magistrates and princes of the age. Even the revolutionary spiritualist Thomas Müntzer and the Anabaptist Balthasar Hubmaier, who castigated Luther and Zwingli as bootlickers, went hat in hand to local political authorities. In the end, Protestant doctrine proved to be as much at home in the territorial reforms of the princes that transformed the cities into their subjects, as it had been in the local city reforms of the early 1520s that opposed those very princely efforts. Some may view such flexibility as damnable hypocrisy. It was in fact the realization of the reformers' original goal. Any ruler willing to defend their doctrine, expose the *Menschensatzungen* of the pope, and depose the papist clergy the reformers were prepared to serve. For them, the first order of business was always to gain sufficient power to establish and maintain the doctrine they held to be true. Once such doctrine was firmly in place, they believed everything else would necessarily follow; as long as their doctrine was not publicly enshrined in law, they knew that nothing they wanted could occur. That is why arguing about church doctrine in the presence of magistrates and princes— whether in formal disputations before city councils, or by letter or appointment with the princes of Saxony and Hesse—became something of a spectacle in the Germany of the 1520s and 1530s.

## SUCCESS

Today growing numbers of historians portray the Reformation as a small part of a much larger and failed burgher revolt against revived feudal authority in the persons of the great German princes. Indeed, "the Reformation" as a viable historical category is today threatened with extinction to the extent that one might wish to apply it to an entire age. According to many, the true contest of the late Middle Ages was not that between Protestants and Catholics, but one between the expansionist territorial states of Europe and the traditionally self-governing villages and towns within and abutting them. The evangelical movement born in the 1520s has accordingly emerged in recent studies as a religious variant on popular communal government, initially very much in the camp of the villages and towns. Had the Reformation kept to this original course, it is argued, when—despite the protestations of its leaders—it appeared to promise a new social and political order for all, then it might have served what at the time may have been a hopeless cause, but also one that history has proved to be far nobler than mere religious reform: the political emancipation of the common man. As it happened, however, Luther and his followers simply folded their tents and peacefully took their place in established burgher society. From such a point of view, the Reformation necessarily appears to have been a failure, becoming after the mid-1520s merely a toy of magistrates and princes, succeeding in its spiritual mission more by coercion than by persuasion, and no longer a true friend of modern democratic ideals.

From another perspective—a more correct one, I believe—the integration of the Reformation into established society, not just in Germany and Switzerland but generally throughout Europe, came about in direct fulfillment of its original design. The public triumph of the Reformation was always the reformers' mission and what most thoughtful people at the time also deemed to be the measure of success. What the reformers wanted above all was a forum in established society from which they could effectively lobby their cause and even shove it down people's throats if they chose. They had no concept of sacrificing their lives in pursuit of a goal as fantastic for sixteenth-century people as social and political equality.

How successful were the reformers in what they set out to do? Let us imagine that we are back again in the fifteenth century, on the streets of the great cities of central Europe that would later turn Protestant—say, Zurich, Strasbourg, Nuremberg, or Geneva.[14] When we look around us, we observe clergy and religious everywhere; they make up 6 to 10 percent of the urban population, and they exercise enormous political as well as spiritual power. They legislate and they tax; they try cases in their very own courts; and they enforce the laws of the church with penances and excommunication.

The church calendar regulates the daily life of the city. About one-third of the year is given over to some kind of religious observance or celebration. There are frequent periods of fasting; on almost a hundred days out of the year in many places a pious Christian may not eat eggs, butter, fat, or meat without special church dispensation.

Monasteries and nunneries are prominent and influential social institutions. The children of society's most powerful citizens reside there. Local aristocrats closely identify with particular churches and chapels, whose walls record their lineage and proclaim their generosity. On the streets, Franciscan and Dominican friars from near and far beg alms from passersby. In the churches the Mass and other liturgies are read in Latin. Images of saints are regularly displayed and on certain holidays their relics are paraded about and venerated. The largest relic collection in northern Europe, containing more than nineteen thousand pieces, actually exists in Wittenberg, soon to be the birthplace of the Reformation. It is the possession of Elector Frederick the Wise, soon to become Luther's protector. It is housed next to the very church on whose doors Martin Luther will post his ninety-five theses. Among its treasures are a piece of the burning bush before which Moses stood, an entire skeleton of one of the innocents massacred by King Herod, a bucket of soot from the fiery furnace through which Shadrach, Meshach, and Abednego trod, milk from the Virgin, and straw from the manger of Jesus.[15]

There is also a booming business at local shrines. Pilgrims gather there by the hundreds, even thousands, many sick, some dying, all in search of a cure or a miracle, but many also out for some needed diversion and entertainment. Several times during the year special preachers arrive to sell letters of indulgence.

We observe many clergy walking the streets with concubines and the children they have fathered, despite their sworn celibacy. Some townspeople curse these women and children as whores and bastards, while others sympathize with such unions and claim they humanize the clergy. Some even claim to feel closer to the clergy who share their experiences as spouses and parents. For its part, the church winks at such relationships after payment of penitential fines.

People complain about the clergy's exemption from taxation and in many instances also from the civil criminal code. We hear people grumble about having to pay for church offices whose occupants actually live and work elsewhere and are never seen in the parishes that support them. Often they are well-to-do students off studying at some university. In some cases they do not even later become clergy, much less serve the parish that has made their education possible. In a few cases it is worse still. The French reformer John Calvin educated himself with such benefices, thanks to the influence of his father, a secretary to a bishop; yet the young Calvin ended up an old Protestant who denounced the church! There is also much concern among townspeople at this time that the church has too much influence over education and culture.

Now let us imagine that we are in these same cities in the 1540s and 1550s, after the Reformation has occurred. We observe few changes in society and politics among the lay population. The same or similar aristocratic families govern as before. But where are the clergy? Overall numbers of clergy and religious have dropped by as much as two-thirds. In some towns, the decrease is astonishing; Rostock, for example, has gone from more than two hundred to thirteen.[16] Religious holidays on which businesses must close have shrunk by one-third. In Nuremberg, the first Protestant city, they have fallen from fifty to twenty. There is a near-total absence of active monasteries and nunneries. Many have been emptied only to enrich princes and lords who confiscated the buildings and endowments. But others have been transformed into hospitals and hospices, and still others made over into educational institutions. Those converted to care for the sick and the needy have kept some of their religious aura; on the surface they seem even to be "Protestant monasteries."[17] But gone are the religious vows and habits, and their endowments are now secularized. A few cloisters do continue virtually unchanged; they house devout old monks and nuns who either cannot be pensioned off, or have no families or friends to care for them in the world. But with their deaths, these cloisters too will close and be converted.

In the churches, worship is now almost completely in the vernacular. In Zurich, the church walls have been stripped bare and whitewashed,

and there is no longer any music to interrupt the congregation's medita-
tion on God's preached Word—this in the town of the most musically
gifted of the Protestant reformers, Zwingli, master of the lute, harp,
viola, flute, reedpipe, cornet, trumpet, dulcimer, and foresthorn. The
only harmony permitted the congregation is the repetition of psalms in
unison.

The laity observe no obligatory fasts; indulgence preachers no longer
appear; and local shrines have been shut down. Anyone found openly
venerating saints, relics, or images is subject to fine and punishment. In
private homes, selections from the New Testament, if not entire New
Testaments and Bibles, are read in translation,[18] and memorizing Scripture is encouraged by the new clergy. In weekly catechism classes
children between twelve and fourteen repeat the lessons of Scripture;
parents are encouraged to be "priests" and "bishops" to their children
and to think of the home also as a "church."

As for the new clergy, they have married rapidly and in large numbers.
Clerical marriage has become as much the mark of the Protestant cleric
as belief in the sole authority of Scripture. An unmarried cleric is deemed
strange; the reformers play cupid for one another in a rush to share the
newly, discovered bliss of married life and to make another public
statement against Rome.[19] The clergy pay taxes unambiguously and are
punished for their crimes in civil courts. Committees composed of laity
and clergy carefully regulate domestic moral life, over which secular
magistrates have the last word. A new moralism also reigns within these
towns, along with a new domestic security and sense of civic purpose.

The placement of limits on the clergy's temporal power and the
broadening of lay authority over religion and culture had been under
way long before the Reformation occurred. But such laicization, which
became commonplace by the end of the sixteenth century, would not
have proceeded with such conviction among the laity nor have cut so
deeply into early modern society had it not been sanctioned and actively
supported by the Reformation in the 1520s and 1530s. Protestants were
not the first to call for limitations on the clergy and an enlargement of
lay spiritual authority, but they did place these issues at the center of
public debate as no other religious movement had before them.

Not all Protestant clergy remained enthusiastic about the new lay
authority in religion. On the streets of sixteenth-century Protestant
towns we can also hear the laity grumble about "new papists" among

the Protestant clergy, men who desire to have again the old coercive disciplinary power over all laity—particularly to be able to ban them at will for behavior they deem unbefitting a Christian.

With the passage of time, the laity too became ambivalent about the Reformation, and a great many proved to be just as reactionary as some of the new clergy. Across Europe more than half of the Reformation's original converts returned to the Catholic fold before the end of the sixteenth century. Whereas one-half of Europe could be counted in the Protestant camp in the mid-sixteenth century, only one-fifth would be found there by the mid-seventeenth century.[20]

Still, measured by the reformers' own stated goals and clear achievements, the Protestant century was a remarkable success. The Reformation gained at this time a permanent legal foundation and institutional form, and its teaching penetrated and shaped the lives of thousands of ordinary people.[21] Its seed-grain was as important as its initial harvest; it set more things in motion during its first century than could then be fully realized—some of which, like religious pluralism, ran contrary to the reformers' own original intentions. And some of its most remarkable innovations would be seized upon more enthusiastically by later generations than by contemporaries, for example, the freedom to divorce and remarry.

When we ask why the Reformation moved so successfully from the private into the public sphere, the most important reason may be one scholars currently tend to ignore. Much recent scholarship explains the Reformation's success as fortuitous and political—the result of the timeliness of its propaganda (that is, an egalitarian spiritual message appearing at a time of social and political upheaval) and the clever manipulation of it by magistrates and princes, who saw in Protestant teaching new opportunities for their own self-aggrandizement.[22] From this point of view, the Reformation's triumph becomes opportunistic rather than genuinely spiritual, and its traditional portrayal as a great religious revolution seems grossly exaggerated. The Protestant reformers, in contrast to their late medieval forerunners, are said to have survived so well because they proved at the time to be exceptionally useful to reigning political authority. But having gained public authority by the favor of magistrates and princes, the reformers soon lost the larger public, particularly the ordinary people in the towns and countryside, who felt betrayed by them after the princes, at the reformers' urging, crushed the Peasants' Revolt of 1525.

There is, however, an argument to be made that the Reformation's success was equally political and spiritual and that the key factors in it were the *political* acumen of the reformers and the *spiritual* credulity of magistrates and princes. The political ordinances of the 1530s and 1540s that raised the Reformation to legal status throughout much of the empire provide a striking testimonial to its success as a spiritual revolt. So literally and piously do these ordinances enshrine the doctrinal teaching of Protestants in law that an unobservant reader might think he had stumbled upon evangelical sermons and pamphlets from the 1520s.[23] The rulers who embraced the Reformation were as naïve about their spiritual lives as they were calculating about their political interests.

A striking example is inheritance practices. Unlike their Catholic counterparts, who early adopted primogeniture, which gave the eldest son all or the lion's share of a father's estate, a majority of Protestant princes clung to the traditional practice of partible inheritance well into the seventeenth century. In other words, they divided their landed wealth more or less equally among their legitimate sons. Such division predictably fragmented and weakened Protestant lands, while Catholic lands, by comparison, thrived. A major reason behind so politically disadvantageous a policy on the part of the Protestant princes was their fidelity to Lutheran marital teaching, which stressed loyalty and love within marriage and the responsibility of parents to care equally for all of their children.[24] Not until the mid-seventeenth century, after the Thirty Years War had made a shambles of Germany, did the Protestant princes, for strictly political reasons, also widely adopt primogeniture. Contrary to a near consensus of modern scholarship on the question, the Reformation may initially have been as much a handicap to the expansion of princely power in Protestant Germany as an aid—because the princes who favored it believed too much in its teaching, not too little.

Over the past three decades scholars have more than answered Bernd Moeller's famous challenge to write an account of the Protestant revolt with more history and less theology in it.[25] The result has been an enormous enrichment of our knowledge of the age of Reformation. Yet we have in the process also come perilously close to obscuring some of the most salient features of this remarkable period of German history. Today we portray a Reformation whose importance lies almost entirely in the indirect political roles it is said to have played. According to leading historians, the Reformation succeeded in its early stages because people misperceived it as being part of a popular, quasi-democratic communal movement in Germany's towns and villages, while in its later stages its success is to be explained by the all-too-willing role it played in building the German territorial states.[26] Such a portrayal has regrettably transformed the most novel and influential event of the first half of the sixteenth century—the public triumph of the Reformation as Germany's most formative spiritual movement—into a mere adjunct of the least successful social movement of the period, the Peasants' Revolt of 1525, and of the period's least novel political development, princely control of Germany's political destiny. While the Peasants' Revolt may have been new in scope, decades of similar protest had preceded it, and it left behind no important or lasting changes in Germany's political and social landscape. And the consolidation of political power by the German princes occurred over centuries, starting in the middle of the fourteenth century and extending well into modern times. The average townsperson and villager living in the 1520s and 1530s did not regard either of these developments as novel. As upheavals in an accustomed way of life, neither peasant revolt nor princely absolutism compares with the revolution in religious institutions that occurred during the first half of the century. When townspeople and villagers in these decades set their generation against the previous one, the most visible and lasting changes in their lives were those brought about by the revolution in religion.

Modern scholars have been remarkably successful in obscuring these salient facts of German history because of a powerful tendency in their thinking to isolate religion from politics and society and to treat it as secondary or epiphenomenal. It is as if the modern separation of church and state had suddenly become a historical canon, rendering religion ineligible to be a major agent of political and social change within a society. There may be grounds for such a point of view in recent Western history, but such a proposition can hardly be argued for late medieval and early modern societies, or for much of the non-Western world today. To approach the sixteenth century with such bias not only narrows our view of history, it also threatens our loss of a movement that gives us great insight into both modern Christianity and modern Germany.

We are, however, getting well ahead of our story. Before we can argue for the Reformation's success and importance, we should first know exactly what the Reformation was, and why it came about. And that involves us in still another continuing quarrel.

# 2. Religious Origins and Social Consequences

W hy might a devout person living in the early sixteenth century have chosen to become a Protestant? That is a far more difficult question than it may at first appear. Explanations of the coming of the Reformation diverge wildly and are even contradictory. At least six different theories are currently debated by modern scholars.

The oldest and best known holds that the laity, while deeply revering the church, had by the fifteenth century become alienated from it because of the clergy's growing immorality and pastoral negligence. The late Catholic church historian Joseph Lortz did much to popularize this point of view. As he nicely summarized it: "Without abuses, hardly a Wycliffe, hardly a Hus."[1] At the root of the abuses Lortz saw the "egoistic spirit" of the Renaissance, which he believed was then giving rise to modern individualism and territorial particularism or nationhood. An all-too-human clergy and laity succumbed to it as easily as everyone else. Among Christians, every group had to have its own festivals, altars, convents, and brotherhoods of the rosary. The failings of the medieval church were thus seen to lie not in its doctrine and liturgy, which in this interpretation remained as wholesome and inerrant as ever in the history of the church, but in human nature itself. Too many ambitious and unprincipled prelates gained high position in the church, and too many poorly educated and immoral priests staffed the parish churches. The result: a church without firm discipline or a clear sense of direction.

A counterthesis, also popular in Catholic circles, portrays the church of the late Middle Ages as a victim of the "propagandistic stereotypes" of would-be reformers. According to this interpretation, the great majority of Catholic clergy were as true as the doctrine they taught. Pervasive clerical corruption and incompetence existed more in the eyes of humanist and Protestant critics than in actual fact. Scholars who hold this point of view defend the deeper spiritual meaning of the church practices seized upon by the church's critics—practices that appear on the surface to have preyed in mercenary fashion on the fears and superstitions of simple laity: flagellant processions, pilgrimages, the selling of indulgences, Masses for the dead, the veneration of relics, and the proliferation of minor saints said to cure everything from sore throats to hemorrhoids.

According to Williams historian Francis Oakley, such practices were more an expression of the vitality of traditional piety than of any deep illness in the church. Far from encouraging only a mechanical and mercenary piety, indulgences acted as incentives to prayer and trust in God. To hostile humanists and Protestants, memorial Masses for departed loved ones may have looked like clerics "feeding on the dead" (*Totenfresserei*), but for pious laypeople they expressed the love of family and friends and nurtured a consoling belief in the continuity of this world with the next. In the end, the worst Oakley can find in the late medieval church is "waning convictions, spiritual sluggishness, and an unsteady sense of purpose."[2]

This argument challenged not only the "abuse theory" of the Reformation's origins; it also countered Johan Huizinga's elegant argument that the culture of the late Middle Ages broke down because of its undisciplined religious exuberance. Huizinga's classic, *The Waning of the Middle Ages*, finds an "enormous unfolding of religion in daily life" that served neither the church nor the laity well. The Parisian reformers Pierre d'Ailly and Jean Gerson decried the endless multiplication of images and paintings, convents and religious orders, festivals and holy days, vigils and fasts, saints and indulgences, hymns and prayers. As the external forms of religion multiplied and emotional intensity increased, the sacred became hopelessly lost in the profane. Folk magic blended with the sacramental mysteries; the lay mind placed the priest's transformation of bread and wine into the body and blood of Christ on a par with a cunning woman's curing of disease. Debauchery proved the most conspicuous companion of pilgrims en route to shrines. People venerated saints especially in their relics and for their ability to protect fields and avert plague. The same breath preached a sermon on the love of one's neighbor and incited Christians to violence against non-Christians.

The result, according to Huizinga, was a love-hate relationship between the church and the laity, as each came to despise the indiscipline of the other, yet also to tolerate and thrive on it, as each side indulged the other's weaknesses for its own gain. Huizinga perceived among the laity of France and the Netherlands, the subjects of his study, a thin line between "ingenuous familiarity" with the church and "conscious infidelity" to it.[3]

By Huizinga's argument, it was a genuine piety perverted by excess— deep and sincere on the one hand, selfish and corrupt on the other— that created a captive audience for the Protestant preachers. Like Lortz, he placed the lion's share of blame for this state of affairs on the clergy, who heedlessly encouraged "religious extravagances" that were only marginally Christian in content. The result was both a degenerate lay piety and the corruption of the church's doctrine and liturgy, as thought and culture fell victim in these centuries to a pervasive spiritual confusion.[4]

As in so many other areas of modern research, the social historians have put forward the most provocative theories about the origins and consequences of the Protestant Reformation. The late French historian Lucien Febvre, the reputed founder of the *Annales* school of French historiography famous for excavating the material life of societies and civilizations, believed that the late medieval church faced a problem far more threatening to its existence than immoral clergy. Febvre saw a different kind of laity emerging from the crises and opportunities of the late Middle Ages. Better educated and more traveled, urbane and curious, these men and women did not accept the world around them as passively as had their lay counterparts in earlier centuries. They also had deep, but different, spiritual needs, a "tremendous appetite for [the] divine" that was left unsatisfied by the "adulterated and miserable fare" provided them by the late medieval church. These laypeople had greater difficulty subjecting themselves to a clergy they often found to be their intellectual and moral inferiors. Neither were they any longer willing to accept unquestioningly church teachings and practices that could give the most pious mind pause.

Febvre was convinced that the laity of the fifteenth and sixteenth centuries would have disposed of much traditional belief and practice even if the clergy had been uniformly saintly and the church completely free of corruption. The laity at this time simply required a new spirituality better suited to urban society and emerging mercantile values—a piety that would allow them to deal as simply and directly with God as they did with one another in their secular and business lives. In Febvre's view, the Protestant reformers quickly perceived this changed situation and were able to offer the laity a religion that many found immediately to be "simple, clear, and fully effective."[5]

Huizinga and Febvre successfully directed the scholarly discussion of late medieval religion away from the church and the clergy and toward the changing world of the laity. To ask first not "What did the church teach the laity?" but rather "Who were the people taught by the church?" has since become standard procedure in the modern study of religion. The radical conclusions to which this shift in focus can lead have been demonstrated by another provocative French historian, Jean Delumeau, who has proposed a "complete rereading" of the religious history of late medieval and early modern Europe.

Delumeau maintains that the Middle Ages were never Christian in any meaningful sense of the term and that the notion of a "Christian Middle Ages" is a myth. The vast majority of people living at the time, he argues, simply knew too little about Christianity to have taken offense at anything its priests may have failed to do on its behalf. Nine-tenths of the population remained semipagan "rustics" and spirit worshipers, and any Christian teaching they might have encountered would soon have been lost in their folklore.[6] When we talk, then, about Christians before the seventeenth century, Delumeau reminds us that we can mean only a tiny minority of well-to-do people—clergy, nobility, and wealthy burghers—at the highest levels of society.

In this vision of the epoch, it was the twin coercive movements of the Reformation and the Counterreformation that converted enough of Europe's semipagan masses to create for the first time a "Christian" Europe. Delumeau thus sees the religious conflicts of late medieval and early modern Europe as being swallowed up in a more fundamental conflict between an educated and powerful elite culture and an illiterate, disenfranchised mass culture. Protestantism and Catholicism were imposed on people by the imperatives of class, politics, and culture, not matters of individual conviction and choice.

More provocative still are the views of the English social historian John Bossy. Like Lortz and Oakley, he fervently defends traditional Catholic teaching; but like Febvre and Delumeau, he is also committed to understanding religion as an expression of social reality. The result is a novel mix of modern Catholic apologetics and the new social history. Under Bossy's approach the Reformation, even modestly understood as a wholesome social protest against church abuses, is stood on its head:

medieval Catholicism becomes the perfect religion of family and society and Protestantism a degenerate by-product of emergent individualism and capitalism. Bossy would jettison the term "Reformation" as a proper category for historical periodization on the grounds of its vagueness and prejudice.[7]

Treating medieval Catholicism as strictly a social phenomenon, Bossy describes it as a religion based on the bonds of kinship and the moral principle of reconciliation. Its basic content was loyalty to one's immediate community (family, town, and church) and the exercise of charity toward all. Its model was Christ, who acquired a human family and made many human friends; and it venerated saints, who, like Christ, worked to unite heaven and earth in a single, continuous community of faith and love. Up to the fourteenth century, the church's basic moral guide had been the Seven Deadly Sins, which ranked the antisocial sins of aversion (pride, envy, and wrath) above those of individual moral failing (sloth, avarice, gluttony, and lust)—another expression of the primacy of community and charity in traditional Catholic teaching (likewise with the sacraments of Penance and Extreme Unction). The priest did not absolve a penitent of his sins until he first reconciled himself with his enemies, and the Last Rites were administered to a dying person only as he agreed to make reparations to those against whom he had sinned during his lifetime. "The state of charity, meaning social integration, was the principal end of the Christian life, [and brotherhood] the most characteristic expression of late medieval Christianity."[8]

Protestantism, by contrast, is said to exalt faith over charity and to make familial and communal bonds secondary to the conscience of each individual Christian. By rejecting the intercession of the saints, Protestants spurned the most ambitious moral goal of the medieval church: its effort to "humanize the social universe" by bringing the world of the dead into communion with that of the living. Especially in its doctrine of justification by faith the social cost of Protestantism became exceedingly high. Ignoring the social dimension of sin, this central Protestant teaching no longer required people to reconcile themselves with their neighbors or to perform any charitable acts in order to be saved. As a result, Bossy believes that the Reformation dissolved the social bonds of religion and left the faithful in doubt and uncertainty, each individual having now to cope with the Almighty by his or her own meager devices.

Protestant reliance on the catechism as the basic tool of religious education is portrayed as having had further detrimental effects on domestic and social life. In Protestant lands, the traditional Seven Deadly Sins, which condemned antisocial behavior above all other, ceased to be the authoritative moral guideline in the instruction of the laity. They were replaced in the Protestant catechism by the Ten Commandments, which instead taught people to think in terms of superior and inferior—those who command and those who obey—and thus to build walls between themselves. "Catechism was well designed to instill obedience and mark out boundaries . . . [but] less well adapted to inspire [among Protestants] a sense of the church as *communitas* . . . or simply the love of one's neighbors."[9] Protestantism thus became a religion of confession rather than one of social practice.

Although Bossy degrades the Reformation in concept, he finds himself respecting it in fact. It was, he believes, one of the most fateful turning points in the history of Western civilization, with consequences not yet fully worked through:

> The instant dissolution [by Protestants] of the multitude of relationships tradition had fostered, as having nothing to do with the salvation of the soul, let alone with the health of the body, was an extraordinary event in the history of Christianity and surely of human society at large. I doubt if we have really measured its consequences. I am not sure that it liberated people from the past in any way that one would want to be liberated from it. . . . There is something to be said for the idea that the dismantling of a social edifice existing in a perpetual present [i.e., traditional Christianity] sharpened anxiety for a congenial past and future.[10]

Bossy's portrayal romanticizes traditional Catholicism, while it caricatures Protestantism. He completely ignores the *contemptus mundi* of cloister piety and culture, arguably the heartbeat of the pre-Tridentine Catholicism he so much admires. An uninformed reader would never suspect from his portrayal that it was traditional Catholicism that taught the world to enclose certain religious for the glory of God, their only contact with family and society being the hole through which their food was shoved each day. Such enclosures were built against the sides of Italian abbeys and churches to house the "walled in" (*muratae*) as late as the fifteenth century. Nor does Bossy devote much attention to the

## An Early Catholic Criticism of Martin Luther

*Luther's "game of heresy" is here portrayed by an anonymous author who claims to be the "true Eckhart," a legendary German hero and also the name of a kindly, popular mountain sprite. Luther's new gospel is said to promise only discontent, rebellion, and an end to the worship of God. Two demons play drums and pipes in praise of Luther, whose new teaching, one claims, destroys all Scripture. Luther himself is portrayed with a raven on his shoulder, the traditional symbol of greed and plunder. He brews his false gospel with the assistance of the devil, who mixes in his own bile and poison for unknowing simple folk. From the great pot of Lutheran heresy rise vapors of falsehood, unbelief, envy, pride, resentment, rebellion, hatred, arrogance, lies, disobedience, error, heresy, blasphemy, lewdness, sensual freedom, division, and disloyalty. An accompanying rhymed text explains the illustration:*

In the year 1520,
Which one now marks in peace,
I have in my simple way forseen
What Luther's teaching promises to bring:
Great rebellion and bloodletting,
Much hatred and strife.
The fear of God will vanish forever,
Together with the whole of Scripture,
And authority will everywhere be despised.
Selfishness will reign supreme.

There is still more evil to befall us,
All from Luther's pot.
I have portrayed it here to warn you
Of the devil's great cunning.
May God also grant with this prophecy

That I prove to be a false prophet.
Still, heed my prophecy well,
Lest great harm come to you;
For if you are not vigilant,
It will prove to be no laughing matter.

So study my drawing as need requires.
In it I portray a bitter death,
For body and soul are here at stake,
And diligence can bring a rich reward.
If you allow this wolf within the fold,
You will find yourself beside an evil guest.
In ten years, ask yourself
Whether my poem was only lies.
My name is the true Eckhart;
I beg you all to be forewarned.

Unknown artist, in *Max Geisberg: The German Single-Leaf Woodcut: 1500–1550*, vol. 4, rev. and ed. by Walter L. Strauss (New York: Hacker Art Books, 1974), p. 1535.

proscriptive side of medieval Christianity. Here was also a religion centering on hierarchy and law, seemingly obsessed with segregating the clergy from the laity and with regulating every aspect of the latter's life, from the practice of sex (including position and frequency) to the conduct of a trade (from profit margins to the days on which businesses might operate). Why did the medieval church deny the Eucharistic cup to the laity, giving them only bread, while the clergy received both bread and wine? Why did the clergy fight so hard to preserve the special privileges and immunities that excluded them from civil jurisdiction and released them from civic responsibilities? What was the church's purpose in forbidding the laity certain foods and proscribing sexual commerce during Lent and other high religious seasons? What did any of this have to do with community, fraternity, and charity? Perhaps the antisocial sins of aversion became primary in the Seven Deadly Sins because the medieval church wanted to enforce obedience to its own increasingly shaky authority. The first and deadliest of them, pride, was also an expression of autonomous behavior, thinking for oneself, questioning tradition—the will to disobey. There is a case to be made for the existence of an unruly lay piety on the eve of the Reformation, one uneasy and discontent, trying too hard to overcome its desperation and fear, and failing to calm consciences and unite communities.[11]

Despite the great diversity of scholarly opinion on the conditions that gave rise to the Reformation, several things may be said in summary. Certainly clerical abuses existed, not the least of which was pastoral neglect of the laity. Delumeau, who does not believe that it made much difference to most people whether they were Protestant or Catholic, estimates that 30 percent to 70 percent of the Catholic clergy, depending on the region in question, did not occupy their offices: "the salvation of whole sections of Christian people was entrusted . . . to a proletariat of temporary vicars."[12]

While many people, perhaps the majority of pious Christians, continued to find traditional belief and practice personally satisfying, many others clearly did not. During the late Middle Ages numerous independent spiritual movements formed outside the church. From the Waldensians in the thirteenth century to the Brothers of the Common Life in the fifteenth, laity and clergy experimented with new forms of piety as they searched for a simpler and more effective spirituality, one believed to be closer to that of Jesus and the first apostles.[13] The evangelical laity of the 1520s and 1530s were heirs to this tradition of religious experimentation. Had they been manipulated into believing and practicing things that were neither true nor relevant to their personal happiness and eternal salvation? Was that why they found traditional piety so unsettling? Their own experience and the sermonizing of Protestant preachers convinced them that indeed they had. A conviction of having made sacrifices in vain for a creed that had little biblical basis, and hence could provide one with only a false sense of security, if any security at all, fueled the Reformation at the grass-roots level. Exposure of such perceived deceit in matters both temporal and spiritual became the key feature of Protestant propaganda and lay endorsements of the new faith. Find a people who believe that they have been invaded in heart and hearth, tricked in matters of conscience and taken advantage of materially as well, and one has found a people ready for reform and revolution.

Beyond its late medieval origins, the most challenging questions about the Reformation today have to do with its evolution through the sixteenth century as it passed from theology into sermon and pamphlet, from sermon and pamphlet into law and public institutions, and then into the daily lives of ordinary people. Although each of these stages of the Reformation's evolution bears a clear relation to the others, each is different in principle and in practice. The Reformation in the hands of the theologians and the pamphleteers is different from the Reformation in the hands of magistrates and princes; and neither can be identified with the Reformation as individual laity embraced it. When the effort is made to define the Reformation as a whole in terms of one or the other of its stages of development, the result has invariably proved to be tendentious and narrow. Those, for example, who would explain the Reformation only by the study of its theology and propaganda simply leave us in the minds of theologians and pamphleteers. Despite the great wealth of Protestant tracts and sermons, pamphlets and broadsheets, such sources are the Reformation in theory only and do not portray a movement of historical consequence. Approached through such sources, the Reformation always appears to have been supremely logical and perhaps too much of a good thing. Correspondingly, those who interpret the Reformation only as an established institution able to impose its spiritual and moral dictates upon the laity confront us with a movement that lacked both a heart and a clear sense of purpose, a Reformation that becomes at best a few failed egalitarian themes, at worst, an impossible dream turned nightmare for an all-too-trusting laity.

The most important question for us today is how, in the end, Protestantism affected the people it touched, how it molded their character. After the new ordinances and institutions had been set in place; after the sermons, pamphlets, and catechism classes had run their course; after the consistories and the visitors had had their say, who was then the Protestant layperson? What, if anything, of Protestant doctrine found a lasting place in the hearts and minds of the laity?

Historians today have a predeliction for evaluating the Reformation's success primarily by focusing on individuals and groups whose exposure to it was brief, intermittent, or only confrontational.[14] In doing so, they stack the deck in advance to find an ugly Protestant and a failed Reformation. At most, such an approach only documents the truism that people resist sudden changes in their accustomed way of life. The only fair measure of the Reformation's legacy for the laity can be the lives of people who grew up with it, so to speak, as with the air they breathe. These are the people it actually influenced for good or ill— those who had contact with it in church, at home, in school, and at work and under circumstances and over periods of time that permitted a thorough acquaintance and an informed response.

# II

# Theology and Propaganda:
## The Reformation Envisioned

# 3. The Revolution of the Pamphleteers

Has too much been made of the Reformation as a religious revolution? Was it a less significant force in sixteenth-century life than we have heretofore believed? Did religious protest and reform actually play only bit parts in the larger sociopolitical drama of early modern Europe?

We cannot readily know what went through the minds of people in the 1520s when they listened to the sermons of Luther and Zwingli for the first time or beheld broadsheet satires of the old church by artists like Hans Sebald Beham and Georg Pencz. It is difficult enough to gauge the religious appeal of Protestantism at mid and late century, when political destinies had become more settled. The confidence with which historians today "decode" the religious history of the past to expose its true political and social meaning calls to mind Lucien Febvre's warning to historians to guard against "psychological anachronism."[1] Before we can even begin to explain the reception of the Reformation among the laity, we must first know what the Reformation was at its inception, when the reformers first envisioned it and an evangelical movement of clergy and laity called on society to reform the church.

The survival of thousands of Protestant pamphlets—our most prolific source for the Reformation—makes it possible to reconstruct the Protestant message as people first heard it. A sizable and growing lay reading public, eager for pamphlets and books on religion and other subjects, had been created by the fifteenth century. For centuries kings and princes in need of skilled bureaucrats had patronized lay education, as had wealthy merchants in need of skilled agents and representatives. Humanists also gave literacy a strong impetus, along with dissenting religious movements from the Waldensians of twelfth-century France to the Hussites of fifteenth-century Bohemia, which urged people to learn to read the New Testament for themselves. The very same centuries that gave us the Black Death, the Hundred Years War, and the Great Schism in the church also produced the greatest boom in lay education and secular culture of the Middle Ages. Between 1300 and 1500, the number of European universities more than tripled, from twenty to seventy, and no fewer than 118 residential colleges were built in France, England, Germany, and Italy to house the growing student populations. This vast new reading public created the market for inexpensive books, which led to the development of printing with movable type. Beginning about 1450 with Johann Gutenberg's shop in Mainz, printing presses came to exist in sixty German cities by 1500 and in more than two hundred Europewide.[2]

From the point of view of the Reformation, it is a great irony of the printing press that its first mass production, in the 1450s, was letters of indulgence and its second the Protestant pamphlets of the 1520s and 1530s.[3] Protestant authors produced perhaps as many as ten thousand different titles by 1550,[4] so many that it has been said, "no books, no Reformation."[5] That, however, is only a half truth. Without print, the Reformation would have been different, and certainly more vulnerable to its enemies; but it still would have occurred, because the culture of the sixteenth century remained overwhelmingly oral. The vast majority of people, probably 90 percent, relied exclusively on the spoken word, not print, for their knowledge and information. Martin Luther described the age aptly when he declared, "the ears alone are the organs of a Christian man."[6] To become a Protestant then required literacy no more than it does today; indeed, the print industry of the sixteenth century enabled Protestant pamphleteers to evangelize as indiscriminately as television does their modern counterparts, addressing the nonliterate along with the literate. Hundreds of the pamphlets that rained down on the laity in the first decades of the Reformation were intended to be read aloud and preached in public as well as pondered in private by readers. Most were short (less than twenty pages), many were sermons, and quite a good many were illustrated—like the single-leaf woodcuts more consciously used to target the nonreading public.

Among the pamphleteers we find the great reformers like Luther and Zwingli, middling clergy and religious barely known to us today, and laymen and laywomen inspired by their own study of Scripture, often under humanist influence. The one thing their pamphlets and sermons unequivocally reveal is their own hearts and minds on the issues of reform. Whether these writings deeply influenced contemporaries or were even understood by them, they clearly attest a transformation through which the authors themselves had gone or were in the process of going. The pamphleteers saw their age as caught up in a true revolution, and their writings are our best evidence of the one revolt without which there could not have been a Reformation of any kind, whether as a spiritual event, a social protest, or an ecclesiopolitical conflict. Without the pamphleteers, few would have know or cared deeply about a Reformation, much less found the leadership and organization to enact it. What was this "revolution of the pamphleteers" that first brought the evangelical movement to life and made it viable in central Europe?

In the pamphlet literature of the 1520s and 1530s, the revolutionary nature of Protestantism is seen to lie in the changes called for in church and society when the authority of Holy Scripture supplants that of reigning church tradition.[7] No early pamphleteer elaborated the consequences of such a critique in greater detail or with more fury than Heinrich von Kettenbach, one of several second-rank figures of the Reformation who deserves to be better known. A Franciscan from Ulm, Kettenbach abandoned his cloister in 1521 to join Luther's movement. In his sermonizing and pamphleteering, we see the Reformation taking its first steps from classroom theology to mainstreet propaganda.

Between 1522 and 1523, Kettenbach preached eight sermons for the benefit of the laity of Ulm, methodically exposing the failings of the old faith. The unifying theme was a play on John 14:6, possibly the pamphleteers' most favored biblical text: "Christ says, 'I am the truth'; He does not say, 'I am custom.' "[8] A rhetorician in the style of Luther, Kettenbach ridiculed the mercurial laws and edicts by which the church operated, claiming that it adopted new rules and regulations every thirty or forty years, depending on pontifical whim. He describes Catholic doctrine as more inconstant and uncertain than the codes of gamblers, usurers, brigands, bathers, poets, and day workers, and he characterizes the church's accretions to Scripture as playing fast and loose with the consciences of simple Christians.[9]

The powerful monastic community in Ulm was not amused by Kettenbach's attacks, and in 1523 it forced his exile from the city. In a sermon circulated immediately thereafter, Kettenbach anathematized forty-three traditional church teachings and practices that, he said, derived from nonbinding "human fables, papal bulls, spiritless laws, and imperial mandates."[10] They included such essential matters as papal authority over Scripture; clerical superiority to the laity and freedom from secular taxation and rents; the power of priests to judge the sins of the laity and to subject them to penances;[11] the power of the pope to canonize saints and promulgate church doctrine; popular religious practices requiring the payment of fees, particularly the selling of indulgences and anniversary Masses; and such external acts of piety as burning candles, revering images, and adoring the host (the doctrine of transubstantiation).[12]

In another pamphlet of the same year (1523), Kettenbach drew no fewer than forty-nine contrasts between the "anti-Christlike" behavior of the pope and the biblical ministry of Jesus—perhaps the most popular tactic of early Protestant propaganda, both pictoral and written.[13] In heated, apocalyptic rhetoric, he urged pious German knights to take up arms against chapters, cloisters, and abbacies, all "plunderers of the bodies, souls, honor, and goods" of kings and noblemen.[14] Elector Frederick the Wise of Saxony, at the time just emerging as Luther's defender, won praise as a ruler who maintained obedience and peace in his land by defying the emperor's edict against Luther and "standing instead by the truth and God's Word."[15] Kettenbach promised a similar political success to the magistrates of Nuremberg, Augsburg, Ulm, and Strasbourg, who then also stood at the crossroads of the Reformation, should they follow the elector's example.

Our pamphleteer did not, however, hold unrealistic expectations of success and was anything but a dreamer. Perceiving the symbiotic relationship between the authority of tradition and the credulity of the laity, he soberly assessed his age's aptitude for reform. Mandatory fasting spoke volumes for him on the deep-rooted, unchristian presumption of both the clergy and the laity. Nowhere in the Gospel did he believe one could find any justification for commanding Christians to fast on pain of excommunication over the forty days of Lent in imitation of Christ; yet abstinence from certain foods was everywhere practiced. "Should we also try to walk on water, raise the dead, and heal the lame?" he asks mockingly. Are people supposed to imitate Christ in these heroic acts as well, and not simply follow his example of charity, patience, and humility? The Gospel recommends fasting only to those who choose it "freely and with a happy heart"; it does not "sear consciences" by commanding people to do what God does not.[16]

At the base of all such false traditions, Kettenbach saw the greed of prelates and the gullibility of the laity. Papal tyranny seemed to him to be a fitting punishment of the laity. "You have raised the pope above me," he has God say to the people:

> I gave the pope to you as a servant, a shepherd in the field; he himself confesses to be a *servus servorum Dei*, a servant of all my servants. But you have made him instead a lord over lords and even over God, even over me [by allowing him to add to and change my Word]. Justly are you now known as "papists" rather than Christians![17]

Lay naïveté seemed boundless to Kettenbach. "The laity set aside Scripture and the Word of God," he complains, "and they heed their clergy, right or wrong. If the clergy in their seductive way were to tell the laity that the devil or an ass is God, they would believe that too."[18] What do the laity do when the clergy flaunt their spiritual superiority over them—when, for example, the clergy claim that their own sexual activity or investments in real estate are qualitatively different from those of the laity, and hence properly subject to more forgiving rules and regulations? The lords and princes of the world compliantly look the other way! Again, it seemed to Kettenbach an appropriate divine punishment of such lay indiligence that so many lords and princes had been rendered religious illiterates by it, "the dumb subjects of the great, raging Babylonian whore [of Rome]."[19] Ordinary people embraced error, superstition, and idolatry even more willingly; they liked to bury themselves in monks' cowls and they readily squandered their children's and grandchildren's inheritances on commemorative Masses, believing that such acts brought them eternal life.[20]

Such experiences left Kettenbach gloomy about the prospects of ever enlightening the laity.

> Faced with death, people are easily drawn into superstition and gross idolatry. No one truly trusts in Jesus Christ for his salvation. . . . But what good does it do to talk about such things? The people prefer to remain in a "Babylonian prison." They are like the Jews in the reign of King Cyrus, when many chose freely and at their own request to remain in the land of the infidels after the king permitted them to return in freedom to the land of their fathers.[21]

When the Protestant pamphleteers decried the old church and its clergy, it was on grounds of deception and greed; when they turned to the shortcomings of the laity, credulity and inertia became new sins.

## Des Bapst erma-
## nung zu seinen
## Tempel knechten.

Seyt nur getröst ir Tempel knecht/
Der Pastorey habn wir güt recht/
Cardinal/ Bischof/ Münch vñ Pfaffen/
Die ich zů meim dienst hab erschaffen/
Hals dis schaff im pferch mit dem bscheid
Das keins geh auff ain frembde weid/
Auff das ir keines werd vergisse
Mit der Euangelischen schrisse/
Das niche den rechten hirten kennen/
Thůt alle lucken jn verkennen/
So bleibens vnterthon vnd willig/
So habt jr simt in schmaltz vñ millich/
Vnd lassen sich willig vnd gern
Als offt jr wölt melcken vnd schern/
Darzu auch gar mengen vñ schinden/
Wie möcht jr besser schäflein finden/
Wann ich sie so in hoher mache
Jn starcken reich/ gwalt/ pomp vñ prache/
Vber König/ Kayser vnd Fürsten/
Die in der welt gunst seind die Fürsten/
Ob die vns gleich sehen inns spul/
Müssens doch darzů schwertzgen still/
Vnd müssen durch die finger sehen
All ding gütlich lassen geschehen.
Derhalben habt vor jn kain scheuch/
Jr keiner setz sich wider euch.
Wer aber das wöle vnterstahn
Den thet ich in den schweren Bann.
Wöle er mit gwale sich wider setzen/
So thů ich ander an jn hetzen/
Die jn vberzihend/ bekriegen/
Denn müsset sich ducken vnd schmiegen/
Kreische wider in schasstal gütwillig/
Gibt zwischt wollen/ täls vnd millich/
Wiewol Teütschland mir ist verkert
Durch den Luther/ der anderst lert/
Vnd nennet vnser Pastorey
Ein möcher gröss vnd schinderey.
Deß sind etlich Fürsten vnd Herr
Den solche lehr zů hertzen gehe/
Wöllen sich nymmer scheeren lassen/
Deß sih ich cramtig vber dmassen.
Mein gwalcwñ schan wirt gar veracht
Vil präcesicks hab ich gemacht

Sie zu her Zihen mit dem har
All ding ist worden offenbar
Hoff es wern etlich meiner glider
Mit der Eisernen ruten wider
Das Teutschland treiben noch zů mal
Jn vnserm Römischen schasstal
Vnd wirt Vns diser duck gerathen
Erst woie wir mengen sieden vñ praten

Den dapele melcken/ schinden vnd schern
Vnd alles laids ergetze werden
Wiewol der Prophet Ezechiel
Sage/ Weh euch hirten Jssahel
Die ir euch habt gewaydet als
Das haupe frost in eurn hals
Mit wollen klaid ir euch auffs bést
Vnd stachend aß das wolgemést

Auff ir waydet ir gar nit mercke
Das schwache habe ir nie gesterckt
Auch habt ir gesuche das verlorn
Je habe gehersihe in gemale vnd zorn
Drost mein herd eiend zersterewe
Das rede auff vns gaistlich leut
Solch ebidung thund gar niche anschten
Mich/ sampe all meinen tempel knechten

Wann vnser Reich nur hie beste
Wer wais wie in sein leben gest
Wir meinen hie die guten tag
So lang vns das gebayen mag
Wer Ohren hat zu hören der hör
Von der lugen sich zur warheit
Vnd sich vom Bapst zu Christo
So bescher im Gott ein selig en

The special failing of laypeople was their readiness to believe what the Bible did not teach and to do what God did not require of them. They had become suckers for religious fantasies, so greedy were they for salvation. The pamphleteers tried above all to demonstrate the human origins of much church teaching and thereby to inculcate in the laity a healthy skepticism and defiance of tradition. Kettenbach attempted to do so by harsh exposure and scolding. Others sought to raise lay self-esteem by satire and ridicule, turning laughter as well as righteous anger against the church.[22]

The most popular publication of this genre was the pamphlet dialogue, and among its practitioners few could claim greater success than Eberlin

---

### THE POPE FLEECES HIS SHEEP

*The pope, sitting at table and counting money, instructs his clergy to keep the Christian laity tightly penned up, so that they remain "subject and compliant" and none may wander off to foreign pastures and be poisoned by the evangelical Scriptures. Then the clergy may continue to milk and shear, butcher and skin them as often as they wish.*

*Kings, emperors, and princes march by pretending not to see the pope's tyranny and abuse, fearing the power of his ban and possible war with him, should they challenge him. The pope notes sadly that "several princes and cities" in Germany have taken up Luther's teaching and are vowing never to be sheared again; they say they have no fear of the papal ban and hold papal authority in contempt. The pope claims to have a secret plan for driving Germany back into the Roman pen, where he will then exact a terrible vengeance.*

*In conclusion, the pope exhorts his clergy to ignore biblical warnings against bad shepherds and "to enjoy good times as long as they last." The moral drawn by the evangelical author:*

> *Let him with ears take all this in,*
> *And turn from lies to God's clear truth,*
> *Away from the pope to Christ,*
> *And God will bestow on him a blessed end.*

Unidentified artist, Vienna, ca. 1530, in *Max Geisberg: The Single-Leaf Woodcut: 1500–1550*, vol. 4, rev. and ed. Walter L. Strauss (New York: Hacker Art Books, 1974), p. 1532.

## WHY GERMAN MINTERS MUST STRIKE NEW COINS DAILY

*Three enemies are said to threaten Germany with financial ruin, if Germans are not vigilant. The first is papal bulls, indulgences, and dispensations, "worthless [spiritual] goods for which the pope takes good money." Prominent in the illustration is an indulgence nailed to the cross in the place of Jesus.*

*Merchants are Germany's second mortal enemy. As the pope sells Germans worthless spiritual goods for their souls, merchants sell them an endless stream of useless foreign goods for their bodies, such things as spices and Italian wines, silks, satins, and linens. The result is widespread desire, envy, and discontent with one's place in life, especially among the German peasantry, who rush to join in such pretense and excess. Encouraged by the merchants to acquire what they cannot afford, people at every social level quickly find themselves deep in debt. Still, the merchants continue to make loans and profiteer, increasing the numbers of impoverished and homeless people who must receive public assistance.*

*Germany's last predator is new habits of dress, the constant refashioning of clothing ("first short, then long, now wide, then narrow") and the influx of new foreign styles with ever increasing, and costly, additions of fur and ornamentation.*

*These three—the pope, merchants, and new customs—threaten Germany's simple, peaceful, ordered way of life. They will surely bring divine wrath and punishment upon the land, the author warns, if Germans continue their spiritual and material folly.*

J. Breu the Elder, in *Max Geisberg: The German Single-Leaf Woodcut: 1500–1550*, vol. 1, rev. and ed. Walter L. Strauss (New York: Hacker Art Books, 1974), p. 323.

# Ein Frag an eynen Müntzer/wahin doch souil Geltz

## kumme das man alltag müntzet: Antwort des selben Müntzers/Von dreyen
### Feinden vnnsers Geltz/wa wir nit acht darauff haben/werden wir den Seckel zum Gelt an.

Wann wir hetten rechten glauben  
Gott vnd gemainen nutz vor augen

Recht Elen/darzü maß vnd gwicht  
Gut frid vñ auch gleich Recht vñ Ghricht

Einerlay Müntz vnd kain falsch Gelt  
So stünd es wol in aller welt.

## Frag an den Müntzer.

Sag lieber Müntzer bist frü früh  
Wa maint das souil gelts hin kum  
Daran Teütsch land groß mangel hat  
Vnd je doch müntzes frü vnd spat  
Nun ist je Silbers nicht vil dran  
Das man müg grün am schmeltzen han  
Auch weil jetz kaur so äntzlich werden  
Das es groß schetz grab in die erden  
Doch ist kain gelt klag all weil sehr  
Das wundert mich vñ manchen mehr

## Antwort des müntzers

Täglich hör ich diß frag vnd klag  
Gib doch die antwort hell am tag  
Wañ wie nit wären sunst als plind  
Vnd sehen vnsers gelts drey sind  
Den Babst/New sitten/frembde rauhe  
Die vnser land erschöpffen gar  
Doch hat der Römisch gureb ein end  
Wa iche wie Teütschen selber wend  
Vom almüsen so wir nit wölln lon  
Werden wir je gelt zum seckel lon

## Der Erste Feindt.

Der Babst kan vns gantz böslich satz  
Die Bullen/Jblaß/Eßenschatzen  
Vmb d3e vnser gut geltz nympt  
Wie zum geschwinden kauffman ziempt

## Der Annder Feindt.

Den andern Feint nun auch verstand  
Der vnser gelt fürt auß dem land  
Ich main den Kauffman der on rü  
Dem vnserm leib so node auch thüt  
Wie s Babsts kaun kunst der sel zugie  
Sonder zu lust vnd hoffart raiche  
Damit nun vns teütsch narren Leiche  
El lancher ley greürtz vnd welschem wein  
Seyden Gummet/sonst ist eben fein  
Dierreet von rotem scharlach gemacht  
Darnach ein yeder pawr jetz tracht  
Der Eltern stat ist gar veracht  
Die vns mit trewen gspart hond  
Das wie so schandtlich jetz verthond  
Die wol sitzend/sei in aine stat  
Kaum aine Kindsch rock vnd hosen hat  
Der paursman trägt ein zwilch Jupp  
für greürtz/was pandel auff sei Jupp  
Kebt rauch/trau se3 pierem most vñ wasser  
Wa nu wie yetz ein soller puasser  
Sagt auff vns flacklein filtz vñ hür  
Wa im für windt vnd kelte gut  
Der hundtwetters man thet jm auch recht  
Elle gro3 vnd nariung was er schlechr  
Von Lande nich nacht der Bürger hand  
Vnd halt man güten vnterschaid

## Der Dritt Feindt.

Jetz kum ich an den dritten Finde  
New sitten der on zal vil sinde  
Damit man treibt ein schentlich prenng  
Jetz kürtz dañ lang/jetz weit dañ eng  
Jetz ist es praut/dañ mache mans schmal  
Daist kain maß jnn vberal  
Was einen setz an ermeln hangt  
Het etwa an jm ein rock gelang  
Jetz läst mans gantz/daß es3 zerschnitten  
Zwerg hang man an andern sitten  
Vnd ist jetz alle vergessen brot  
Drumb sich man allenthalb groß nodt  
Dañ aine hoffart werde kain tail  
Da bey man doch mache schulden vil  
Die werden nicht zu danck bezalt  
Wirdt eine drey jar tranck oder alt  
Hilff Gott so hat ee nit mer leben  
E Mañ müß jn pfand jnn spital geben  
Darnit triebt yederman beschwerde  
Der gemain/vnd aigen seckel glert  
Vnd kan zu letst anders werden drauß  
Daß 3 os me müssen lan von hauß  
Sonst der vberfluß wirde gspart  
Ein Teütscher sich des andern nart  
Vnd wer brauchet Lande grawßo vñ twut  
So würd d3en sachen noch wol rat

Ein yeder nach sein gut vnd stand  
Pfuch pfuch es ist ein grosse schand  
Das so sich jetz hat alle verkert  
Vnd besem übel nymande wert  
Was aine jetz jar vnd tag gewan  
Henckt er ons nals dem Lai sack an  
Das übrig müß sein gar verschlempe  
Kaine überfluß sich nymande schempe  
Ja wen es gält ein güldin slon

¶ Wolffgang Resch Formschneyder.

von Günzburg, after Luther the most prolific Protestant pamphleteer of the early 1520s and almost as popular at the time, despite the fact that he is little known today. An outstanding example of his talent is his explanation of Germany's impoverishment: *I Wonder Why There Is No Money in the Land.* A discussion by three lay travelers and a character named Psitacus (Eberlin's stand-in), the pamphlet does not blame Germany's problems solely on the church. Endemic warfare is also said to play a role, along with merchants, who corrupt society by their materialism and example of gain without work, despoiling people in more subtle ways than soldiers do by high markups and exorbitant interest rates. Eberlin, like Kettenbach an ex-Franciscan, believed nonetheless that the clergy had a special talent for misrule. More adept at deception and self-aggrandizement than soldiers and merchants, they actually managed to be revered and praised by those they impoverished. One of the travelers, Jörg Laicher of Rottenburg, explains how the clergy do it:

> In all lands, cities, villages, manors, and houses, in all seasons, by every means, at every opportunity, God and his saints come begging to us, crying out, "Give, Give!" Moved by their cries, we turn over to them our property and our lives. . . . We thus find ourselves supporting not only God and his saints, but their many servants as well, an entire culture of beggars . . . priests, monks, and nuns in uncountable numbers. And all of them want to lead a life of pleasure and abundance in princely pomp and circumstance, without having to work for it. Such a life requires much property and many goods, which they claim they deserve because they are God's servants. So filled with the good life are they that they think they can emulate God; from their great abundance of piety and holiness, they say they can make us holy as well when they favor us. They claim to possess an inexhaustible supply of indulgences on which they draw to redeem souls from purgatory on payment of a small fee. They even have special books that allow them to calculate the number of hours a soul must spend in purgatory. One such book, written by the Franciscan Caspar Schatzgeyer, informs us that our Lord God has created a 546-acre field that is heaven. Therein is found inexpressible joy, and space enough for a great throng of people. One also finds there fields and meadows, houses and manors, and fair rents and taxes to support divine services. It is known as the blessed isles (*Insule fortunate*), and

those who reside there receive back one hundredfold what they have given on earth to the saints. Who among us would not surrender all his possessions on earth to gain in return a hundredfold [in heaven]?[23]

According to Psitacus and Jörg Laicher, the clergy gain their advantage by convincing the laity that God and his servants require very special accommodations while they are on earth.

> *Psitacus.* Because God is the supreme prince and lord, [the clergy say] he and his servants must have the very best house on earth. Once we agree to this, the beggars' dance begins. . . .
>
> [*Jörg.*] Even though God very rarely stays the night with us, and his saints or their relics visit us perhaps only once a year (they prefer to lodge with a priest or at the inn), God nonetheless must have a house unlike any other, while many poor families live in broken-down shacks. Just look at God's house! How wide, how high, how towering like a mountain castle! And furnished with a separate choir and costly Venetian stained glass! So many beautiful pictures on the walls and more iron and lead throughout than the straws in a peasant's hut! How stately are the chairs in the choir for the gossiping, drunken priests, while those for the congregation are cheap and plain! The altars are made of precious stone, have golden panels, and are draped with fine cloth. There are pewter and brass candlesticks, lecterns with lattices, and many columns, banners, and decorated doors.
>
> [*Psitacus.*] How unnecessary are all these things!
>
> [*Jörg.*] But they are [just the beginning]. One must also have Massbooks, songbooks, crosses, monstrances of silver, little fonts for oil, special receptacles for the sacrament, baptismal fonts, lavish cloths, choir coats, and white choir dresses made of fine linen, leather, silk, and damask. Then there are the special utensils for the Mass, silk stripes for the left arm of the priest who celebrates the Mass, also silk scarves and choir caps.[24]

The clergy are relentless, the three travelers complain. They encircle the laity with churches so numerous that one seems to stand at every mile, two or three in every village, while along the back roads chapels appear everywhere. Every peasant wants his own little stone or wooden "saint house" at the edge of his vineyard or field. The clergy either own the choicest properties or exact rents from them. And they charge the laity fees for prayers, baptisms, confirmations, burials, and intercession on behalf of sick children. Even on a short pleasure walk one bumps into the almsboxes that dot the land, each decorated with the image of some fearsome guardian saint like Saint Quirin, who protects one from gout, if properly honored. Plague saints also abound, like Saint Anthony, the founder of monasticism, who will save one from "Saint Anthony's fire" (a contemporary description of erysipelas, an often fatal complication of a streptococcal infection that leaves the skin inflamed), if his order is given a pig. Then there is Saint Wendel, the patron saint of shepherds, who watches over sheep in exchange for sheep. Should a layman join a confraternity, he has still more religious fees to pay. Meanwhile, mendicants swarm about the laity demanding money, wine, beer, peas, corn, clothes, cheese, and eggs, and promising most temptingly "great [spiritual] freedom and indulgence" in return. Presently, the Saint Peter's indulgence, whose proceeds go to the rebuilding of Saint Peter's church in Rome, is "scooping up all the money in the land."[25]

At the end of the dialogue, Jörg Laicher concludes that God, his saints, and their clerical servants "own us." "They have taken the things of our world over into theirs, so that everything of ours has become theirs." Zingk of Renfelden, another fictitious traveler, agrees:

> We now have a God who does us no good. He takes away our property and endangers our lives. Frequently he forbids us to eat eggs, butter, and meat, sends us off to die in his wars, and excommunicates and damns us eternally over one unpaid groschen. Either our God is no God at all, or he is not the true God. For a true God does good things for his servants and protects and saves them.[26]

Thus were the three travelers brought to the brink of atheism by the malpractices of the medieval church. But such a conclusion could not be the final word for a pamphleteer of the Reformation. So at story's end we find Zingk appealing from the "false God" of tradition to the true God of Scripture, as he summarizes Luther's teaching about salvation by faith:

> I know of a true God about whom I have learned in an old Book. He does many good things freely for his people and he takes nothing in return. He forgives their sins. His son died for them. He permits his people to eat whatever they have whenever they need it. His servants

are devout and honorable . . . [and] he asks of them only that they be at peace and love one another. . . . I will therefore embrace this God and let the old God go. For our God is . . . surely not the true old God. The Bible is older than our God's book [i.e., canon law], and the biblical God is older than our God. Therefore, I find the biblical God to be the true God.[27]

As a *literary event*, the revolution envisioned by the pamphleteers was a revolt of ordinary laypeople newly impervious to spiritual deceit against those who would defraud them. This image was conveyed to the public not only in pamphlets featuring educated laity capable of formal theological debate. Spiritually enlightened shoemakers, bakers, cooks, spoonmakers, bellsmiths, carpenters, and haymakers also take leading roles in the pamphlets, challenging readers and auditors with a folksier logic and oratory.

Hans Sachs, the famous Nuremberg shoemaker and Meistersinger, especially brought ordinary people to speech on behalf of the Reformation. In four dialogues composed in 1524, he put the new Protestant gospel in the mouths of Nuremberg laity. The first featured a debate between a canon and a shoemaker on a subject close to Sachs's heart as a layman supporting Luther: the laity's awakened sense of spiritual equality with the clergy.

The learned canon lectures the shoemaker, who had earlier dared to correct the clergy and even to criticize the pope—an allusion to a poem Sachs had written in 1523 in praise of Luther, *The Wittenberg Nightingale*. In response, the shoemaker declares it his right and duty as a baptized Christian "to rebuke any sinful brother, whether he is an ordained cleric or not." When the canon retorts that no mere layman, unordained and lacking clerical rank, is qualified to interpret Scripture, the shoemaker appeals to his baptism and an inner calling. "From what university did St. John, who writes so eloquently about God, come," he asks; "was he not a mere fisherman?"[28]

On the basis of his own reading of Scripture, the shoemaker not only criticizes the behavior of the clergy, but spurns as well the veneration of saints, fasting, the sacrament of Penance, and the authority of church councils (excepting that of the original apostles in Jerusalem). Warned by the canon "not to despise good old custom" ("gut alte gewonhait sol man nicht verachten"), the shoemaker sounds the trumpet charge of the pamphleteers: "In the fourteenth chapter of John's Gospel, Christ says: 'I am the way, the truth, and the life'; he does not say, 'I am custom. . . .' We must stand by the truth, which is the Word of God and God himself . . . for custom comes from men and passes away with them."[29]

The major reformers, too, portrayed the laity as superior in moral character and spiritual insight to the clergy of Rome. Interjecting himself into a local conflict, the Swiss reformer Zwingli praised an "unlettered bellsmith" named Hans Füssli, who had incurred the wrath of a learned Strasbourg schoolmaster and canon lawyer, Jerome Gebwiler. In a brief preface to Füssli's 1524 pamphlet critique of traditional religion, a work that paralleled Zwingli's own theological tome of the previous year, the *Sixty-Seven Articles*,[30] Zwingli wrote,

> Behold, pious Christian [reader], how our heavenly father likes to conceal his divine light and wisdom from the wise and the learned (Matt. 11) and reveal it to those who are like children. In this way, he destroys the wisdom of the wise and casts aside the understanding of the learned (Isa. 29:14). Our God favors the lowly multitude so that he may shame the wise. Here a mere bellsmith, totally lacking in speech and understanding save for what God and his mother have given him, challenges an old schoolmaster long versed in many arts, most notably, canon twaddle or, as it is also called, canon law. The faithful heart will discern which of the two has better understood divine truth and more truly interpreted God's Word. Here we also see the reason that the world's powerful lords persecute the teaching of Christ. After Christ was murdered, it was fishermen who proclaimed him to the world and made him more widely known than he had been in his own lifetime. And when all of the fishermen have been driven away, the bellsmiths, millers, glassmakers, cloth cutters, shoemakers, and tailors will continue to teach us about Christ. They are already doing so, just as the fishermen once did. So, dear students, if you want to learn about the pope and rhetoric, stay with Gebwiler, for Hans Füssli knows nothing about such things; but if you want to hear God's truth clearly stated, forsake the orator [Gebwiler] and sit at the feet of this bellsmith.[31]

Such themes saturate the pamphlet literature of the early Reformation. Their clear purpose was to reflect and to engender lay spiritual self-confidence and a sense of equality with the clergy. Another pamphleteer of the 1520s, Hans Steigmeyer, declared the laity "more experienced in the teaching of Holy Scripture than all who wear miters," and he envisioned an imminent fulfillment of the prophecies of Isa. 29:14 ("God will destroy the wisdom of the wise and cast aside the understanding of the learned") and John 6:46 ("God will directly teach all people his truth"). In a striking denouement, Steigmeyer has a monk not only praise a baker's demonstrated expertise in Scripture, but also proclaim his conversion to the "Christian order of the laity" and a life of working in the world with his hands.[32]

In the Protestant pamphlet literature of the 1520s, the laity refuse any longer to allow the church to treat them "like children"; they declare themselves to be of age and henceforth their own teachers. We find a spoonmaker, blessed with a peaceful conscience (the reward of "honest work"), instructing a Franciscan friar made anxious by Luther's "enlightenment of the common man." Never again, he assures the friar, will the clergy treat the laity like "blind mice" or "bears with rings in their noses"; there will be no more "hopping to fairy tales."[33] An anonymous, self-described "Prague Hussite" cites among forty condemned tenets of Luther to which he also subscribes "that the priests and monks have used hell/purgatory, confession/penance, and human laws to frighten simple people into giving them their money, just as parents frighten children into obedience by telling them the bogeyman is hiding behind the door."[34] A judge in Schwabach recounts his public rebuke of a priest for being absent from his post and failing to teach God's Word; though admittedly a mere "subject and sheep" in the church and no ordained cleric, this layman claims it his right as a Christian to teach interested laity the truth of the Bible in the privacy of his own home.[35] Then there is the haymaker who assures a lumberjack that his vocation is a true spiritual work and that he need not, as the clergy have instructed him to do, join a religious confraternity or perform some other religious good works in order to be saved.[36] In both contrived and autobiographical pamphlets, we find sons and daughters defending their flight from cloisters and instructing their still traditional parents in the tenets of the new faith.[37]

The pamphlets of the early Reformation thus portray a Christendom in which all spiritual distinction between the clergy and the laity and the learned and the simple was fast vanishing. The new authority of Scripture had rendered the church's traditional coercive power (that is,

its rulings, statutes, and threats of excommunication) no more frightening to the laity than the "hiss of a goose."[38] In Christ, the laity protest,
there are no spiritual levels among believers, no marks of superiority
whatsoever, only the common baptism all share alike.[39] "We, the sheep,
have the right to judge the doctrine and preaching of our shepherds,"
concludes another pamphlet, whose title proclaims: *The Clergy's Power Is
Despised, Their Craft a Joke; Their Lies Ignored, Their Pretense Exposed; Right Is
Now as God Makes It.*[40]

So it was that, in an age that prized stability and feared tumult, the
Protestant pamphleteers attempted to enlighten and embolden a laity
they deemed instinctively cautious and chronically credulous. How successful were they? Do pamphlet conquests reflect real victories?

The pamphleteers themselves were of two minds about their impact.
Already in the 1520s, some believed that their assaults on tradition were
so successful that the brakes had to be applied quickly to avoid religious
anarchy. Eberlin von Günzburg condemned as worse than the papists
the new "delirious evangelicals," who, having convinced themselves of
the all-sufficiency of the new doctrine, "abandoned all discipline and
decency . . . and preached only revolution and bigotry."[41] By the end of
the decade, the course of the Reformation deeply disturbed even Luther
himself. Reading official reports of spiritual laxity, ignorance, and indifference throughout Saxony, he concluded that the common man had
learned nothing so much from his Gospel as how to abuse the freedom
it gave him.[42]

In the 1530s, spiritual discipline (*Zucht und Ordnung*) came to replace
spiritual equality at the top of the reformers' agenda. The great Lutheran
churchmen of the period, Johannes Bugenhagen and Johannes Brenz, especially made it their watchword, stressing both the necessity of discipline and its compatibility with evangelical freedom in the model church
ordinances they wrote in 1531 and 1533, respectively.[43] What a startling
revelation it must have been for the Lutheran preachers of Augsburg in
the mid-thirties when, after having prepared a statement on evangelical
"orthodoxy" to rebuke growing numbers of Protestant radicals (particularly Anabaptists), they found themselves having to defend not only the
new evangelical doctrines, but the most ancient Christian teachings as
well—such staples as the Trinity, the Incarnation, original sin, salvation
by faith alone, the necessity of good works, infant baptism, the true presence of Christ in the Eucharist, and, most ominous of all, the "orderly

creation" of faith through external religious services—the latter item "against those who say that the preaching of the Gospel and the administration of the sacraments contribute nothing to salvation."[44]

The Protestant assault on tradition in the 1520s had stimulated both socioreligious utopianism and spiritual apathy among the laity of Augsburg, problems that would plague the new faith almost everywhere for the remainder of the century. Ironically, the longest article of the new Augsburg creed pleaded for communal spiritual unity—the hallmark of evangelical congregations a scant decade earlier. Article nine of the creed asks all children of God to take part in the community of faith by hearing the Word and receiving the sacrament, and explains, "Christian doctrine, admonition, punishment, and exhortation should be truly observed and constantly exercised; we say this against the many who today reject or avoid the external community of the church, obedience to the Gospel, and Christian discipline."[45] The final article of the Augsburg creed ominously defended the right of secular government to enforce upon the citizenry a proper moral and religious behavior.

In 1537, Nuremberg Protestant leaders Andreas Osiander and Lazarus Spengler reported disruptions in their city brought on by the new Protestant domestic reforms. According to Osiander, people in Nuremberg were marrying not only within relationships long forbidden by the church—as Lutheran teaching permitted them to do—but many "false saints" ignored traditional kinship barriers to sex and marriage altogether, threatening Nuremberg with the spectacle of "incestuous whoring and adultery" among the closest family members. Spengler reports rumors from outside the city that Nurembergers "marry each other like dogs, without discretion . . . judgment, and differentiation among the degrees of relationship between them." Faced with such license and criticism, the city fathers had little choice but to reimpose traditional marriage practices, thereby postponing liberal changes in Nuremberg's marital laws until the last quarter of the century.[46]

Another, more positive, claim of evangelical success appears in the highly propagandistic pamphlet "letters from hell." An outstanding late example of this popular genre, circulated in 1538, reports a conversation among the deceased popes Leo X (1513–1521), who had excommunicated Luther, and Clement VII (1523–1534) and the recently arrived Cardinal Spinola. The cardinal brought them the "bad news" of the world, most distressing of which was the inexorable advance of the Lutherans throughout Europe. Not only had Germany and England fallen, Spinola reports, but Protestantism was making steady progress in Italy as well: "the Italian people and our own preachers everywhere press for reforms like those of the Lutherans." Pilgrims no longer come to Rome, nor do people any longer buy indulgences. "Save for a few religious, poor widows, and soul sisters, the people no longer believe in such things." Purgatory, too, has fallen victim to Protestant criticism. "Oh, that is bad news indeed, truly an eternal disaster," groans Pope Clement; "without purgatory, woe to the clergy; they will now have to work with shovels and axes!" Pope Leo recommends brute force against the church's enemies ("strike, kill, burn"), while Pope Clement recalls how effectively he had bribed his enemies with benefices. But Spinola assures them that the church of the 1530s can no longer enforce its will in such traditional ways; the Protestants are too clever and have become too many, and the power of patronage—as Clement's successor, Pope Paul III (1534–1549), was sadly learning—is no match for the new reform sentiment.[47]

Contrary to this rosy picture of success, which many pamphleteers paint at least for rhetorical purposes, others indicate that the Reformation did not in fact readily overturn tradition; the spiritually conservative continued overwhelmingly to outnumber the eager converts. Nuremberg may serve again as a case in point. In another of his dialogues in 1524, Hans Sachs subjected a zealous Lutheran (Peter) to the criticism of a moderate evangelical (Hans) and a traditional Catholic (Ulrich, Peter's father-in-law). The pair accuse Peter of conveying the impression that the new faith consists of little else than abusive ridicule of tradition— a bigoted mocking of the religious importance previously attached by pious Christians to prayer, saints, fasting, confession, pilgrimages, the Mass, indulgences, good works, and vigils and Masses for the dead. Hans warns that such self-righteous dismissals of tradition, regardless of the truth of the criticism, only causes people to dig in their heels. He advises that it is

> better to give unknowing people some consoling words about Christ. Tell them that Christ's death is the one work of our salvation, that our heavenly Father has given Christ all power in heaven and on earth, that we should obey Christ and do what he commands, and that in those things which Christ leaves us free to do, no one in heaven or on earth may forbid us.[48]

This more positive approach, it is argued, has the better chance of softening hearts still loyal to tradition.

Such comments convey the impression that the ordinary layperson was not in truth the bold, perceptive knight of faith depicted in the pamphlets and woodcuts of the 1520s, but rather one who had to be carefully weaned and cajoled away from the old to the new, inclined in his or her innermost self to cling tenaciously to tradition and custom. The Protestant clergy of Nuremberg concurred in that judgment. In the year of Sachs's pamphlet, they circulated for the benefit of the laity a massively detailed justification of the changes undertaken in the traditional services of the local churches, obviously anticipating resistance and complaints. Among the discarded traditional practices were the Latin Mass ("pure blasphemy"), anniversary Masses (the product of "clerical greed" and "shameful lay ignorance"); funeral Masses ("if the common man properly understood these, he would not give a 'good morning' for one"); singing vigils for the dead ("if the common man only understood these, he would not pay a dollar for a year's worth"); purgatory ("it is nothing"); and the *Salve Regina*, consecrated salt, and holy water (a "mockery of Christ"). Nor would the laity in Nuremberg any longer hear the singing of matins and compline—canonical hours said neither to honor God nor to aid the souls of one's neighbors.[49]

The new Lutheran clergy also expressed a disinclination to force such changes on the laity without their understanding and consent. For this reason, they claim to have preached against church abuses and human teachings (*menschensatzungen*) for a full two years before finally taking decisive action. Nevertheless, the pastors ominously acknowledge that "love and patience" in these matters had gotten them nowhere with their detractors, who interpreted their charity as weakness and only intensified their efforts to keep Nurembergers within the old church.[50] The following year (1525) the clergy prepared a still more massive summary of their case against tradition. On the heels of an imperial diet in the city, they presented officials with a 210-page, 23-article statement that dwarfed the 74-page, 10-article account previously composed for the local laity.[51] No more than the ordinary layman did Nuremberg officials find evangelical reforms easy and self-evident. If numerous external changes in religious practice came about comparatively quickly in the city, lasting internal ones occurred only slowly over decades.

In fact the Reformation never did become the unqualified success and boon to society that its inventors had hoped it would be. Neither was it the complete failure and scourge of society that its enemies envisioned and present-day historians again allege. Contrary to the gloomy reports of pamphleteers in the heat of battle, religious utopianism, spiritual apathy, mindless loyalty to tradition, and coerced conformity were not the only lay responses to the new Protestant gospel. Amid these extremes, laity in Protestant lands also opted for moderate and workable reforms—and in sufficient numbers to win the contest with tradition in more than one-third of the Holy Roman Empire's cities and towns. And the new religious establishment they created proved to be as capable of continuity with tradition as criticism and correction of it.

In 1524, as Nuremberg was becoming the first imperial city to turn Protestant, Lazarus Spengler, the powerful secretary of the city council, portrayed the middle ground of reform in a pamphlet defense of the changes then underway in the city's religious life. Although he was as moderate a Protestant as one will find in the sixteenth century, his name had earlier appeared on the papal bull *Exsurge Domine* (1520), which first threatened Luther with excommunication. Spengler had not in fact been an original conspirator of the Reformation, but he had gotten on the wrong side of Luther's great opponent Johannes Eck, who played a key role in the drafting of that famous bull. In Spengler, Nuremberg Catholics faced a tough, but still fair-minded, Protestant critic.

To beseiged Catholics, who saw their world crumbling before their eyes, the Reformation appeared to be religiously anarchic and to threaten civil disorder as well. In an effort to reverse the tide of reform, they presented the city council with eight reasoned arguments, which can be briefly summarized.

1. If, as the Lutherans allege, the gospel as they preach and teach it is the gospel as it should always have been preached and taught, then the church fathers and the church councils have erred and our forebears in the faith, thousands upon thousands of people, did not live and die as true Christians.

2. Had the church in fact been so long in error, God would not have preserved it for so many centuries.

3. Luther and his followers interpret Scripture according to their own pleasure, with no respect for the ancient fathers.

4. The new faith brings forth much that is Christian, necessary,

and good, especially when it condemns clerical abuses; but like all heretics, the Lutherans mix poison with the good.

5. Because Luther's teaching has been condemned and forbidden both by the pope [the bull *Exsurge Domine*] and the emperor [the Edict of Worms], it lacks legality and moral sanction and should not be preached.

6. Having thrown off tradition and law in religion, the Lutherans inspire others to defy human authority as well; their teaching encourages disobedience and awakens rebellion in subjects.

7. The new faith does not bring about any moral improvement of society.

8. The new faith exalts the authority of Scripture alone and suppresses tradition.[52]

Where Catholic critics saw only rebellion, Spengler perceived allegiance to the truth, which he refused to equate with majority belief, the writings of the church fathers, or the decrees of church councils. Viewing opposition to the Reformation as understandable, if misplaced, loyalty to "parental superstition and idolatry," he pleaded a new version of the pamphleteer's leitmotif: "Christ teaches us to *honor* our father and our mother, not to trust and believe in them, for we are saved only by our trust in him."[53] No more than he would equate numbers of believers with truth was Spengler prepared to identify custom and antiquity with it. The Jews, he pointed out, are older than the Christians, and Islam has been a religion longer than Germany has been Christian, yet who in Christian Nuremberg would dare claim that Jews and Muslims are nearer the truth than Christians? "As the popular proverb holds, what has been in error for a hundred years has never had an hour's worth of truth."[54] Spengler accused the defenders of tradition of wanting to mix "uncertain human doctrines, statutes, and opinions" with God's Word and truth. For security's sake, the shaky authority of tradition had to be replaced by the "complete clarity" of Scripture.[55] For the same reason, he explained, evangelicals defy the religious edicts of popes and emperors; such decrees can no more measure God's truth and bind consciences than mere numbers and custom do. The line of spiritual authority in the end runs directly from conscience to the Word of God.[56]

Responding to the charge that Protestant religious disobedience was inspiring social and political revolt, Spengler laid the blame for the rebelliousness of the age squarely at the feet of the rulers themselves. The reason so many secular and ecclesiastical lords now oppose the Reformation, he claims, is that the gospel it preaches unmasks their deceit, corruption, and abuse of their subjects.[57] By exposing such misrule, the reformers have both invited their own persecution and laid a foundation for a more just and moral society.

If the latter seemed little in evidence to Nuremberg's Catholic apologists, Spengler hastened to point out that these were the same people who would have Nurembergers believe that a person is devout if he endows a cloister, buys Masses for the dead, decorates a church with silver-framed paintings and images, goes on pilgrimages, prays to saints, buys indulgences, and lights candles. The Reformation, he concluded, had at least taught people that true piety did not consist in such things, but was an internal matter of the heart which only God could judge.

> I will concede that the Word of God has not yet brought forth any [moral] fruit or improvement. Still, everyone must admit that we are better off having been shown the true path to salvation through the preaching of the clear Word of God than we would be if we remained forever in the old error and ignorance of doing many external works and believing them to be good.[58]

The revolution of the pamphleteers was the Reformation in blueprint only, not in actual fact. Still, they envisioned no utopia, either in an ecclesioreligious or in a sociopolitical sense. The confluence of Christian "mind set" and egalitarian communal government that some today claim to have been the original goal of the Reformation tells us far more about the political dreams of contemporary historians than it does about those of the Protestant reformers, who, from Luther to Calvin, grudgingly recognized the human and political limits of reform. The pamphleteers of the early Reformation hoped to establish in church and society two modest but far-reaching principles: the spiritual equality of the laity with the clergy and the inalienable right of either to subject tradition to the test of Scripture and draw the logical conclusions. And they believed that once these principles were secure, the societies in which they lived might, in time, to the extent that it was humanly and politically possible, become true cities of God.

# 4. Evangelizing
# the Real World

Spiritual changes are also embodied; they have a preexisting material matrix and concurrent material effects. The soul's salvation also engages the mundane issues of individual and social life. The Reformation's struggle for souls took place as much on the battlefields of body and property, money and politics, society and culture as within individual hearts and minds. For the Protestant apologists, the quest for a God-fearing church went hand in hand with a search for a godly society. Espousing biblical ideals was not enough; their criticism and propaganda had also to confront church and society as they actually existed and were likely to remain. Being themselves products of the societies they wished to change, the reformers' teaching naturally reflected contemporary cultural values and concerns as well as the newfound biblical norms by which they hoped to reform them. Particularly as they began to anticipate victory, they addressed their propaganda to real-life problems. The pamphleteers, in other words, must be recognized as (auto)biographers and social commentators as well as propagandists; they tell true stories as well as preach, and they expound real lives along with the books of the Bible.

In this chapter we meet a less theological and idealistic "revolution of the pamphleteers," one more down to earth and prepared to reach its goals by negotiation and compromise. Much might change in religious belief and practice in the sixteenth century, but in this age there was not going to be a political and social revolution in God's name—of that reigning magistrates and princes early apprised overzealous reformers. So we also find many Protestant sermons, tracts, and pamphlets that are less searching lights and guiding beacons than mirrors of contemporary society as it actually was and of the Reformation as it was necessarily going to be: not blueprints for the New Jerusalem, but a program of reform for the real world.

Religious protest at this time also had a deeply personal, but nonspiritual, side. People turned Protestant not only because of what traditional religion had done to their souls, but also because of its impact on their material lives. Early series of pamphlets, examined in the section that follows, reveal many of the social and economic problems of the era and, more importantly, demonstrate how quickly the pamphleteers learned to address these issues along with the more urgent ones (in their view) of religious reform. In the early years of the Reformation, before a Protestant "orthodoxy" had been created, individual laity and clergy had their own personal sense of who they were spiritually and what the religious conflict was really about. A second series of pamphlets considers some contemporary lay and clerical self-images, which became as important to the reform's initial success as the idealistic biblical models of Christian life. Finally, we will look at the budding Protestant establishment in a pamphlet projection of what a reformed society should realistically entail.

## 1. SOCIAL AND ECONOMIC PROBLEMS

Protestants at first took positions of dissent on purely spiritual and ecclesiastical matters, arguing over such things as the power of indulgences, the authority of tradition, the place of the pope, the role of good works in salvation, and the right of the clergy to marry. But religious ideology quickly found itself face to face with nonspiritual issues that had not been at the forefront of the Reformation's original agenda. Finding themselves under the suspicious eye of political authority, Protestant spokesmen had time and again to restate the purpose of their reforms, clarifying their ideals and making the social, economic, and political content of their teaching explicit. In 1523, Heinrich von Kettenbach, the Franciscan friar turned Lutheran pamphleteer, shared with the laity of Ulm his views on the decisions posed for them by the coming of the Reformation. During his brief ministry in the city, he acted as spiritual adviser to a pious old woman, whose traditional faith had been shaken by the Protestants. The woman first came to him for guidance after the city's evangelical chaplain instructed her to stop buying church candles, the habit of a lifetime, and to give the money instead, which only amounted to seven pennies a week, to the city's poor and to her own children and relatives. The chaplain also challenged her decision to invest her life savings, a tidy fifty gulden, in an anniversary Mass in her own memory after she died, though the "worthy spiritual fathers" had long assured her that she could not do a better work.[1]

Brother Heinrich scolded the old woman for falling so willingly into a "Babylonian captivity" of costly superstition, and he regretted the hold popular piety continued to have over the consciences of Ulm's laity.

> Such great honor is paid to the "gods" [that is, to pilgrim shrines, sculpted images, paintings, and the saints], but, as Jeremiah says, it is all done in vain, for such things help no one, neither the one who venerates them nor those he seeks to aid through them. It is the same with all pilgrimages, images, paintings, and saints throughout the whole world; they are the ways the devil makes light of the fate decreed by God, as people [who are sick and fear death] are made to believe that such things will heal and save them.[2]

He also accused the old woman of robbing her relatives of their rightful inheritance and taking needed assistance away from the poor by foolishly devoting her savings to a memorial Mass. While the souls of the departed are presumably administered to in purgatory and here on earth priests and monks enjoy good wine purchased from the largess of such lay endowments, the poor of Christ go visibly hungry on the streets of Ulm.[3] Have you listened carefully at Mass? he demands of the old woman; do you know what you are buying with your savings? Although she has attended Mass daily lifelong, she admits that it is something she has never really understood, because it is sung in Latin. She can recall only the words "seculum seculorum" and "quantus quantus thomas scarioth," each repeated three times. The realization that she has invested so much of herself in something she does not comprehend moves her to ask Brother Heinrich why priests are not trained to conduct services in the languages the laity speak. And why are the clergy also exempt from many taxes she must pay?

> How is it, Brother Heinrich, that you monks and priests are free from taxes, tolls, and other payments, while I, a poor wife, spin at my wheel by the light of the moon till almost midnight and yet I am not free from such? . . . And if Christ has really freed you from them, why did he himself pay tribute to Caesar?[4]

Kettenbach assured the old woman that priests were beginning to conduct services in the vernacular—he mentions the recent experiments in Basel by the reformer Johannes Oecolampadius, who had begun to read the Epistle and the Gospel in German—despite political opposition everywhere to a vernacular Gospel because of its feared revolutionary impact on simple folk.[5] He further assured her that clerical immunity from taxation had been opposed by a succession of distinguished thinkers since the thirteenth century, citing among the forerunners of Luther—Emperor Frederick II, William of Ockham, and John Hus.[6]

Torn between the "old doctrine" she suspects, but says she cannot hate, and the "new doctrine"[7] she finds attractive, but hesitates to embrace, the old woman confessed what must have been a common experience at this time for both the many devout converts to Protestantism and those driven to religious indifference by the religious conflict. "Brother Heinrich," she asks, "how can I find peace of conscience? I suffer so much in my heart, and I find no release from my suffering and anxiety in confession, prayer, the Mass, pilgrimages, or penance—in no work under the sun."[8] Kettenbach assured her that the peace she sought would come only through a "right true faith" in Christ, who makes people righteous by his own perfect righteousness so that they need not anxiously seek salvation by donations to images and saints or by going on pilgrimages.[9]

Suspended between the old religion and the new, the old woman experienced a religious disillusionment probably typical of that which gave birth to the Reformation as a popular lay movement. Lay awareness of clerical abuse and sensitivity to empty ritual became the emotional soil in which Protestant sermons and propaganda took root and flourished. The changes brought about by the Reformation in popular religious practice alone were a major upheaval in the world as people then knew it, regardless of whether they were pious Christians or personally embraced the Reformation. Devout aristocratic families long closely identified with local churches,[10] as well as ordinary laypeople whose social status and economic condition did not change dramatically over a lifetime, must have watched in shock as laws were proposed, debated, and passed that progressively ended or severely limited such traditional practices as fasting, penance, the veneration of saints, relics, and images, indulgences, pilgrimages and shrines, Masses for the dead, belief in purgatory, Latin Mass and liturgy, numerous ceremonies, festivals, and holidays, cloisters, mendicants, and celibate clergy.

The Reformation was not a social revolution in the sense that it led to a reordering of traditional social classes and estates. Despite urban and peasant rebellions during its early decades, the larger process of territorial political centralization, already under way in the fifteenth century, continued throughout the sixteenth. In the cities and towns, the customary social divisions and tensions also persisted. The Reformation did not directly challenge or affect any of these developments. It did, however, indirectly affect the larger political landscape of Europe, for as religious and political loyalties became territorially intertwined, opposing groups identified its religious message, positively or negatively, with their own economic or political self-interest.[11] Still, the major social impact of the Reformation lay in its successful displacement of the traditional religious beliefs and practices that had given daily life security and meaning for Christians during the greater part of the Middle Ages.[12]

The simple cessation of Masses for the dead immediately created novel legal and moral problems for cities and towns. Were new Protestant executors of last wills and testaments any longer bound to respect the wishes of deceased Catholics—even their own parents and relatives—who had, during their lifetimes, in good faith endowed Masses in their own memory? What of the many who, like Kettenbach's old woman, had pledged their life savings, only to discover from Protestant preachers that such pledges were useless? Could they or, after their death, their heirs conscientiously break testaments sworn in good conscience before God and man and divert such endowments to other purposes?

As the exodus of monks and nuns from cloisters began in the 1520s, the propriety of breaking monastic vows had posed a similar problem within clerical ranks. The basic Protestant position on that question had been that celibate vows could bind no one indefinitely, inasmuch as they lacked a clear basis in Scripture and manifestly contradicted human nature.[13] The release of laity, both living and dead, from their testamentary vows was now defended by a similar argument. The Lutheran reformer of Altenburg, Wenceslaus Linck, addressed the question in a popular pamphlet in 1524, in which he sought support for the immediate redistribution of the endowments of Catholic churches and cloisters. Linck depicted God-fearing, ethical, and rational testators as people who refused to endow vigils, churches, Masses, images, organs, or bells in their own memory, because they recognized that such endowments contradicted God's commandment and the teaching of Christ and only increased idolatry and abetted clerical profiteering.[14] Responsible testators remembered their primary obligation to their children, relatives, and the poor. Linck went so far as to instruct the executors of last wills and testaments to alter or "emend" a bequest in which the testator had acted against God's will either through human frailty or by the (mis)guidance of clerical advisers.

> The form and the execution of the will should proceed less according to the words and more according to the intention of the deceased, which should be completely conformed to Christian faith and the will of God. Therefore, let the executor consider first the will and law of God instead of the words, writings, and opinions of the testator.[15]

The executor was thus left free to adjust the will of a deceased person to changed historical circumstances in good conscience.

> Let me take an example. Suppose that someone has left money to churches, cloisters, and the like, even though God has commanded no one to do so and such is done against his will. It is still possible to make the gift serve God's will and not oppose it. When a situation arises in which God has clearly commanded people to help one another, we should not hesitate to turn to that purpose the money that has been willed to churches, cloisters, and the like. For example, when there is a famine and poor people suffer want, it is clear that such endowments should not be used for the purpose designated by the testator, but rather given over to that ordained by God. Funds should be taken freely from churches and cloisters to support the poor to whom we are obligated by both divine and natural law. And any goods and treasure left over should be placed in a common chest and there held until a need for them again arises.[16]

Protestant rejection of the monastic life not only entailed such redefinition of the legal status of church endowments. It also encouraged new attitudes to work and the poor that found their way into the new city ordinances. Linck addressed this subject in an influential pamphlet reflective of the kinds of changes magistrates had long wanted to make in the laws and which the Protestant leaders now strongly supported. It bore the title *On Work and Begging: How One Should Deal with Laziness and Make Everyone Work* (1523). Aware of the widespread resentment of begging in Altenburg, Linck's purpose was to advise the burgomaster and city council on their continuing responsibility to the poor. In doing so, he presented to them a peculiar theology of work, according to which hard work becomes God's special remedy (*Artzney, heylsame büsse*) for humankind's fallen condition, a necessary pain and penance by which people make their way back to God and become more like the people God originally intended them to be.[17] By contrast, the devil's favorite temptation is said to be a life free from all work and effort (*zu mussigkeit reitzen und von arbeyt abwenden*), which happened also to be fallen man's innermost natural inclination. But it is the religious, Linck argued, who make such idleness their special preoccupation. More than any others they are the ones who "strive to escape all of the burdens common to humankind . . . to live above the law . . . free from the usual work and punishments that other men and women must bear."[18] Indeed, Linck makes avoidance of work the devilish motivation behind all of the world's deceit, thievery, tyranny, simony, profiteering, usury, accumulation of benefices, monopolies, and begging.[19]

He carefully distinguished professional itinerant beggars from the deserving local poor. The former are described as people who demand everything from, yet offer nothing to, the communities through which they pass, and Linck advised Altenburg's magistrates against assisting them in any way whatsoever, unless the city fathers believed they had wealth to spare.[20] Among such beggars, mendicant friars are the least tolerable, for unlike other foreign beggars, who base their appeal on such actual misfortune and visible need as illness or blindness, the friars expect handouts on the grounds of their claim to superior spirituality.[21]

The new rule of charity in reformed Altenburg instructed magistrates to render assistance only to truly needy members of the local community, who gave clear evidence of a will to work but were unable to do so because of circumstances beyond their control. In most instances charity was to be given only for a short duration and in the expectation of rehabilitation and, in some cases, repayment (charity came in the form of interest-free loans as well as handouts).

> It is just as when one member of the body becomes sick and cannot perform its customary function for the welfare of others. When this happens, the other members help the sick member regain its strength, or at least make sure that it does not completely deteriorate. . . . All who bear common burdens share with one another both good and

bad, fortune and injury, profit and trouble; for they are one body, whether it be a city, a village, a parish, a house, or another such assembly.[22]

As every community had a moral obligation to its own poor, the Protestants of Altenburg believed that there was no moral justification for any community to allow its poor to wander about burdening the limited resources of other communities. As a way to resolve the political conflicts created by the Reformation, the Diet of Augsburg (1555) later allowed each ruler to choose the religious confession of his land (*cuius regio, eius religio*). In the early 1520s, Linck wanted each community or territory to become the custodian of all of the poor within its borders (a kind of *cuius regio, eius pauperi* doctrine), to solve the problems created by itinerant begging. He extended this principle also to individuals. Each individual had an obligation to remember his relatives and friends in a last will and testament, just as a bishop is responsible for the people within his own diocese. "Orderly love begins with oneself—not that one should love only one's own person, but that one should look first to those who are members of one's own family or group."[23] Itinerant begging, with its attendant crimes and social problems, existed solely because of the unconscionable failure of communities to meet the basic material needs of their most vulnerable members.[24]

As leaders of a religious reform movement opposed to organized or entrepreneurial begging, the reformers understandably involved themselves in shaping legislation for the poor generally. Linck's views gave a Lutheran blessing to the rationalization of welfare then underway in German cities. New ordinances created moral and need tests for applicants, identifying badges for the qualified poor, and a system of loans for the temporarily unemployed, the underpaid, and those who had become economically paralyzed because of too many children.[25] Linck also countered growing callousness to poor people by reminding magistrates of their abiding responsibility to them.

Protestant religious protest against monastic and mendicant begging drew the reformers not only into secular discussions of welfare reform. They also became deeply involved in long-standing controversies over the propriety of tithing and usury and, with the approach of the year 1525, the economic plight of the German peasantry as well. Another Lutheran pamphleteer, the reformer of the town of Eisenach, Jacob

Strauss, argued so forcefully on biblical grounds against honoring contracts bearing interest of any kind that critics accused him of encouraging people to ignore their fair debts. According to Strauss, when poor simple folk enter usurious contracts "in ignorance of the Gospel, having been deceived by . . . priests, scholastics, and monks," they are not beholden to honor those contracts, once the true circumstances have been made known to them.[26] This was heady doctrine in 1523, when peasant unrest was building, and it seemed to identify the Reformation with utopian social protest. On the eve of the great Peasants' Revolt of 1525, Memmingen peasant leaders appealed directly to Luther and to the Bible in support of their sacred right to determine which tithes they would pay.[27]

Although Protestants opposed usury and the use of tithes and endowments for the support of unworthy clergy, they never intended to invalidate feudal contracts or encourage people to withhold fixed secular taxes. But the line between religious and sociopolitical injustice was blurred in the early sixteenth century. As the peasants' protest grew and revolt became imminent, the reformers rushed to defend the right of both lords and clergy to derive their income from the sweat of others, that is, from customary tithes and taxes (*Zehend, tribut oder schatzung*). Although the New Testament did not directly command them, Christians were said to make such payments freely to rulers on the basis of Old Testament examples and in fulfillment of their Christian duty to support temporal authority and order.[28] It was also emphasized that those who pay tithes and taxes to secular governments should expect their money to be used to further God's honor and word, preserve the law of the land, and support the poor.[29]

Chastened by criticism from Luther and Philipp Melanchthon, who felt the pressure of high political authority, Jacob Strauss in the end publicly recast his arguments against usury: if peaceful protest and petition failed to end usurious contracts, he declared, the common man had no recourse but to suffer the economic injustice, because Christians could not properly take the law into their own hands.[30] In the wake of the Peasants' Revolt, Protestant preachers, under the firm orders of their rulers, everywhere proclaimed "Christian freedom" a purely spiritual affair, entailing no release from the traditional bonds of serfdom.

Whether it was by choice or by necessity, out of deep belief or for the sake of public order, the religious reformers found themselves wrestling with basic social problems—from the validity of last wills and testaments to contracts, the conditions of public assistance, and the legitimacy of secular and religious taxes. The social extension of the Reformation proved both irrepressible and immense.

## 2. CONTEMPORARY SELF-IMAGES

A devout Protestant was no casual creation. People who left the old religion for the new either had spiritual needs the church did not fulfill or religious grievances it failed in their minds to redress, or both. What were the specific personal reasons given for turning Protestant? The pamphlets of Nuremberg layman Hans Sachs again provide a clue to the laity's spiritual self-perception at this time and their attitudes to the clergy. And ex-Franciscan Eberlin von Günzburg has much to say about the discontents within traditional clerical ranks, the source of the new Protestant leadership. From very different backgrounds their comments delineate the role played by changing cultural and religious values in burgher and clerical circles at the height of the Reformation.

In 1524, Sachs wrote a lively exposé of monastic vows by two outraged laymen. Despite the anticlerical title—*A Conversation About the Illusory Works of the Cloistered and the Vows by Which They Blaspheme the Blood of Christ and Believe Themselves to Be Holy*—the drama says more about the audacious self-confidence inspired in the laity by the Reformation than it does about the shortcomings of the traditional religious orders. Three speakers appear: Brother Heinrich, a Franciscan monk; Peter, a Lutheran baker; and Hans, a shoemaker, who speaks for the author. As in Protestant pamphlets generally, ordinary people here attain an unusual prominence as authorities on Christian doctrine and as examples of virtuous living.[31]

The dialogue opens with the appearance of Brother Heinrich, who comes begging candles. Peter quotes to him Deuteronomy 15 ("There shall be no beggars among you") and declares that he gives alms only to the local poor who are willing to work as best they can. Thus rebuked, Brother Heinrich calls Peter a "Lutheran," but Peter protests that he is simply "evangelical." Brother Heinrich then recites the Bible's admonitions to charity so impressively that Peter is moved to offer him a penny. To Peter's surprise, he refuses to take it on the grounds that Franciscan vows prevent him from so much as touching money. Whereupon Peter and Hans interrogate Brother Heinrich thoroughly on each of his vows, beginning with poverty.

Hans points out that although the friars take no money directly, they have powerful patrons outside the cloister, who make it possible for their order to amass great wealth, which they then use to buy cardinals' hats and build cloisters rivaling princely estates. As Peter puts it, "You profiteer, but under your hoods." The friars and monks, who are healthy and able to work, thus impoverish ordinary laity by diverting charity from the truly needy and the sick to themselves.[32] Peter here directs his protest as much against aristocratic lords and merchants as against the cloisters they patronize—a long standing alliance of wealth and piety that he claims harms ordinary people. Had Sachs known his church history better, his protagonists might also have cited to Brother Heinrich the *Testament* (1226) of St. Francis of Assisi, the founder of the Franciscan Order, who enjoined its members "to give a good example and avoid idleness" by learning a secular trade and begging only when work was unavailable to them.[33]

Unbending, Brother Heinrich hastens to point out that the Bible permits the spiritual worker a just reward (Matthew 10) and that cloisters do provide free meals daily to the needy poor. True, the cloisters dispense "spiritual goods," like vigils and Masses for the dead, more liberally to the laity than they do material goods, but that is only because they have spiritual goods in much greater abundance. Astonished by this apology, Peter interjects that the food the poor receive at the cloisters amounts only to the scraps the monks themselves will not eat, and their touted spiritual goods are "sold," not given away: anniversary Masses and other memorial sacraments require endowments.[34]

As for celibacy, the second vow of the religious, Brother Heinrich marshals his own list of the physical trials and sacrifices the cloistered must endure. Monks wear inferior clothing held together by rope; they have no linens; they go barefoot or wear clumsy wooden shoes, are tonsured, forego bathing, have no feather beds on which to sleep, take half of their meals without meat, have no pewter dishes from which to eat, and are bound to practice silence and spend up to five hours a day standing and kneeling in choir. Plus they must rise early in the morning for matins.

Flabbergasted again by such argument, Peter responds to the friar's litany with heartfelt emotion—the kind that turned smoldering resentment against the church into open revolt in the 1520s: "I and my fellow workers must labor all day and we eat poorly. Rarely are we in bed at matins, and if we are, my children sing matins to me. I live in a much harder order than you."[35] Only a brief passing comment made in a contrived dialogue, but in fact an oration on the anticlericalism of the age!

Turning to the final religious vow, obedience, Hans and Peter scold Brother Heinrich for feigning a higher obedience than that of ordinary Christians. Scripture, they maintain, subjects Christians to only two vows: a profession of faith all make (or have made for them) at their baptism and an oath of allegiance to secular government (Romans 13, Matthew 22); no higher vow exists for the religious life. In claiming allegiance to a higher vow, the religious simply seek to escape the subjection to secular rule that is the lot of ordinary men and women and avoid taxes, rents, and other burdens of civic life.[36] In this way the clergy actually become less obedient to God and man than the laity. In a sarcastic comment on the funeral customs of the day, Peter says the religious have become so arrogant that they try to clothe the laity in their habit at the approach of death.

> The Franciscans have a shortcut [to perfection for the laity]; they put a gray hood on one who is dying and make a monk out of him, then they shave and bathe him, so that he may pass as one who is "full" [*voller*, drunkard], I mean as one who is "perfect" [*volkommner*], into heaven—yes, like a cow into a mousehole.[37]

Brother Heinrich assures Peter and Hans that if it's true, as they say, that his vows won't get him to heaven, he'll hang up his cowl on a fencepost and throw stones at it. Peter and Hans urge him to forsake the cloister. But Brother Heinrich says he is too old for that even if he wanted to, and he knows no other work; he has been a monk too long. At that, Hans promises to send him a hatchet with which he can work in the world with his own hands and discover for the first time in his life the meaning of true poverty, chastity and obedience to God.[38]

At dialogue's end, then, the common labor of a baker and a shoemaker is declared more God-pleasing than the works done under celibate vows. Two ordinary, Bible-wise laymen are presented as being more religious in their daily work than the most observant members of the church's most exemplary order.

At the opposite pole from the radiant, secular self-esteem of Sachs's laity, we find the near self-hatred of Eberlin von Günzburg's clergy. Eberlin, a Franciscan friar who converted to Lutheranism between 1521 and 1522, distributed *The Lamentations of Seven Pious but Disconsolate Priests Who No One Can Comfort* in May 1521, a pamphlet that pretends to be a transcript of a conversation among seven priests who gather in secret to discuss the most burdensome aspects of the priesthood.

For the first priest, celibacy is that burden. In graphic detail he recounts his own unsuccessful struggle against the demons of sex: his sensuous dreams, nocturnal emissions, masturbation, lechery, and finally adultery with a married woman, which became doubly grievous to his conscience because he continued to befriend her cuckolded husband throughout the affair. Guilt-ridden, he left her and took a concubine. But that relationship brought him no relief from sin, because it too was illegal, and he forced his lover to practice birth control. She died, and he took another concubine with whom he claims to have lived for twenty years and by whom he has had seventeen children. Church authority, the priest points out, disapproves of the arrangement, but the bishop tolerates his concubine as long as he pays the prescribed penitential fee or "whore tax" (*hurenzinss*). "Our bishop might better accept my having ten whores than one wife." The laity, too, tolerate clerical concubines, "the way stableboys become accustomed to dung."[39] This priest feels deeply that his life contradicts both his conscience and the gospel he preaches; and he personally agonizes over the hardships his children must face because of the stigma of illegitimacy.

> Thus am I entangled: on the one hand, I cannot live without a wife; on the other, I am not permitted to have a wife. So I am forced to live a publicly shameful life to the detriment of my soul and my honor and to the damnation of many who take offense at me [namely, by refusing to receive the sacraments from his hands]. How shall I preach about chastity and promiscuity, adultery and knavish behavior, when my whore goes to church and is seen on the streets and my bastards sit before my eyes? How shall I read the Mass under such circumstances?[40]

In a companion pamphlet of the same year, Eberlin, commenting very probably on his own personal experience under vows, described the celibate life as a daily nagging of conscience and unrest of mind, by which all joy becomes suffering, all consolation saddening, all sweetness bitter. The celibate regime, he cries, dulls and deadens the human senses, hardens the heart, and restrains natural honesty leaving one in the end in so uncivil and inhumane a state, and so guilt-ridden and remorseful, that one hates salvation and the good in one's life and longs for misfortune.[41] Clerical marriage, not surprisingly, was one of the first and most successful reforms in Saxony and Switzerland, as prominent a part of the Protestant agenda as justification by faith. And the depth of the resentment over enforced celibacy explains why the leadership of the Reformation came so freely out of traditional clerical ranks.[42]

Eberlin's second priest is disconsolate over the richness of his benefice (*pfrunden gut oder Pfaffen narung*). He believes that the clergy, like noblemen, lead idle lives and live off the "bloody sweat" of poor working people in violation of the Bible's command to earn one's living by one's own hands. His discomfort is only intensified by his congregation's acceptance of clerical idleness; some of his parishioners even encourage their children to become priests so that they, too, might have an easy and secure life. And they ridicule priests who work with their hands as "peasant priests" (*buren pfaffen*).

This priest resents even more the fact that he is supported by usury, the ill-gotten gain with which rich people endow benefices for the clergy and try to buy their way into heaven. And he also finds his conscience burdened by church laws that divide up clerical territory, granting local monopolies for certain religious services within a region, a kind of extortion.[43] Like the first priest, this one, too, both resents himself and senses his parishioners' resentment of him.

> I should teach people to work, yet I remain idle. I must teach them to befriend one another freely, yet I make them pay for their baptism. I should teach them to live securely and trust God for their daily bread, like the birds in the air, yet my own nourishment is assured sixfold.[44]

Fraudulent religious services (*tempeldienst*) weigh most heavily on the conscience of the third priest. He regards the Mass as helpful neither to the living nor to the dead, and the special vigils, Masses, and eternal flames (candles) for the dead to be absolutely useless, the laity's trust in them folly. By such deceptive rites Christian services become "more insane" than those of pagans.[45] This priest, like his fellows, feels trapped in a profession he no longer respects, yet cannot leave without economic consequences he lacks the courage to face.

The fourth priest bemoans the failure of traditional preaching. The laity are now better educated and no longer believe the "good sermon books" mandated by the church from which he preaches.[46] Although both his conscience and "the common laity" demand biblical preaching from him, he fears violence against his person should he preach in the new evangelical manner. He is damned whichever way he turns. "If I do not preach [the Bible], I cannot in good conscience remain a pastor. Yet, if I do preach Christian truth, I contradict my own life, risk punishment from ecclesiastical and secular authorities, and incur the wrath of worldly wisdom and piety."[47]

For the fifth priest, the clergy's loss of honor and respect has become the great burden of office. "When one today hears the word 'priest,' " he laments, "it brings to mind a soulless, godless man who is drunken, lazy, greedy, quarrelsome, defensive, whorish, and adulterous"; no longer can he show himself tonsured in public without fear of being assaulted by his flock.[48] Reform-minded clergy everywhere have their hands tied. They take counsel at their peril from the writings of apostate reformers like Luther, Melanchthon, or Andreas Karlstadt. But neither can they turn for guidance to their clerical superiors, the monasteries, or the universities, "for they would be the first to persecute us, if they knew who we were." Despite his obvious discontent, this priest, too, trembles at the prospect of leaving the priesthood. "Who then will feed me? I cannot work, and I am ashamed to beg; I have become accustomed to a good life, and a priest's fare is not bad."[49]

The sixth priest is so convinced of imminent persecution, he thinks it a miracle that the laity have not yet stoned the clergy. He recalls the warning of his great uncle, also a priest, to his father when the two discussed sending him into the priesthood: "it would be better to drown the boy than to let him become a priest, for before forty years have passed, dogs will be urinating on us priests."[50]

The final disconsolate priest in Eberlin's drama turns out actually to be a priest's helper, who discovers to his great dismay that even innocent bystanders like himself must suffer the opprobrium of the present anti-clerical climate.

In a companion piece, Eberlin proposed temporary measures short of overt Protestantism for each of the afflicted priests. For those burdened

by celibacy he recommended a secret marriage.[51] Priests disturbed by
ill-funded benefices may concentrate on the many good things an honest
priest still can do, such as reading and teaching the Bible, avenging the
exploited, monitoring taxes and the practices of the marketplace, and
correcting, binding, and illuminating books. Priests who find themselves
in positions of authority can perform many useful chores and set examples of diligence. As pastors, they can avoid past errors, omit wrongful
services, and enlighten religious devotion when opportunities to do so
arise.[52] Priests wishing to eliminate certain practices altogether are advised to approach that goal with patience, remembering how the early
church accommodated the weak, tolerating pagan and Jewish celebrations, such as Lammas (originally a pagan harvest festival that became
the Christian celebration of Saint Peter's deliverance from prison), New
Year's Day, and All Saint's Day, as well as non-Christian practices like
planting linden trees near churches and carrying banners in processions.[53]
As for priests' discontent with traditional sermons, nothing prevents
them from preaching the Gospel and defending it when others contradict
or attack it.

In the end Eberlin counseled against clerical despair and cynicism.
Trustworthy bishops with reform at heart did exist, though their official
position forced them to proceed cautiously and at times appear to oppose
reform.[54] Those fearful of attack by outraged laity Eberlin consoled by
pointing out Luther's condemnation of such tactics; most laity still stood
ready to protect "patient, friendly, and honorable priests." As for the
unfortunate priests' helpers compromised by their masters' reputations,
Eberlin advised flight and a search for better employment.[55]

## 3. A REALISTIC REFORM

The temptation to carry evangelical ideals to unrealistic conclusions was
real enough in the 1520s. But Protestant spokesmen also understood
that attacks on ecclesiastical wealth could not be extended to the rich
generally, nor criticism of mendicants to all of the poor. To be rich was
not necessarily to be irreformably papist, nor was being impoverished
and on welfare necessarily to live unjustly off the sweat of others. As
there were unconscionable lords and undeserving beggars, there were

also godly rich and godly poor, and the reformers weighed their criticism accordingly. On the whole, they recommended neither abject accommodation to the socioeconomic status quo nor, much less, communalistic social engineering. They sought instead a middle position short of social tumult on the one hand, and efforts to erect a New Jerusalem on the other.

A case in point is Hans Sachs's third dialogue of 1524: *The Argument of the Romanists Against the Profiteering and Other Public Offenses of the Christian Community [of Nuremberg]*, composed with both the city's confessional divisions and the incipient Peasants' Revolt in the countryside very much in mind. The pamphlet appeared at a crucial point in the Reformation's ascendancy in Nuremberg, a city in which, at the turn of the century, one of ten people was a priest, a monk, a nun, or a friar. In the period between the second Nuremberg Reichstag (February 1524) and the public disputation that made the Reformation official there (March 1525), the city dissolved its monasteries; required the clergy to assume the normal responsibilities of citizenship; abolished fasting, the cult of the saints, and many traditional holy days; introduced Luther's German Mass; and recognized clerical marriage. Beneath the obvious propaganda of both Catholic and Protestant spokesmen—a prominent feature of Sachs's pamphlet—lies a detailed report on the moral and social problems of contemporary Nuremberg, which the city's Catholic critics (the "Romanists") attributed almost entirely to the Reformation. Writing as a spokesman for the growing Protestant majority, Sachs attempted to answer such criticism.

As Sachs sized up Nuremberg Catholics, they had failed to refute evangelical doctrine by argument and so now sought instead to undermine it by focusing on the moral failings of the many in the city who professed it. By shifting criticism from doctrine to life, these apologists hoped to dissuade the wavering from turning Protestant.[56] Two speakers appear in the dialogue: Romanus, the Catholic critic, and Reichenburger, a well-to-do evangelical citizen.

Romanus indicts the Protestant citizenry of Nuremberg both high and low, both lay and clerical, for a variety of moral and social failings, but above all for greed and profiteering, faults he claims Protestants have one-sidedly and hypocritically ascribed to the Catholic clergy alone. He declares of the Protestants that, despite their vaunted reforms,

I still find no good works among you. Indeed, you permit your bodies to do as they please. It is now customary [in Nuremberg] not to go to confession, fast, pray, attend church, give alms, or make pilgrimages. You also eat meat [whenever you wish] and flee the cloisters. You continue unashamedly such heathen offenses as greed, adultery, whoring, enmity, rebelliousness, anger, factions, envy, hatred, backbiting, murder, dishonesty, idle amusements, blasphemy, drunkenness, dancing, pride, fornication, gambling, and disobedience. From such fruits one must judge that you are not Christians, but heathen.[57]

Romanus dwells especially on continuing economic crimes and injustice. Protestant merchants, he charges, buy futures on wine, grain, and salt and hoard these staples purely for individual use and profit. Deceptive sales abound as inferior or spoiled goods are marketed as whole, and throughout the city false weights, measures, and accounting are in use. Spices are controlled by monopolies. Merchants and publishers cleverly exploit workers, especially pieceworkers; falsely accusing them of inferior work that forces them to sell their products at a loss, they pay them less than fair wages. Against such practices workers have no defense, for many have loans to repay and fear nothing so much as the loss of their jobs. Romanus also finds trade riddled with usury. When one buys something on credit over a six-month period, he complains, one must pay an additional 5 or 6 percent, though the fifth chapter of Matthew's Gospel teaches that one should give freely to a needy neighbor.[58]

Romanus's list of injustices seems endless. He cites the city's harsh treatment of the indebted poor, who are cast into prison and have their few remaining possessions confiscated. In the law courts, false witnessing and swearing of oaths are commonplace, and the law invariably takes the side of the rich: "where there is money, there is a lawyer and a favorable verdict; where there is no money, there is neither a lawyer nor an acquittal." All such practices contradict the Bible, which teaches patience with the poor (Deut. 24) and instructs creditors to tear up their unpaid bills (Isa. 58), return their notes, and take nothing from them by force (Exod. 16). "The Gospel talks everywhere only of love, love, love."[59] If a Reformation had occurred in Nuremberg, Romanus could find no positive evidence of it in the moral behavior of the citizenry.

In response, Reichenburger defended the society the Protestants were creating. He agrees that hoarding staple goods for personal gain is unchristian; and he too opposes the exploitation of workers. Still, he does not believe that defiant workers—those who cannot be paid enough when they are needed, yet refuse to turn a hand once hired—should go unpunished.[60] He agrees that lending should serve a neighbor's need and not reap unconscionable profits; but he is just as quick to point out that a lender could profit at least 5 or 6 percent over a six-month period from the money a borrower denies him for investment—an argument with sound legal grounds in late medieval economic practice. Nor does Reichenburger find it regrettable that the poor are dealt with harshly, certainly not in the case of chronic debtors (*böser zaler*), drunks, gamblers, and whores, who use what they have to ill purpose and ignore all overtures to straighten out their lives.[61]

In defense of the Protestant work ethic, Reichenburger asserts that one can be rich and still not place one's heart in riches. True Christians are good stewards of their possessions and know they take nothing with them when they die; thus they do not confuse wealth with godliness. And they are prepared to live without their possessions should God will it, while continuing to help the deserving poor as long as they have the means to do so.[62]

That there are charitable as well as selfish rich in Nuremberg Reichenburger attributes to the Reformation, claiming that many had begun to use their wealth in a Christian way since the Gospel became clear to them. By contrast, he strongly opposes unrestricted charity to the poor,[63] a policy he believes creates many idle and useless people, and he defends the city's decision to deny alms to mendicants. Turning the tables completely on the Reformation's critics, he traces the city's limited moral transformation not to any failure of evangelical teaching, but to the persistence of "the lying doctrine and human commandments" of the old church—an accusation Romanus quickly recognizes to be a homiletical coverup of the city's immorality for which he, Romanus, would just as unfairly hold the Reformation responsible.[64]

In conclusion, Reichenburger lectured Romanus on the lunacy of expecting too much of society on this side of eternity, the impossible moral ideals to which the old church so liked to subject Christians. "You keep asking for signs, signs—signs of the worship of God and the labor of love. Don't you understand that the kingdom of God is invisible, that one cannot say, 'Behold, it is here, it is there?' It is a kingdom within the heart."[65]

Scholars have interpreted Sachs's dialogue as evidence of the Reformation's accommodation to reigning burgher morality and established political power on the eve of the Peasants' Revolt—a restriction of reform to a benign spiritual sphere and the surrender of controversial social and political goals in exchange for respectability and security.[66] But Reichenburger is more accurately seen as one who speaks for a movement that was trying to be realistic about people and society and cognizant of the disruptive consequences of unworkable moral, social, and political ideals. He does not believe that such recognition means acquiescence to injustice or any stinting of generosity toward the poor. Yet he is convinced that a religion teaching human perfectibility and expecting the Christianization of society will neither deeply influence the real world nor survive long within it.

Here, then, was a reformation that refused to sanction utopian standards in either the private or the public sphere; the communal conscience no more than the individual conscience was to be burdened by impossible ideals. Far from distancing the Reformation from worthy moral and social goals, Sachs merely rejected efforts to hitch it to ideals that society was not in his view obliged to pursue and incapable of attaining even if it did. Particularly for a layman like Sachs, the godly society had above all to be a viable society.

To ask of the first Protestants, as some present-day historians do, that in the fragile world of the 1520s they champion social reforms on the scale of a twentieth-century egalitarian society is simply to demand that they forfeit their own vision of reform and die for the truths we hold to be self-evident. By such criticism we burden the past with our own bad conscience and blame it for failing to realize our dreams.

# III

# From Propaganda to Law:
## The Reformation Enacted

# 5. Gaining a Big Stick: Ordinance and Catechism

W hether in the sixteenth century or in the twentieth, the first and most important measure of a reform's success must be its ability to become law. Even then many people still may not take its teaching to heart. But few of the unconvinced will ever do so if a reform fails to gain legal status and a presence in reigning institutions. Before a reform can become a public moral force, it must become legal. Institutionalization brings with it the opportunity to inculcate methodically one's values in the young, both at church and at school, and thereby to shape the behavior of future generations. Enshrined in law, a reform can change people's behavior—even if they begrudge the change.

Despite the insatiable ambition and abiding discontent of reformers, they probably accomplish all they can reasonably expect once their programs have been mandated by law. As their reforms become the law of the land, they take on a life of their own, beyond the control of their creators. To reformers in any age, the experience is both exhilarating and demoralizing—exhilarating because their ideals at last gain the force of mandate; but demoralizing because those ideals are now at the mercy of the common man. Success brings both triumph and a new vulnerability.

To enshrine reform in law obviously requires political support, which in turn depends on a ruler's conviction that reform also serves his own interest. If a regime is reluctant or opposed to reform and can neither be converted nor overturned, then reformers must find ways to coopt and cultivate it. Whether in the end rulers support reform out of true belief and perhaps at their own political risk, or accept it only grudgingly with an eye to making it serve their own political ends, the reigning "establishment" is as necessary to a reform's success as the reformers themselves. Rulers, therefore, become as much a target of reformist propaganda as the masses at large, and the reformers' relationships with the ruling class are equally many and diverse.

The revolution wrought by Protestant pamphleteers gained structure and respectability through the favor of magistrates and princes. New political and moral ordinances gave the Reformation a public face. Without them, the Reformation would have existed only in the hearts of its followers—a crushed rebellion barely remembered. But once evangelical doctrine became law, the "human traditions" decried by the pamphleteers as unbiblical and ungodly became illegal and impracticable as well. Henceforth, in Protestant lands any who publicly embraced such teachings could expect rebuke and punishment. Having long spoken loudly without a big stick, the reformers, as the new clerical elite, found themselves able to speak softly, confident of the support of their new political ally. For the many laity who had found Luther's gospel of faith and love an appealing transformation of traditional religious belief and practice, its newfound legality gave new life to their long-restrained if not quite defeated piety.

## MAGISTRATES AS BELIEVERS

Already in the fifteenth century German princes had gained a reputation for being virtual "popes" within their realms. They controlled or influenced much of public religious life, from the sale of indulgences (from which they took a cut of the profits) to the appointment of local high clergy. Such secular involvement in religion only increased with the success of the Reformation. In Protestant territories, lay-clerical courts or consistories, under the firm control of secular magistrates or princely agents, displaced the traditional ecclesiastical courts and episcopal authorities that had regulated moral behavior and religious orthodoxy during the Middle Ages.[1] As pamphleteers, the reformers had urged secular rulers to intervene in the reform of the church; now, as a new clerical establishment, the same reformers elevated their rulers to de facto high spiritual office.

This was particularly true of Martin Luther. Instinctively he knew that church and state should stay at arm's length; but he also recognized that his reforms could succeed only if the two embraced. His solution was imaginative, if in the end ineffective. During the early years of the Reformation, when the need for sure protectors and strong internal discipline became matters of life and death for the young Protestant churches, Luther appealed directly to the German princes to act on behalf of reform as "emergency bishops" (*Notbischöfe*). He chose that phrase carefully, stressing the exceptional nature of a ruler's role in religious reform and linking this exalted title not to his secular office, but to his membership in the church.[2] Theoretically a ruler would serve the purpose of reform, but in such a way that he could not lay claim to it. The sacred and the profane would thus be both interdependent and distinct.

Such a fine distinction was lost on the Swiss Reformation. In Zurich, unlike Wittenberg, theocratic impulses, derived from Old Testament examples of cooperation between prophets and kings, and the Swiss republican political tradition led to far greater cohesion between the new church and the old state and between the true Christian and the good citizen. Zwingli treated rulers like biblical kings; they were "servants of God in the place of God under the guidance of Christ,"[3] a definition that magnified magisterial authority and clerical compliance. In Zurich, the magistrates had as primary and abiding a responsibility for religion as did the clergy.

Despite Luther's desire to keep politics and religion distinct in Germany, princely power and clerical ambition prevented it. Luther's theological distinctions notwithstanding, magistrates in Lutheran lands came to play as great a role in shaping religious life as they did in Switzerland. In Württemberg during the 1530s, the subjects of the Lutheran prince addressed him as "tutor of the church" (*nutricius ecclesiae*), and he exercised broad powers over religion through a loyal consistory composed of noblemen, burghers, and theologians. The prince financed the parish churches, educated their clergy, and monitored the purity of doctrine and worship.[4] The new clergy stood their ground as best they could, reminding rulers of their subservience to the Word of God. At times they did so subtly, especially when a local ruler was involved. But when the ruler in question was distant and unlikely to strike, the new clergy could sound like Old Testament prophets facing down Pharaoh. For example, during the confessional standoff of the mid-1530s, after the emperor had suspended his efforts to force Protestant lands back into the Catholic fold, rumors circulated in Württemberg that he planned to break the truce and attack Protestant cities. Responding to such rumors, the Württemberg reformer Johannes Brenz denounced the apparent imperial and papal plot with the dire warning, "You may strangle our people and burn our books, but the gospel of Jesus Christ . . . which is pure and clear among us, cries out in defiance of all human power: 'Do not tread on me!' . . . The emperor may be the most powerful man on earth, but everyone knows there is a majesty in heaven that excels all human and earthly majesty."[5]

From Wittenberg, Luther's loyal colleague Philipp Melanchthon, a famed educator and author of the major Lutheran confessions, admonished Saxon princes and lords in much the same vein, urging them to eradicate "by God's command" the idolatry of traditional religion and to set true doctrine in its place, defying any bishop or prince who might dare to stand in their way.[6] In 1546, when the Lutheran elector John Frederick of Saxony was under the imperial ban and Protestants were on the verge of defeat by imperial armies (John Frederick became the emperor's prisoner in April 1547), the Saxon reformer Nicholas of Amsdorf put the following prayer in the mouth of his embattled prince:

> My fight is against false doctrine. . . . Inasmuch as both the emperor and the pope are seeking to destroy the true preaching of God's Word and replace pure doctrine and the true worship of God with lies and idolatry, we [princes] must spare no sacrifice to spoil their terrible plans. For the sake of our subjects and posterity [we must] risk all that we have on behalf of God's dear Word and Name.[7]

The struggle between church and state for political sovereignty reached far back into the Middle Ages and historically had been fought out locally as well as nationally and internationally. Of course the politicians involved, from urban magistrates, to regional lords, to kings and emperors, had their own personal reasons for wanting to wear miters. Still, a very great part of the arguments in defense of the Reformation propounded by spokesmen for the new Protestant regimes reiterated the arguments of the pamphleteers virtually verbatim. From city halls to royal palaces the political speech of the age became infused with the propaganda of the pamphlet wars of the 1520s, particularly the appeal to Scripture as a weapon against entrenched tradition. When, for example, Elector Frederick the Wise and Crown Prince John Frederick of Saxony met leaders of the Saxon clergy in Weimar in 1525, there to create the Wittenberg Reformation ordinance of that year, the rulers proclaimed the first duty of the clergy to be preaching the Gospel "pure, clean, and clear [*lauter, rein, und klar*], without any admixture of human doctrines."[8] The first article of the comprehensive Frankfurt reform ordinance of 1525 issued the same directive: that city preachers "proclaim the Word of God and holy Gospel unmixed with human statements, by which [preaching] the people shall be made strong and set free."[9]

At roughly the same time (1524) religious conflict in Brandenburg forced Margrave Casimir to hold discussions with Protestant and Catholic apologists on twenty-five disputed issues, both petty and paramount, a virtual master list of the pamphlet debates. It would strike us today as more than strange if the governors of the various American states spent days debating with theologians the following laundry list of doctrinal topics:

> the proper number of sacraments; annual confession and communion; auricular confession; the reservation of certain sins for higher church authority to absolve; the denial of the Eucharistic cup to the laity; the church's alteration of Christ's words of institution in the sacrament of the Eucharist; the display of the Eucharistic elements in monstrances; endowed Masses for the living and the dead; holding the Mass in Latin; baptizing children with Latin formulas; forbidding priests to have wives; the degrees of kinship alleged to impede marriage without papal dispensation; the right of monks and nuns to leave their cloisters and marry; whether the mere preaching of God's Word and administration of the sacraments made one a pastor and a priest; whether faith in Christ sufficed for salvation; whether the will was free in salvation; the efficacy of prayer to the Virgin Mary; whether her image should appear in the churches; the propriety of certain religious ceremonies; whether religious holidays and fast days should be mandated; fasting regulations; whether one must obey papal, episcopal, and conciliar decrees that lack the support of Scripture; whether the Bible is its own best interpreter; and whether the Roman church or its councils may properly be called "the holy Christian Church."

That the mighty margrave of Brandenburg should have to ponder such matters attests the success of the pamphleteers in bringing the religious conflict into the highest circles of government. And the margrave's directive for its resolution at the end of the debate indicates that he not only shared their concerns, but had learned well from them, for he invoked their test of Scripture:

## A Christian Testament and Blessed Death of the Holy Confessor of Christ and His Gospel, John Frederick, Duke of Saxony [1503–1554].

*Behold, I am about to die, but God will be with you and bring you again into the land of your fathers. Genesis 48.*

*I have been taught and truly believe that a time is set for every person to die; it is written that God has determined the time for each. I know now that the time set for me has come, that the day and the hour are now.*

*As a creature before my Creator and a servant before his Lord, I am prepared to die. I await the hour of my death freely and happily as a Christian who stands by the Gospel in faith in Christ, not like a Jew, a Turk, a papist, a Mamluk, an Interimist, an Adiaphorist, an Osiandrist, a Caritatist,\* or an unbeliever. Moreover, as did that true man of God, the patriarch Jacob, on his deathbed, so do I now on mine confess with both my heart and my tongue that I die as one recognized to be a man and friend of God and an enemy of the pope, the Antichrist, having for my part, as the apostle says, fought the good fight, finished the race, and kept the faith.*

*I have already sent my wife, the princess, home to the Lord in heaven, where I will soon see her again. I now end my life on this, my last day, to leave the world behind and go to my Father, where the crown of righteousness awaits me, and which the Lord, the righteous Judge, will bestow on me [when] that day [of judgment comes]. And O you young princes, my dear sons, do not grieve for me without hope. It is true that your beloved mother is in heaven and that within three hours I will be with her. But this should not cause you to despair or to be dejected, for I have ordered and arranged another father for you.\*\**

*Inasmuch as I am a poor, dispossessed prince and am unable to leave you great wealth, property, cities, land, and people, I ask in my testament that you be aware that I do bequeath you a good reputation and a gracious God. I know that the God and Father of our Lord Jesus Christ will be with you. Be confident that God will richly restore to you some of the land and inheritance of your ancestors that was taken from me because of my confession and imprisonment.\*\*\* God will return you to the land of your fathers and give you both temporal and eternal life. May the angel of God, Jesus Christ, who has saved me from all evil, bless you, his dear children. I now commend you to him as I go to my God. Amen.*

\*The last four terms refer to intra-Lutheran heresies of the liberal faction; the duke places himself squarely in the camp of the orthodox wing of the new church.

\*\*That is, he has appointed a guardian for them, to whom they owe the allegiance and obedience that sons owe to a father.

\*\*\*A reference to his capture and imprisonment by the emperor in 1547, when he was forced to surrender his electoral possessions around Wittenberg.

Ein Chriſtlich Teſtament vnnd Seliges Abſterben des Heiligen Confeſſoris oder Bekenners Chriſti vnnd ſeines Euangelij / Johann Friedrichs Hertzog zu Sachſſen.

Gebruckt zu Magdeburgl durch Pancratz Kempff.

---

Pancratz Kempf, Nuremberg, in *The German Single-Leaf Woodcut, 1550–1600: A Pictorial Catalogue*, vol. 2, ed. Walter L. Strauss (New York: Abaris Books, 1975), p. 503.

It is the sincere command of his Grace that throughout his kingdom and in all of his lands the holy Gospel and divine Word of the Old and New Testaments shall be preached clearly and purely, according to a right and true understanding, and that nothing contrary shall be preached that might lead the community of the Christian people into error and faction.[10]

When Landgrave Philip of Hesse suppressed Hessian cloisters in the late 1520s, he justified his action by appeal to still another favored motif of the pamphleteers: the work ethic of Saint Paul. According to this moral principle, Christians are forbidden to lead idle lives (*unordig sein*) and must earn their daily bread with their own hands. "What else is it not to work, yet still to live well," asks the landgrave's mandate, "but to have a good, lazy life for oneself? And it remains such even though one brightens it up, or, more fittingly, covers it up with long useless prayers and songs in choir that most do not understand."[11] Claiming fully three-quarters of the cloistered on his land to be foreigners and declaring cloistered life to be "unchristian," Philip suppressed Hessian monasteries and nunneries "for the sake of the honor of God, Christ, and the Gospel and out of love for one's neighbor." He viewed his action as a fulfillment of the Diet of Speyer's imperial order to rulers in 1526 to settle the religious divisions within their lands "so as to be able to answer for their actions before God and the emperor."[12] The landgrave believed he could answer before God.

Pamphleteer rhetoric also became law in the Brunswick reform ordinance of 1531, prepared by the Wittenberg pastor Johannes Bugenhagen. It gave special attention to the "human works" and superstitions that the pamphleteers took such delight in exposing. Declaring it the devil's work when people believe sin to exist where there is none and deem things holy that clearly are not,[13] the ordinance condemned numerous "contrivances" of the old church for masquerading as God's will and fostering superstition in the place of faith, among them the staple practices of popular Catholicism:

[In the old church people] do not place their hearts and faith in God, but rather in cowls, special foods, holy water, holy candles, consecrated herbs, indulgences, prized little prayers, precious Friday fasting, confraternities, the pilgrimage of Saint James, the rosary, and observances, rules, and clothing, none of which God has ever commanded. . . . The more holy water we had, the more poltergeists; we warded off thunder with candles and herbs and practiced magic with herbs in our beds and in the cellar by the beer, unaware that all of these things were contrived against the grace of our Lord Jesus Christ, who alone takes away our sin, and also against Christian prayer, by which we should call out to our dear Father through Christ for all our bodily and spiritual needs. For that is what will help us, not water, candles, and herbs.[14]

The 1533 Brandenburg/Nuremberg ordinance, composed by the Lutheran pastor Johannes Brenz, also complained about "false, fabricated sins," such as eating meat on Fridays, cutting wood on religious holidays, touching the consecrated Eucharistic cup, "and other such foolishness," while it dismissed as "unnecessary and childish" the elaborate funeral Masses. The ordinance devoted one of its articles to "human doctrines that terrify, burden, and hold consciences captive" by commanding people to do what God has not.[15] When the official Basel confession of 1534 recalled the city's introduction of the Reformation in 1529, it described it as "the complete removal or reform of every abuse, error, and perverted worship of God that lacked a basis in divine Truth."[16]

In 1537, Augsburg's burgomaster and city council defended their removal of traditional religious teaching and ceremonies from local churches to the Catholic emperor, who of course strongly opposed such changes. In doing so they stressed their responsibility as lay Christian rulers. Appealing to "the holy divine biblical Scriptures," they declared that "it falls to us, the magistrates, at the risk of our soul's salvation, to remove and in no way to tolerate or permit to continue what has been shown in divine Scripture to be against God and his holy Word."[17] The city's new moral ordinance of the same year declared it to be the magistrates' Christian duty not only to eradicate harmful ceremonies from the house of God, but to remove "all gods and idolatry" from the hearts of their subjects as well, so that each might lead an enlightened and blameless Christian life within the community of God.[18] To this end, a variety of punishments was established "in body, life, honor, and/or property" for any who attempted to reinstate discarded traditional practices or who was found to be "dilatory or negligent in hearing the preaching of the Word, attending the teaching of the holy Gospel [catechism], or joining in other Christian church practices."[19]

Just how deeply the new religious message might penetrate the policies and rhetoric of rulers, whose piety could be as profound as their political opportunism, can be seen in the response of Elizabeth, duchess of Brunswick/Lüneburg, to the failure of the ecumenical discussions held in Regensburg in 1541. When, after a year of talks, it became clear that neither the reunion of Protestants and Catholics nor a desired reform of traditional practices would be forthcoming, the duchess issued her own reform mandate, directing that the Word of God be unambiguously preached throughout her kingdom and all false and misleading doctrine eradicated. She asks rhetorically,

> Have we not in the past been shamefully led astray from the Gospel and the truth by human commandments and teaching? What did we know about catechism, that is, the moral and religious training of children, before the Gospel reappeared? What did we know about the correct celebration of the Eucharist? When did anyone teach us correctly about the forgiveness of sins, justification, truly good works, and the holy cross? Did not the clergy go about preaching pure fables? Had it not reached the point that forgiveness of sins was being sold for money in a remarkable insult to the merit of Christ? If any would deny this, let him tell us why the indulgence has been so widespread in Germany. Those who would be the heads and regents of the church should long ago have found ways to control such horrible errors and false worship of God. But, alas, no such leadership has been forthcoming, and we poor people go about now as sheep without a shepherd.[20]

In lieu of clerical leadership, the duchess declared the responsibility for church reform to rest with rulers, each to act individually within his or her realm. As her mandate puts it,

> It has always belonged to the office of magistrate to maintain God's Word and true divine services and to protect the common good. Why else would Holy Scripture call those who hold political office and rule over people "gods"? They are so called because they must act in God's place to maintain and promote his Word and true worship, govern society by good and honorable laws, and reward people who are good and punish those who are bad.[21]

On many a specific measure the hot polemics of the pamphleteers reappear in the leaden legal wording of the reform ordinances. An early, comprehensive, and detailed example is the 1523 Elbogen ordinance regulating church and worship. In it the sermon gained priority over the Mass, while traditional processions around the church and the sprinkling of holy water and holy salt were abolished as "ceremonies that divert the people from the true worship of God, which consists of faith and trust in him through his holy Gospel." Laity wishing to receive the Eucharist in both kinds were henceforth to receive it that way—a rejection of the traditional spiritual distinction between the clergy, who received both bread and wine, and the laity, who received only bread. A prior private confession also ceased to be a condition for receiving the sacrament in Elbogen. The ordinance further permitted the local parish to appoint a preacher of its own choosing, provided he could be independently endowed and sworn to preach "the clear, bright, and pure Gospel." The ordinance forbade funeral and anniversary Masses, first on the grounds that "the people, especially the common folk, place more belief and trust in the external ceremonies of burial and remembrance of departed souls than they do in the suffering and re-demption of Christ," and second because the rich hold an unfair advan-tage over the poor in obtaining such Masses. Accusing the church of discriminating against the poor when it sells cemetery plots, the ordi-nance declared the cemetery to be the property of the civic community. Nor might a pastor any longer act against the will of the congregation (*wider ain gemain*), whose members are said to share in the governance of the church, inasmuch as the common body of churchgoers (*gemain kirchmenge*) are "the stewards of the church's material needs" as the pastor is "the keeper of its divine secrets." The ordinance further directed that the sacrament of Baptism henceforth be conducted in German and no longer in Latin, "so that it is not received lightly and in ignorance, as has happened in the past." Also, the pastor was left free to read or to omit the canonical hours. Finally, the Elbogen ordinance obligated the magistrates to provide a sure income for the pastor drawn from the tithe, the priest's penny (paid four times a year), and the city's mill tax, while allowing him also to continue to collect an additional fee for blessing marriages.[22]

Cities and towns that remained solidly Catholic in faith and practice also felt the impact of the pamphleteers. Without embracing the new evangelical doctrines, some shared and acted on a number of the reform-ers' criticisms of the church and the clergy. A case in point is the city of Regensburg, whose 1524 reform decree provides an example of the early Counterreformation response to Protestantism. The magistrates' overriding concern at the time was the sheer number of clergy in the city, whose ranks they sought to thin. They also wanted certain clerical activities to be better regulated, especially the spiritual services for which the laity were taxed or paid fees. The decree directed priests to "proclaim the gospel in the old manner" (*der alten manier*), that is, according to the ancient church councils and the teaching of the magisterial church fathers (saints Augustine, Gregory, and Jerome)—an echo of the imperial mandate of 9 February 1524. Priests were further ordered to wear proper dress, lead honorable lives, and desist from all "commercial activity" (*kauffmanshendel*), while the decree instructed papal legates to take immediate action against offensive clerical behavior. For their part, bishops were admonished not to appoint absentee or unskilled clergy or to ordain any priest who had not first been examined and found fit. The decree further forbade the ordination of new priests and any increase in the number of Masses said by present ones, unless and until outside private funds were obtained to support them. Priests failing to meet their spiritual responsibilities were threatened with the loss of their benefices, while those who had taken wives had to appear before the bishop for punishment. Priests also fell immediately under the city's sumptuary laws, and any convicted of a crime in the city could no longer escape civil punishment by merely paying a fine.

Regarding other clergy in the region, the Regensburg decree confined monks to their cloisters and permitted them to perform religious services within the parish churches only if they came from impoverished cloisters and those involved returned each night to their cloisters. Only with advance permission and by direct invitation might an indulgence preacher any longer enter the city. In an attempt to reduce the number of occasions on which religious festivals might disrupt everyday life, celebrations of saints' days were confined to the locale of each saint's shrine. In an effort to discourage the inflation of episcopal staffs, the Regensburg decree made bishops responsible for provisioning their assistants' every need beyond their basic living expenses. It further condemned simony (the buying or selling of church offices) along with the bestowal of benefices on "soothsayers and magicians," apparently a pejorative description of disreputable clerics. Annual episcopal visitations were demanded and territorial synods (*National Concilia*) scheduled to meet every three years.

As for popular religious practice, the Regensburg decree took steps in an arguably Protestant direction. It made funeral Masses optional, no longer something priests, who profited from them, might dictate to the laity. It prohibited clerical enforcement of fasting laws by excommunication (*nicht beym Bann*) and punishment of the community at large by interdict when a citizen happened to kill a priest. The church's right to collect parochial tithes (*pensionen*) and tithes for the maintenance of benefices (*gotsgaben*) was rescinded. And no longer did the laity have to pay a set fee to have sins absolved (*Beychtgelt*); they had only to give to the church "what came freely from a good will." Nor could the clergy any longer withhold the sacrament from the laity "for any fault"; only murderers, heretics, and the excommunicated could henceforth be turned away. Finally, Regensburg's decree forbade the church to deny a Christian burial to any who had failed to receive the Last Rites, if the person in question was known to have made an Easter confession.[23]

Such reforms addressed long-standing grievances made all the more intolerable to the laity by pamphleteer criticism. Yet they left the Mass and other central teachings of the church firmly in place. By correcting serious church abuses while at the same time affirming its basic doctrines, reform decrees like Regensburg's saved the church from the Reformation in numerous communites during the 1520s and 1530s and set a model for later Tridentine reforms.

Where communities embraced both the new theology of the Reformation and its criticism of traditional church practice, the evolution of the pamphleteers' revolt into a new religious culture could be rapid and thorough. The city of Frankfurt is a case in point. Its reform ordinance of 1525 required the clergy either to marry or to live alone; prohibited mendicant begging and preaching; closed cloisters; declared monks and nuns free to depart their cloisters at will; subjected the clergy to the same civic duties and taxes as the laity; and transferred all income from canceled clerical testaments, benefices, confraternities, and commemorative vigils to a communal treasury or common chest to be dispensed to the needy or for other purposes as the government decreed.[24]

Likewise, the Bern ordinance of 1528 proscribed all religious ceremonies and practices lacking a clear foundation in Scripture and threatened to deprive any cleric who disagreed of his benefice. Describing regional bishops as "self-seeking" and denouncing them for having placed a "burdensome yoke" on their lay charges, the ordinance released cathedral deans and the agents of the bishop's fisc from their oaths of allegiance to episcopal authority; then it rebound them to the new Protestant regime, thereby "converting" by decree the entire standing ecclesiastical bureaucracy! The ordinance further provided for the gradual removal of the Mass and images from city churches, and it mandated the elevation of the sermon to the high point of worship. Among other important provisions were the abolition of Masses for the dead; the dissolution of confraternities (with a promise to negotiate fair compensation for confiscated endowments); an end to obligatory fasting (but with a ten-pound fine for any "ostentatious gluttony" on the traditional fast days!); the barring of new recruits from the cloisters (thus ensuring the cloisters' demise on the deaths of those still remaining within them); and, finally, the freedom of all clergy and religious, monks and nuns as well as priests, to renounce their vows and marry freely.[25]

The 1534 Basel confession of faith also treated tradition harshly. Distinguishing "what is and what is not commanded by God," it placed auricular confession, the prohibition of foods, Lenten fasting, religious holidays, the veneration of saints and images, clerical celibacy, and "similar human creations" among the uncommanded.[26] When in the mid 1530s the magistrates of Augsburg acted to reform religious practice, it must have seemed to contemporaries that the pamphleteers of the previous decade had suddenly become the city's legislators and policemen. Gone from the service of worship was "the papist Mass with its horrible ceremonies," the invocation of the saints, and the veneration of images. Tough new disciplinary measures put an end to what the magistrates called the clergy's "loose living . . . with . . . women and their many other depravities committed with impunity against God . . . and the soul's salvation under the pretense of their famous immunities (*der berümbpten Freyheiten*), scandalous to the common citizenry . . . and [threatening] the peace, profit, and well-being of every citizen."[27] A concurrent report to the emperor by startled Augsburg Catholics complained that the magistrates had "maliciously forbidden" the Mass and the traditional rite of baptism along with other sacraments and revered old customs and ceremonies; they even blockaded the churches and cloisters and removed panels, images, and altars from them, along with their *monumenta* and *epitaphia* to the dead. In addition, Catholics in the city endured repeated insults to their faith in the new Protestant sermons.[28]

In such reform ordinances as those described above, the pamphleteers' image of enlightened laypeople as "spiritual authorities" attained its fullest expression within the new Protestant regimes: the lay magistrates defined a new religious orthodoxy and legally enforced it. They did so with the advice and consent of the new clergy, who also helped implement the new measures. But the end result, like the process itself, was strictly a civil one. Devout Protestant magistrates, like the pamphleteers before them, also vacillated between contradictory images of their subjects. On the one hand, they viewed them as enlightened and sharing their own outrage at clerical abuse; on the other, they believed them to be willing victims of corrupt custom and to require stiff fines and punishments to break away from the bad habits of the past.

The magistrates also understood well the overweening ambition of the new clergy. They took care to dictate the degree and pace of change to them as well, ensuring in the process that the outcome would be neither tumult from below nor a theocracy from above. The Reformation in ordinance and mandate was accordingly more the work of a community's magistrates than of its clergy.

Modern historians err, however, when they portray the Reformation as the abject servant of the German princes. Since the fourteenth century, the princes had been steadily consolidating their power and centralizing their realms; their success was the major political development of the fifteenth and sixteenth centuries. Modern historians understandably prefer to view religious revolt as part and parcel of a larger political process, for it has usually been such in the modern world. But it was not the German magistrates and princes who first created the religious revolt and manipulated it to their advantage at the expense of politically hapless reformers. Rather, it was the evangelical preachers and their congregations who forced upon magistrates and princes a new religious order—creating a situation from which at the outset many magistrates and princes had little to gain personally and out of which they could see coming only division and turmoil within their realms. The magistrates and princes who chose to support Protestant reforms were the real novelties of the age. The portrayal of Protestant clerics as helplessly bullied by or shamelessly toadying to the state is a false caricature of current scholarship. Although politicians had put clerics in their pockets many times before, the Reformation presented the unusual if far from unprecedented phenomenon of politicians being successfully instructed by clerics. The success of the Reformation, not the continuing steady march of German absolutism, was the big story of the sixteenth century, the century's most dramatic and enduring break with the past.


## BENDING THE TWIG

As the political ordinances of the new Protestant regimes turned pamphlet criticism into law, the religious catechisms of the new Protestant schools and churches made pamphlet polemics and ideals a child's language. Like the ordinance, the catechism too was a true civics lesson, only with a more prominent religious underpinning. As the law addressed the willfulness of adult citizens and subjects, the catechism grappled with a child's penchant for autonomy. None in authority believed that either inclination had to be taught; all saw children and adults as driven by nature to place their own desires above the best interests of society and to evade higher authority whenever possible. Love of self began even before birth, passed on from parents to child at conception "like gout or plague."[29]

In the minds of secular magistrates and clerical catechists alike, self-mastery and good order—internal control and external security—were what most people needed lifelong from their very first breath. Neither, they believed, came naturally; the one had to be carefully inculcated by parents, teachers, and preachers at home, in school, and at church, while government had firmly to impose the other. For its part, the Protestant catechism addressed two interconnected and deeply felt concerns of parents at this time: the anxiety and disruption created in the lives of their children by their animal passion and self-will (*eigenwil*) and the anarchy that threatened society at large if such forces were not harnessed early in life.

The catechism took both defensive and offensive stances. On the one hand, the catechist sought to give children a sense of security and purpose in their lives regardless of their actions; at the same time, however, he wanted to instill in them a sense of shame for immoral behavior and fear of its consequences—to his mind the essential conditions of ethical behavior. So he held before them both a loving God and an avenging one. To instill morality and nurture a civic consciousness, he directs his wards to the behavior that befits social beings and children of God. From the conduct of rulers in governing their realms to the activities of children at home and in school, the catechist frankly discusses right and wrong. Contrary to some current scholarship, which describes the Reformation in ordinance and catechism as an "uninviting attempt to substitute uniformity, routine, and obedience for autonomy in the exercise of one's religion,"[30] the Protestant catechism was far more a lesson in good breeding and citizenship than an exercise in conformity and bigotry.

A case in point is the Nuremberg *Catechism or Children's Sermons* of 1533 already alluded to, possibly the most popular catechism of the Reformation. Composed by the Nuremberg reformer Andreas Osiander, these homilies elaborated Luther's *Small Catechism* (1529) for an audience of "young children," specifically twelve- to fourteen-year-olds who were preparing for their first Communion. The sermons elaborated the Ten Commandments, the Apostles' Creed, the Lord's Prayer, and the sacraments of Baptism and the Eucharist.[31] While inspired by Luther, the sermons were made necessary by the large number of children coming each year to their first Communion in Nuremberg. The city's Sebald and Lorenz churches alone confirmed twelve hundred annually, far too many for the small number of pastors in the city to provide individual instruction. On the Sundays, holidays, and designated workdays when the catechism was preached, the service began with the recitation of an article of faith, to which a specially prepared sermon was then addressed. By mid-century, the Nuremberg *Catechism* was widely in use across central and northern Europe, including England, where in 1548 Archbishop Thomas Cranmer, who had earlier married Osiander's niece, had it translated into English for use as a handbook by English priests.[32]

"Gather round, you children," the catechist invites, "and listen to me. I will teach you the fear of the Lord [Ps. 111:10]. Who among you desires a good life and wants to have many happy days? Then let him guard his tongue from evil and his lips from falsehood, turn away from evil and do good, seek peace and pursue it [Ps. 34:12–15]." By "fear of the Lord" the catechist meant two things: the recognition of the existence of an almighty God who does good for those who are good and punishes all who are not, and the resolve to do nothing to offend him, but everything to please him by keeping his commandments to the best of one's ability. "Then will you become fine, capable people, who can be of use to others and do a lot of good."[33]

The catechist's concern throughout is less with theory and doctrine than with the practical application of biblical teaching to the child's everyday life. The goal is to empower children morally so that they might readily say no to the things that tempt them and serve those around them with true charity of spirit, abilities no one in the sixteenth century believed to be simply inherent in human nature, but gained only through careful training.

In a less noble vein, the catechist also intended to eliminate all spiritual competition for the child's heart and mind. This aim becomes particularly clear in the exposition of the Ten Commandments, by far the largest part of the catechism. One or more contemporary vices tempting the young are discussed with each commandment. The first commandment ("I am the Lord your God; you shall have no other gods"), for example, is presented as a warning against devoting oneself to things that have no lasting power over one's life and destiny, remembering that whatever one most fears, trusts, and loves becomes one's God. Among the "false gods" said to beckon perniciously to the youth of Nuremberg is astrology, a supposedly "scientific" body of knowledge the catechist feared would lead the young to believe the stars more powerful than God. Tyrants are another false god; fearing their power, people deny even God's Word to gain their favor. Then there is the love of money and trust in one's own works, which the catechist declares "the greatest idolatry on earth." Finally, children are said to face daily the temptation of gluttony and drunkenness, which turn their bellies into gods—together with sexual promiscuity probably the most alluring of the "idols" then tempting Nuremberg's twelve- to fourteen-year-olds.[34]

Among the ways God's name is taken in vain (the second commandment) the catechist cites three sins afflicting Nuremberg children: cursing, frivolous talk about God, and invoking God's name in "magical formulas." With the sacramental magic of the Roman church as much in mind as the spells cast by ordinary conjurers, the catechist condemned all magic as "idle deception and lies contrived by scamps (*bösen buben*) to fool simple folk." But if the length of the catechist's commentary is any measure, casual cursing posed a greater danger to the souls of Nuremberg young. "Not only do men and boys do it," he complains;

"women and girls do it as well. Even small children curse, and in the most horrible manner! They curse not only when they are angry, but also when something good happens to them. Today people curse for no particular reason at all, as if cursing were a virtue and to curse some kind of blessing."[35]

The ungodly sinful works said to break the third commandment ("Remember the Sabbath") were closer still to the world of young teenagers. The catechist berates the youth who does not go to church on Sunday or pray to God, but prefers instead to sleep late, wander about idly, go dancing, gamble, get drunk, whore, quarrel, and revile and fight with others even on the Sabbath.[36]

The catechist devotes twice the attention given each of the three previous commandments to the fourth ("Honor your father and mother"). The reason is apparently that he extends this commandment to all adult authority in a child's life, or what he calls "the most important people on earth, fathers and mothers and all authority (*alle obrigkeit*)." In addition to a child's parents, the catechist cites as authorities his guardians, schoolteachers, pastors, magistrates, and the masters to whom children are apprenticed or with whom they take employment as servants. Children are instructed to fear, obey, love, and respect each of these authorities as they would their own parents; as it shows "great contempt" on the part of a child to think himself wiser than his parents, no less, the catechist warns, does that child sin who scorns those who stand in their place outside the home.[37]

The catechist's exposition of the fourth commandment reveals more about contemporary notions of parenthood and parental responsibility than it does about the nature and duties of childhood. The reason children owe such loyalty and obedience to adults is the enormous good adults do for them, exceeding, it is claimed, any good children can later do for them in return.[38] Parents give their children life and, from mother's milk to father's income, the sustenance without which they would die in childhood. Children also have their parents to thank that they have a fatherland, citizenship, and an inheritance. And adults baptize them and rear them as Christians, "so that they do not grow up eternally lost . . . like hundreds of thousands of unbaptized Jews." From the same adult world children learn self-discipline, so that they may become "fine, peaceful, civil people" (*feine, fridliche burgerliche leut*). They also gain there the skills they need for all kinds of work, from manual labor to highly technical trades and professions (*feine kunst*), so that they can support themselves and live independently when they are grown. All of this having been said, the catechist, like the pamphleteers before him, hastens to point out that to honor and obey adult authority does not mean that children should place their every faith and trust in it; no child is obliged to heed any adult who commands or asks something contrary to God's will.[39]

The catechist cites only one contemporary example of widespread disobedience on the part of Nuremberg youth: marrying without parental knowledge and consent. Throughout the sixteenth century efforts to discipline marriage by putting an end to the illicit sex and secret marriages of the young ran counter to forces more elemental and resilient than society's laws. Nonetheless, the catechist, speaking from keen observation, if not out of his own experience, warns his teenagers of the folly of such willful unions: "Marriage is such a dangerous, tedious, and wretched state when it has not been well prepared (*wol geret*); for then you must be plagued by it and know lifelong a misfortune from which only death saves you."[40]

In commentary on the fifth commandment ("You shall not kill")— and later on the fifth article of the Apostles' Creed—the catechist defines for Nuremberg children the basic moral axiom by which they are to live: never have lasting enemies of one's own creation. Peace is to be made immediately with any person, peer or adult, whom a child might have "killed" by hateful thoughts or words spoken falsely or in anger. "Christ teaches that the very best and most necessary worship of God is to keep God's commandment and be reconciled with one's neighbor (Matt. 5:23)."[41] In this ethic of reconciliation lay humankind's peace with itself and with God. According to the fifth article of the Apostles' Creed ("Forgive us our trespasses," Matt. 6:14), God has promised to forgive people as they forgive one another. He intended the act of human forgiveness to be a model rather than a condition of salvation. By such forgiveness God accommodates himself to human weakness and enables people to comprehend his nature and plan for their lives. As the catechist explains, it is neither right nor credible that God should forgive those who themselves will not forgive others. "For although it is difficult for us to forgive others, it is much easier for us to do so than to believe that God forgives our own sin."[42] Hence the importance of moral reconciliation; when people forgive one another, they also come to understand how God forgives them, and in the process they create peace and unity around themselves, without which the world could not continue. By God's masterful design, then, the most basic ethical behavior—making friends—bridges time and eternity.

A twentieth-century reader might have expected a Reformation cate-chist to pass quietly over the sixth commandment ("You shall not commit adultery"), lest the subject matter awaken adolescent lust. To the contrary, his wards are said most urgently to require a discussion of this commandment, because "several godless madmen" in Nuremberg, who go unnamed, have maintained that the commandment condemns only adultery and allows premarital sex—information that must surely have riveted the catechist's youthful audience.[43] The catechist makes short shrift of such argument: not only is whoring as forbidden as adultery, but chastity until marriage is God's universal rule. Not only must youth forego all sexual activity; they must also avoid all suggestive talk and suppress all sexual thoughts as well.[44] Nor shall they place themselves in situations conducive to sexual feelings, for example, where "excessive eating and drinking, idleness, and dancing" occur.

With the exposition of the seventh commandment ("You shall not steal"), the Nuremberg *Catechism* becomes a true civics lesson. To incul-cate in the young a sense of ethics in business and professional life, the catechist apprises them of the many ways those in positions of trust or authority abuse their office. A ruler, for example, becomes a "thief" by taking more in taxes than is required to protect his subjects, thereby bringing financial ruin upon them. And government also steals when it directs public revenues to private use, or fails to staff its offices with honest and competent civil servants, or allows basic institutions and services, from schools to water fountains, to go neglected.[45]

Lawyers are said to steal by encouraging unwinnable suits and by cleverly undermining good suits solely for the sake of a fee. Judges break the seventh commandment when pursuit of their own gain guides their rulings. Then there is the enormous thievery of merchants, who charge exorbitant prices, sell defective goods, and use false weights and mea-sures. They cleverly buy goods cheaply knowing secretly they will soon rise in price, and they sell at high price goods whose price they know will soon plunge. To force regular suppliers to sell them goods and materials at less than fair market value, merchants falsely claim that they can get the items in question more cheaply elsewhere. They especially exploit poor, dependent pieceworkers; claiming not to need their services at all, they force them to work at unfair wages. At the other end of their business, they rig prices and create monopolies, forcing their customers also to pay whatever they choose to charge.[46]

Laborers and workers steal too, by poor workmanship, false claims of quality, and demands for greater pay than they deserve. Free peasants steal by laziness and inattention to their work, and by selling their crops and animals for more than they are worth. Domestic servants compound a similar kind of thievery by disloyalty to their masters and lords.[47]

The catechist ends this particular lesson on a happy note; he assures his tutees and their parents that the seventh commandment forbids no one from becoming a success in life. God permits everyone to make enough money to care for their offspring and provide for their own comfort in old age.[48]

The moral of the eighth commandment ("You shall not bear false witness") is the value of a good name and reputation, "the most important thing a person can have in life." Because bearing false witness not only harms individuals, but corrupts the process of justice as well, it threatens to undermine society as a whole. Slander is still worse; whereas a false witness can be fought in court, one who ruins reputations by gossip and innuendo does so with impunity.[49] Hence a child must learn early in life how to control his tongue.

The sermon on the final commandment ("You shall not covet") challenges children to look directly into the darkness of their own souls.

> Pay no mind, my dear children, to unknowing people who say that little infants are without sin. We all sense and experience that we are by nature filled with evil desires. We like everything that gives pleasure to the flesh and we flee everything that harms the body. Such desire [and aversion] can also be detected in infants in the cradle, and even in their mother's womb. When an infant is uncomfortable, hungry, and thirsty, or too cold or too hot, it kicks, thrashes, and cries. It acts this way when one shows it something pretty and then quickly takes it away, or if one refuses to give it something it has its mind set on. That is a clear sign that the infant in the cradle and in the mother's womb is full of evil desires and as much a sinner as those who are old.[50]

Much current scholarship has zeroed in on such comments to expose the dark side of Protestant child-rearing. Gerald Strauss, for example, devotes virtually his entire discussion of the Nuremberg *Catechism* to its "harping" on congenital sinfulness, which he claims a modern person cannot read "without wincing."[51] A fair-minded reader may wince even more at so tendentious a portrayal of this complex and constructive catechism, which actually devotes fewer than two of its seventy-three double-columned pages in the modern reprint edition to the subject of original sin. For the sixteenth-century catechist, confronting the enemy within—and no one then doubted his existence—was as vital a part of the maturation process as schooling and work.

The ninth commandment was also supposed to teach the young to be content with their station in life. In this regard, the catechist cites a surprising contemporary example of the corrupting power of sinful desire in domestic Nuremberg, but one the children of the city must have witnessed frequently: competition among families for good maids and servants. Bidding wars are said to break out as households attempt to entice good help away from others! The result, according to the catechist, is the perversion of the city's domestic servants, who flatter themselves into believing that no one can pay them enough for their services or deserves to have them for long.[52]

Unlike modern pedagogues, the Nuremberg catechist believed that fear and shame had a positive role to play in properly bending the twig. He concludes each of his lessons with a dire warning for transgressors. Those, for example, who would take God's name in vain are reminded that "the Lord is one who punishes in earnest, and when he does, he sends death, famine, poverty, and war, also terrible, savage wild animals, robbers, and murderers, by which our sins are repaid."[53] Breaking the Sabbath invites lifelong impoverishment, so that one might never again know a day of rest. According to the catechist, God spares some this fate in life only to inflict a worse punishment in eternity—apparently a warning to affluent children, who might think themselves immune from missing a meal.

In defense of the fourth commandment, the catechist reminds his tutees of a harsh Old Testament remedy for chronically disobedient children: stoning [Deut. 21:18–21]! Exactly what might a disobedient child bring upon himself?

One [person] loses a leg, the other an arm, still another an eye. A horse runs down this one, another falls into water and drowns. Youths

## PROFITEERING, HOARDING, AND DECEIT

*This broadsheet claims fraud and deceit to be pervasive in 1530s society. Merchants are said to hoard staples until their price triples, while poor men, women, and children starve to death in the meantime. Christians are portrayed as surpassing the Jews in profiteering on loans, while the law turns a blind eye to their unjust dealings. While many people harm their communities in these ways without remorse, others are said to hang themselves. Swindlers and cheats are everywhere, offering their false love, counsel, friendship, and money. Unknowingly drinking adulterated wine, pregnant women have premature births. The art of disguising imperfections in manufactured goods has been perfected. On every scale there is a heavy thumb, and counterfeit money is commonplace.*

> The entire world is now faithless,
> Brotherly love blind and dead,
> Everyone deceives. . . .
> False clergy come and go———
> Monks, priests, beguines, and beghards. . . .
> Copper passes for gold,
> Mouse dung is mixed with pepper,
> Furs are dyed. . . .
> Spoiled herring is laced with fresh. . . .
> He who can save himself
> From such deceit is surely blessed.
> The child deceives its parents when it can,
> The parents in turn the child,
> The host the guest,
> The guest the host,
> People false, disloyal, demeaning one another!
> One sees them everywhere.

Unidentified Artist, Gotha, ca. 1535, in *Max Geisberg: The Single-Leaf Woodcut: 1500–1550*, vol. 4, rev. and ed. Walter L. Strauss (New York: Hacker Art Books, 1974), p. 1538.

# Vom wucher. Furkauff vnd Tryegerey.

Dem soll man greyffen zů der hauben
Vnd yhm die zecken wol ab klauben
Der hinder sich kaufft inn sein hauß
Als wein vnd korn im gantzen land
Vnd förchtet weder sünd noch schand
Damit ein arm man nichs nit find
Vnd hungers sterb mit weyb vnd kind
Darumb man hat so vil thewre
Ists ferne groß/ noch grösser hewre
Kun galt der wein kaum zehen pfunde
Jnn ein Monat es darzů kumot
Das er yetz giltet dreyssig gern
Als geschicht mit weytzen/rocken/kern
Jch will vom vbernutz nit schreyben
Den man mit zinß vnd gyle thůt treiben
Mit leyhe/bleesßkauff/vñ mit borgen
Manche ein pfunde gwinne ein morgen
Mer dann es ein Jar thůn sole
Man leyhet yetz ein müintz vmb golt
Fur zehen schreybt man eylff ins bůch
Gar leydlich wer der Juden gsůch
Aber sie mögen nit mer bleyben
Die Christen Juden/ sie vertreiben
Mit Juden spieß die selben rennen
Jch kenn vil die ich nit will nennen
Die treyben doch wild kauffmanschatz
Vnd schweygt darzů all recht vnd gsatz
Vil sich gegen dem hagel neygen
Die lachent auff den reyffen zeygen

Doch geschicht dargegen auch gar dick
Das mancher henckt sich an ein strick
Wer reych wirt mit schaden der gemeyn
Der ist ein narr/ doch nit allein
Betrieger seinde vnd felscher vil
Wachen auff alle zeyt vnd zil
Falsch lieb/ falsch rat/ falsch freind/falsch
Vol vntrew ist yetz die gantz welt    ( gelt
Brüderlich lieb ist blind vnd tode
Auff betrogenheyt ein yeder gohe
Darmit er nichts hab on verlust
Ob hundert schon verderben sunst
Kein erbarkeyt sich man mer art
Man laßt es vber die Seelen gart
Das man eins dings möcht kummen ab
Voraus left man den wein nit bleyben
Groß falscheyt thůt man mit jm dreyben
Salpeter/ schwebel/ todtenbein
Weydäsch/ senff/ milch/ vil kraut vnrein
Stoßt man zum spünten inn das faß
Die schwangern frawen drincken das
Das sie vor zeyt genesen dick
Vnd sehen ein ellend anblick
Man helt kein massen vnd gewichte
Die elen sind kurtz zůgerichte
Der tůchlad můß gantz finster sein
Das man nit sech des tůches schein
Die vile einer thůt sehen an
Vnd gunafftet den laden an

Dieweyl gibt man die wag ein truck
Das sie sich zů der erden bucke
Vnd fragen eins wie vil man heysch
Falsch gelt ist worden yetz gemein
Vnd falscher raht/ falsch geystlicheyt
Münch/ priester/ begein/ nolbrüder trie
Vil wölff gen yetz in schaffen kleyde
Für golt man kupffer yetz zů rist
Meißdreck man vnder pfeffer nlsche
Man kan das belgwerck alles verbern
Vnd thut es auff das schlechtest gerben
Das es behelt gar wenig har
Wan mans kaum tregt ein viertel Jar
Die faulen hering man vermisch
Das man sie verkauff fur gar frisch
All gassen sind fürkeuffer voll
Kremer werck treiben schmeckt gar wol
Mit handtirn will sich yeder nern
Darmit er müssig mög spaciern
Drumb bleybt kein war in jrem were
Mit falsch mans zu vertreiben gere
Selig on zweyffel ist der man
Der sich vor falsch yetz hüten kan
Das kind sein eltern treuge so es mag
Die eltern thuns auch wie ich sag
Der wirt den gast/ der gast den wirt
Falsch/ vntrew/ bschiß/ man vberal spirt.

are killed on the streets, at play, or in war. When one [attempts to] set up house [on one's own], he goes to ruin,[54] and because of his poverty he must flee to the protection of others. If he has sunk so low that he lies and steals, he can expect to be hanged, or banished and have to live among strangers, where no one trusts him and there is no one to whom he can turn for help. That is the true punishment for those who disobey [their parents] in their youth.[55]

The consequences of whoring and adultery are said to be even more disastrous both for the individuals involved and for society as a whole. Illegitimate children "have little luck [in life] and little blessing from God, for the world regards them as unfit for any honorable work." The offspring of whoring and premarital sex are said to grow up with neither the discipline nor the skills to gain a secure place in life: "they see, hear, and learn nothing good [from their unwed parents]; a bad, ill-bred, uncivilized people sprout up from such children and commit every sin and offense. Then God must come and punish everyone for it with famine, war, and death, until everything is destroyed."[56] An equally harsh fate is said to await those who succeed in gaining what they covet:

> If you force your neighbor from his house or room, you will be sick in it, or otherwise go to ruin when you occupy it. If you force him from his garden or field, hail will destroy it and deprive you of its harvest. If you take another's cattle, they will die on you. Nowhere is there any good fortune for one who covets and strives after the things that belong to others.[57]

The catechist attaches to the seventh article of the Creed ("Deliver us from evil") a grander description still of the psychological chain reaction triggered within a person by unrepented sin. One can only wonder what went through the minds of the twelve- to fourteen-year-olds who heard the following recitation. If they were not amused by the obvious exaggeration, it must have instilled in them a keen sense of vigilance. Sinful desire is said to beget a bad conscience, from which fear, sadness, terror, and timidity follow until a person "deteriorates daily, his heart declining with his disorderly nature." Then follow hunger, thirst, passion, apathy, and fatigue, every kind of illness, and eventually death. In such a state, one soon loses his mind and becomes an easy prey of the devil, succumbing to idolatry, sorcery, heresy, error, and every kind of false doctrine. And these things in turn plunge him into hatred, anger, quarreling, cheating, rapine, robbery, insult, abusive words, blows, killing, lies, deception, war, and every corruption. And because God will not let such things go unpunished, he soon unleashes the devil, who then poisons the air, causes storms, fires, and floods, drives some people mad, possesses others, breaks one man's neck, and causes others to drown, die in fires, or fall to their death.[58]

Such horror stories were intended to catch and hold the attention of the young, so that they might take to heart advice designed to preserve their bodies and save their souls. Although the stories echo tactics roundly condemned by the pamphleteers when the old church employed them, the catechist knew they served his purpose well, which was not to terrify children gratuitously, or to take from them their own minds and wills, but to console and strengthen them in the new faith. A modern parent who has prepared a child to resist abduction—the modern version of ultimate evil and calamity in a child's life—can appreciate the positive role that fear-inspired vigilance may play in saving a child. The ultimate objective of the catechist, as stated at the outset, was to create "fine, capable people, who can be of use to others and do a lot of good." Whatever misgivings a modern reader may have about his methods or the values of his age, we must concede that he understood well the complexity of his task and that it was a noble one.

Particularly in the *Catechism*'s distinctively "Christian" parts—the exposition of the Apostles' Creed and the Lord's Prayer—the mighty and merciful God of Reformation theology comes to center stage, a perfect caring and giving Father who offers only good things to his children and from whom each may only receive. The sermon on the third commandment, for example, explains why God requires people to worship him by "resting on the Sabbath." It is a paradigm lesson in salvation by faith rather than by works, making clear the peculiar nature of the Protestant God as one who desires from his people only their trust.

Our God is so rich and powerful that he has no need of our services and good deeds for himself; and he is so friendly and gracious that he does good things freely for everyone. . . . "You could do me no greater service [he says to his children] than to come to me and let me do good things for you. Then you will recognize in me your gracious father and come to trust and love me as children should a father."[59]

The catechist elaborates the portrayal of God as perfect father exactly where one might expect him to: in commentary on the first article of the Lord's Prayer ("Our Father who is in heaven"), which magnifies in God the qualities of the good earthly parent.

> Behold [children] how dear every father on earth holds his children. They rear them with the greatest diligence, feed and clothe them, work for their sake, teach them, arrange schooling for them, save up an inheritance for them, and concern themselves with their every welfare. When their children are bad and must be punished, fathers still love them and suffer on their behalf. And if their children only amend their lives and never do that wrong again, their fathers rejoice, forgive them, and forget everything. So also, and even more so, does our dear Lord God in heaven rejoice, forgive, and forget.[60]

God is portrayed not only as a perfect, self-giving father; he is also, as the Creed proclaims, "the Father Almighty," one for whom absolutely nothing is ever impossible, regardless of the odds. The child who understands such omnipotence should weather any storm and never again know incapacitating despair or hopelessness:

> No one is so sick that God cannot make him well. No one is so poor that he cannot make him rich. No one is so simple that he cannot make him wise. No one is so despised that he cannot bring him honor. There is no sinner so great that he cannot make him devout. Nor is anyone so faithless that he cannot make him believe. Nothing is so incredible that God cannot make it happen, if he chooses.[61] One should therefore trust only in him and know that all things are in his power.[62]

Even when a child found himself suffering undeservedly, the catechist would have him understand that it is all part of God's plan and purpose for his life ("Thy will be done on earth") and that he should take hope also from such unfairness. "When God sends you illness, poverty, undeserved shame or suffering, and persecution, take it, my dear children, as a sign that he loves you."[63]

As an additional piece of protective armor against the many perceived enemies and temptations that threaten the young, the Lutheran catechist handed down choice polemics against both the old church and competing Protestant sects (Zwinglians and Anabaptists), who are said to be "certainly not Christians."[64] In commentary on the first commandment, for example, he explains how people turn the true God into a false idol by imagining him to be other than the Bible says he is, "as when we believe that God would sooner save a man in a cowl than one dressed in other, honest clothing, or that he is pleased by a service of worship which he neither enjoins nor commands."[65] Then there are those who treat God as if he were some human lord who expects many good works from people, "[commanding them] to make sacrifices, light candles, decorate pictures, go on pilgrimages, or perform the other hypocritical works and false worship of him that we were previously persuaded and deceived into doing."[66] The catechist extends his list in commentary on the seventh commandment (against stealing), which priests and bishops are said to transgress by "vigils and Masses for the dead, anniversary Masses, indulgences, confraternities, pilgrimages, and other such trickery."[67]

The revolution of the pamphleteers lived on in such polemics. But anti-Catholic propaganda was not the catechist's main concern, and it plays a very small part in the *Catechism*. At this point in the Reformation's evolution, the reformers had indoctrination, not propaganda, on their minds; instilling the truth in new converts and in the young now held priority over any further exposés of the old church and competing Protestant confessions. A great divide separated the polemics of the pamphleteers from the lessons of the catechists. No longer outsiders propagating the heretical beliefs of a minority, Protestants now became the new insiders, challenged to shape the young according to the doctrines a majority now professed to believe. Exposure of the old church naturally gave way to defining the new, and the catechism replaced the pamphlet as the voice of the Reformation.

If the Reformation in theology and pamphlet had occasionally been idealistic, the Reformation in ordinance and catechism was strictly down to earth. It focused on what could be done at the moment, no longer on what might exist in the best of worlds. In the laws and lessons of the new Protestant regimes and churches, the Reformation began to pass out of the hands of the magistrates and the preachers and into those of ordinary people.

# 6. Luther's
# Political Legacy

Reforms and revolutions create leaders who articulate common grievances and shared ideals and enter the fray personally in an exemplary way. Although such men and women stand out in history as individuals, their successes rarely come from having discovered something previously unknown to their contemporaries. It lies rather in their ability—often in spite of themselves—to speak for many. Great leaders know no more nor feel any more deeply than those they lead; they are admired and followed because they express with unique clarity and force what many have long known and felt. It is this ability to embody and represent charismatically the wishes of others that makes them leaders. Such men and women are, of course, distinct individuals in their own right; but in the public mind they come to epitomize a cause much larger than themselves. In the stories of their lives the issues of an entire age come into focus and, in this sense, their biographies become the history of society itself.

Martin Luther was such a leader. He became uniquely identified in the public mind with the German Reformation because his own spiritual dissatisfactions and his aspiration for reform were also those of his contemporaries. One-third of all books sold in Germany in the early 1520s were by Martin Luther. By turning now to Luther's political philosophy at midstream in this study, we catch the Reformation at its most articulate and, for both its contemporary critics and its modern ones, its most controversial point: its impact on politics and society.

It would be difficult to find a sixteenth-century figure whose political philosophy has received more adverse criticism from modern scholars than Martin Luther's. Today the Reformation he led is identified with a political system that knew only privileged lords and disenfranchised subjects; a virtual scholarly consensus holds his political teaching responsible for a fateful inculcation of political passivity in the German people. Was the Reformation in ordinance and catechism a perversion of the revolt of the pamphleteers, with political absolutism, even modern fascism, its terrible distant legacy?

The serious scholarly case against Luther began in the nineteenth century with the German sociologist Ernst Troeltsch, who characterized the Lutheran ethic as one of internal faith and "aloofness from the world," a "kind of quietism" that permitted society and politics to go their own way. Because he viewed existing political institutions as established by God (Rom. 13:1), Luther is said to have instilled in his followers an uncritical approach to government by teaching "religious obedience and humble submission." Troeltsch believed that Luther sanctioned and even glorified unconditional obedience to reigning political authority.[1]

Several generations of scholars have since echoed this thesis. In a major survey of early modern political thought, Quentin Skinner declares Luther's key concepts to be the purely inward nature of the "spiritual kingdom" of the church and the divine origin of reigning political institutions—teachings said to undermine the church's ability to oppose political authority, while at the same time exalting secular government as a "direct reflection of God's will and providence." The result: political passivity on the part of his followers even in the face of manifest tyrants. As is well known, in the 1520s Luther refused to countenance Saxon political resistance of higher imperial authority; only after the emperor rejected the Lutheran Augsburg Confession (1530) and threatened to suppress the Reformation by armed force did Luther approve the Saxon princes' resort to arms against the emperor and the pope. Still, for Skinner, as for Troeltsch, the die had been cast in the previous decade, when Luther collaborated with the princes and counseled his followers to obey higher political authority unconditionally; Lutheran political theory was thus destined to play a "vital role" in legitimating the emerging absolutist monarchies of northern Europe.[2]

Still more recently, Swiss historian Peter Blickle has developed such deterministic thinking about Luther's political impact in more provocative directions. According to Blickle, quasi-democratic communal forms of government (*Gemeindeversammlungen*) struggled to maintain themselves in both town and countryside in the centuries between 1300 and 1800. Having emerged in the wake of the disruptions brought about in the old feudal order by the great demographic crisis of the fourteenth century (the Black Death), these new forms of government are said to have had some remarkable features: elective public offices; an economy that was both individual and collective; lords who were mindful of local interests and prepared to cooperate with their subjects instead of merely dominating them; and central administrations willing to integrate local communities into larger territorial government as fully enfranchised members.[3] The result was a neighborly society with a healthy respect for freedom and self-determination—somewhat akin to early New England town government.

Unfortunately, according to Blickle, the organization of communities on such principles struck at the heart of the traditional feudal state order, which was based on the inequality of its members. Hence, in the late fifteenth century rulers adopted a policy of territorial demarcation and internal control designed to end independent communal government once and for all. Privatizing previously free common lands and installing special agents to oversee the villages and towns on their lands, they progressively subjected the common man—identified broadly with the masses of nonnoble, nonclerical peasants and burghers in town and countryside—to a uniform code of law.[4]

So it was, according to Blickle, that in the century and a half between 1500 and 1650, the period of Protestantism's rise to power, German political absolutism was fixed. During the age of Reformation, a political system developed that divided people into two basic groups: the few who ruled and presumed themselves to be superior by birth, and the masses they ruled and presumed to be their inferiors. On the land and in the towns, the common man protested this development both by petition and by revolt, as he attempted in vain to defend his political maturity. Viewed thus from below, the political history of the Reformation becomes the story of the defeat of Germany's only contemporary alternative to autocratic government. When the Peasants' Revolt failed in 1525, the last great offensive on behalf of communal government had occurred, and Germany, for all practical purposes, lost its last chance before the twentieth century to establish a democratic form of state government.[5]

When it is asked how so appealing a prospect could have been so thoroughly dashed at this time, Blickle lays the blame squarely at the feet of the Reformation. Having ridden the communal movement to initial victory in church reform, the reformers betrayed it for still greater gain, and among them, none was more guilty of such betrayal than Luther.[6] In an important pamphlet of 1523, Luther had defended a community's right to organize and direct its own spiritual life, in Blickle's view, a "whopping endorsement" of communal equality and autonomy.[7] But the Peasants' Revolt so terrified Luther that in its wake he set the Reformation on a completely contrary course that ended up sanctioning the sovereignty of Germany's rulers not only politically, but spiritually as well. Here the "regressive" side of Luther's thought is said to have triumphed tragically over the "emancipatory," as the great reformer directly assisted the suppression of political principles he himself had earlier championed. The betrayal was of one piece, Blickle believes, with the later "absolutistic" formula of the Peace of Augsburg (1555) proclaimed throughout the Holy Roman Empire: "each region, its own religion" (*cuius regio, eius religio*)—as deems the ruler, so must believe the land.[8]

Blickle blames the great reformer's retreat simply on his conservatism; in the end Luther could not envision a social and political order different from the one in which he had grown up. The Reformation's point of no return is set in 1526, when Luther solicited the princes' assistance in the creation and enforcement of new church ordinances. "Hereafter there was to be no more talk of a Reformation on the basis of a [spiritually and politically] mature community." Luther would henceforth portray church and state as two interdependent kingdoms in so close a working relationship that the state could not but be rendered "sacrosanct" to its subjects and "unassailable" by them: "the only obstacle [Luther] placed before a ruler tempted to become a tyrant was the ruler's private conscience."[9]

Like Bernd Moeller before him, Blickle champions the Swiss reformer Zwingli as the more socially and politically progressive of the two great theologians. Unlike Luther, Zwingli is said to have believed that faith in the Gospel implied "a total change in social and political life," although neither Luther, Zwingli, or Bucer ever seriously pursued such an unrealistic goal, much less achieved it. Unencumbered by Luther's inflexible dialectic between law (the province of the ruler) and Gospel (the province of the church), which, Blickle claims, denied religion a constructive role in Saxon politics, Zwingli was theoretically in a better position to make Christianity directly relevant to Zurich's social and political life.

Blickle also believes that Zwingli provided his followers with clearer guidelines for political resistance. "Christian princes must govern by laws that are not against God," Zwingli wrote, "[for without such laws] people will not submit to princely authority and unrest will follow."[10] Whereas Luther only wished for Christian rulers, Zwingli is said to have demanded the recodification of secular law to ensure government's conformity with divine law—"a Christianizing of positive law and thereby of the state." From the point of view of Zwingli's supposedly more progressive theology, Blickle even views the Peasants' Revolt as an "unfolding of the Reformation itself."[11]

## THE TWO KINGDOMS

Between 1520 and 1525, Luther confronted two mortal threats to his Reformation: on the one hand, outright political suppression by the emperor and Saxon rulers loyal to the old church; on the other, incipient socioreligious utopianism among some of his own followers that threatened to make the Reformation politically intolerable to rulers generally. The two-kingdoms doctrine (*zwei Reiche Lehre*) originated and developed as a response to these threats. According to this famous doctrine, two distinct spheres of human life exist, one temporal and one spiritual, each ruled by a divinely appointed authority, the one responsible for all that pertains to the life of the body, the other for all that pertains to the life of the soul; and neither may properly challenge the other's sphere of jurisdiction. But inasmuch as each still needs the other to fulfill its responsibilities, their proper relationship must be one of mutual cooperation.

The first manifestations of this new political vision came in 1520 when Luther appealed to the German nobility to rescue conscience and Christendom from the tyranny of "human doctrines." In an *Open Letter to the Christian Nobility of the German Nation*, he condemned as "human laws and inventions" all papal claims to superiority over secular government, Holy Scripture, and church councils. By such claims, Luther pointed out, Rome had long successfully walled itself off from effective criticism by the three forces capable of forcing change on the church. In rebuttal, Luther declared laypeople and priests, princes and bishops—all so-called "temporals" and "spirituals"—to be of the same Christian estate, "all true priests, bishops, and popes." And on the basis of such shared spiritual authority, and in the absence of episcopal leadership willing to reform, he urged the Christian nobility of Germany, as representatives of the Christian laity, to seize the initiative, convene a council, and reform the church themselves.[12]

In May 1523, Luther found himself again defending lay reform initiatives, this time on behalf of a rebellious evangelical congregation in the Thuringian town of Leisnig. Laity there had taken it upon themselves to appoint a pastor and to write ordinances for worship that conformed to their new evangelical beliefs. In doing so, they defied the local Cistercian cloister, which traditionally regulated the spiritual life of the town and made all clerical appointments to the parish church. When the Leisnig evangelicals wrote to Luther for his support, he responded by declaring it both the right and the duty of a Christian congregation or community (*versamlung, gemeine*)—in distinction from "the people" or the "masses" at large (*das volck, die menge*)—to defend itself against the tyranny of "human law, principle, tradition, custom, or habit,"[13] by which he meant Catholic religious practice.

Both his exhortation to the German nobility and this defense of the Leisnig congregation came at a time in which Luther believed the budding evangelical movement to be at grave risk. On the one hand, he saw conscience and Christendom under assault, on the other a traditional clerical leadership that either could not or would not respond on their behalf. Such circumstances, he believed, rendered the official distinction between the clergy and the laity secondary to their spiritual equality, which in Luther's scheme empowered the laity to act decisively on behalf of reform, whether they were the nobility, as in 1520, or a local congregation, as in 1523.

At the outset of the Reformation, popes, bishops, and cathedral chapters had been the chief obstacles to change. After the condemnation of Luther by the Diet of Worms in 1521, lay authority, too, became such an obstacle. At this point oppressive *Menschensatzungen* presuming to speak as God's Word began to pour forth from hostile imperial and ducal courts as well. In 1523, Duke George, invoking the Edict of Worms, proscribed the printing and reading of Luther's works throughout ducal Saxony, including Luther's recently published translation of the New Testament, copies of which were confiscated and burned. In Bavaria, Duke Wilhelm IV issued a similar decree, as did Duke Joachim I in Brandenburg.

In pained awareness of these changed circumstances Luther prepared perhaps his most definitive statement of the two-kingdoms doctrine. It came in a treatise entitled *On Temporal Authority: To What Extent It Should Be Obeyed* (1523). Here he professed a need to "change tactics" in light of the way lords and princes had abused his earlier charge to them to exercise their Christian office on behalf of the church. They now needed to be instructed "in what they may not do" to the church, and docile and trusting laity needed more than ever to be rescued from perverse *political* leadership.

> God . . . has made our rulers mad; they actually think they can do whatever they please and order their subjects to follow them in it. Their subjects, in turn, make the mistake of believing that they must obey whatever their rulers command. It has now gone so far that the rulers order people to get rid of certain books and to believe and conform to whatever they prescribe [as if it were God's truth]. They have thereby presumptuously set themselves in God's place, lording it over people's consciences and faith and schooling the Holy Spirit according to their own crack-brained ideas.[14]

Even previously friendly evangelical rulers are said to exceed their divine mandate in the exercise of their power. A notorious example was Margrave Casimir of Brandenburg. In the face of determined Catholic resistance to reform and ominous peasant clamor for it, he subjected Protestant clergy on his lands to the strictest control, dictating "clarifications" of evangelical doctrine to them in the name of law and order.[15] Having urged the Christian laity to cleanse the temple of God, Luther suddenly found rulers attempting to lay claim to it. As he had earlier opposed the "human doctrines" of the pope, he now exposed those of self-aggrandizing secular authority. A large section of his treatise *On Temporal Authority* was devoted to a discussion of the distinction between spiritual and temporal government and the strict limits God placed on the latter. Specifically, Luther criticized a secular government's presumption to rule over people's souls by forbidding them to read his writings and the New Testament:

> Temporal government has laws that extend no farther than to life and property and external affairs on earth, for God cannot and will not permit anyone but himself to rule over the soul or guide it, kill

Duke George of Saxony, Luther's great political adversary, ca. 1533. Hans Brosamer, in *Max Geisberg: The German Single-Leaf Woodcut: 1500–1550*, vol. 1, rev. and
ed. Walter L. Strauss (New York: Hacker Art Books, 1974), p. 775.

it or give it life, bind it or loose it, judge it or condemn it. . . . If, therefore, your prince or temporal ruler commands you to side with the pope, to believe thus and so, or to get rid of certain books, you should say . . . "Gracious sir, I owe you obedience in body and property; command me within the limits of your authority on earth, and I will obey. But if you command me to believe or to get rid of certain books, I will not obey; for then you are a tyrant and overreach yourself and give orders where you have neither the right nor the authority to do so."[16]

If thwarting political suppression of the Reformation was one motive of the two-kingdoms doctrine, saving it from the enthusiasm and idealism of its supporters and fellow travelers was the other. Like the lords and princes, ordinary laity too could abuse evangelical freedom in the name of Christ and place the reform in jeopardy.[17] During the early 1520s, Luther contended with three radical movements that threatened his own. The first was the popular revolutionary spiritualism of several original supporters—Andreas Karlstadt, the so-called Zwickau prophets, and his greatest rival in these early years, Thomas Müntzer. Luther considered them all to be dangerous fanatics chasing sociopolitical dreams no society could ever hope to realize.[18] Then there were the "ranting and raving" Anabaptists, pacifistic and separatist, "who wanted to rule the world by the Gospel and abolish all temporal law and sword."[19] Finally, most ominous of all, was incipient peasant insurrection against clerical and secular landlords, which Luther along with the vast majority of his contemporaries associated with the bigotry and idealism of some of his own followers. A Lutheran pastor, Christoph Schappeler, coauthored the famous Twelve Articles of the Memmingen peasants, which became a banner for many lesser peasant revolts. In 1522, hoping to nip trouble in the bud, Luther devoted a special treatise to the subject of revolt, both evangelical and peasant, in which he emphatically disassociated himself and his reform from revolutionary political tactics and utopian social goals.[20]

To the Luther of the 1520s, the great enemies of the age were the advocates of absolute cultural uniformity, whose aim was to identify church and state and collapse religion and society together. On the one hand, they were the magistrates and princes who treated the church and the soul as also their wards; on the other, they were the evangelical fanatics who wanted to rule the world by the Sermon on the Mount, as the pope had earlier aspired to do by canon law. As long as those in power viewed the sacred and the civic as coextensive realms, society would only oscillate between attempts by each side to dominate the other. So Luther not only proclaimed the limits of temporal authority in the seminal political tract of 1523; he also made the Christian's duty to respect and obey rightful government a major topic of discussion. If God did not intend magistrates and princes to rule over souls, he had unambiguously set them over bodies and property. And if rulers had limits on their authority, so too did Christians on their ideals.

Not only did Luther refuse to share the Anabaptist and Spiritualist vision of an egalitarian Christian society beyond coercion and servitude, he considered the very notion fantastical and a certain road to civil strife and destruction; and despite their occasionally more idealistic rhetoric, Zwingli and Bucer in the end agreed. While it may be theoretically true that Christians have no need of coercive government, inasmuch as one may presume that they will do naturally what is right, Luther warns that "no one is by nature Christian or righteous ... [and] among thousands [who profess Christianity] there is scarcely a single true Christian to be found."[21] And the many nominal Christians need the discipline of the law and the protection of the magistrate's sword as much as the multitude of non-Christians. For their part, the tiny minority of true Christians who "govern themselves according to love and tolerate no injustice toward their neighbors"[22] encourage and assist their government so that their neighbors may enjoy the blessings of peace, order, and justice. True Christians even become hangmen and soldiers, Luther insists, willingly killing and maiming people, so that their neighbor's bodies and property may remain safe.[23] Declaring service to God and neighbor to be more characteristic of Christians than of any other people, Luther concluded that "the temporal sword and authority ... belong more appropriately to Christians than to any other people on earth."[24]

By so distinguishing two separate and autonomous, yet still vitally interdependent spheres in which God is served on earth—the one inward and for the salvation of the soul, the other external and for the safety of the body—Luther believed he had resolved a major dilemma of his age. The doctrine of the two kingdoms made it possible for one to be both a true Christian and an active citizen of the world without having to forego the one for the other, subject the one to the other, or transform the one into the other. Luther boasts of the Christian's ability, by his new definition, to serve his neighbor selflessly through the political institutions of secular society:

> In this way the two come together nicely: at one and the same time you satisfy God's kingdom inwardly and the kingdom of the world outwardly. You suffer evil and injustice [on your own behalf because you do not avenge yourself or seek your own gain], and yet at the same time you punish evil and injustice [by avenging your neighbor and improving his lot in life through the offices of the state]; you do not resist evil [as Christ commanded], and yet, at the same time, you do resist evil.[25]

The doctrine of the two kingdoms was not intended to be a theoretical basis for transforming society by high Christian ideals or for bringing about a new egalitarian social order. Luther never doubted that such aspirations only laid a path to religious folly and civil anarchy. He did, however, believe that peace and order would reign on earth and justice freely flow if existing administrative and judicial offices faithfully exercised their divine mandate to protect the righteous and punish the wicked. Problems of governance were seen to be problems of political will and personnel, not of political structure. When Christians entered government, they did so not as the prophets of a new order, but as the hangmen, constables, and judges of the established regime. For Luther, to hold secular society to a perfection it could not attain, and had not been commanded by God to attain, would prove in the end to be as destructive of civil society as the church's attempt to hold people to laws and works beyond human ability and God's law had proved to be for individual Christians. Hence, Luther's condemnation of those who wanted to "mix the two kingdoms" by imposing Christian norms on the world. The "heavenly prophet" Karlstadt he deemed a reverse pope, that is, one who would have people *not* do what God has said they might—in distinction from the pope, who rather commands people to do what God has not.[26] Luther also criticized peasants who demanded material goods and political freedom as "Christian rights." In an instructive application of the two-kingdoms doctrine on the eve of the Peasants' Revolt, he instructed the peasants of Swabia to "drop the name of Christ":

Your name and title must be those of people who fight because they
will not and ought not endure wrong or evil according to the teaching
of nature (*wie das die natur gibt*). You should have that name and let
the name of Christ alone, for those are the kinds of works you are
doing. If, however, you will . . . keep the name of Christian, then I
must . . . count . . . you as enemies who would destroy or hinder my
gospel more than the pope and the emperor have so far done, since
in the name of the Gospel you are acting against it.[27]

Luther spoke out no less emphatically when society's divinely appointed hangmen presumed also to be its shepherds. He instructed his
followers to disobey any ruler who commanded them to act against
conscience and the Word of God, and he exhorted evangelical pastors
to "rebuke boldly and openly" any ruler who despised God's Word and
treated the community he ruled "as if it were his pig or dog." "God's
Word has appointed rulers, made them 'gods,' and subjected everything
[on earth] to them; therefore, they shall not despise his Word . . . but
be subject to it and let it judge, rebuke, mold, and master them."[28]
Because of the moral authority of the pastor's office and the pastor's
equality with rulers as co-defenders of the kingdom of God, Luther did
not view such criticism as seditious. And he sincerely believed that
economic injustice and social disorder threatened to undo God's kingdom as much as the suppression of the Gospel.[29]

Luther was a good example of his own advice. According to a contemporary critic, he failed in his efforts to calm rising peasant discontent
because of the severity with which he censured the injustice of rulers.
Upon learning of his criticism, the peasants only believed their grievances
to be all the more justified and became even more aroused against their
lords.[30] Not only did Luther rebuke rulers in numerous pamphlets and
tracts, he also regularly instructed them in peacetime through the mail.
He wrote more than one thousand letters to political authorities high
and low, involving himself in basic issues of social, economic, and political
policy as well as in matters more narrowly affecting the church.[31] That
in the process he acquiesced in policies that strengthened Saxon rulers,
and may even have been used by them, seems less striking today than
his remarkable ability to preserve so well, with their assistance, the
essential features of his reform.

## A Protestant Warning to Peasants
## on the Eve of the Great Revolt of 1525

*The peasantry is here sympathetically portrayed as a "poor common ass," on whose back ride political tyrants and profiteering merchants. A third cruel rider, spiritual hypocrisy (the Roman church), has, however, been thrown to the ground, thanks to the Reformation's rediscovery of God's Word. The church at least, it is claimed, will no longer easily exploit the common man. Fallen spiritual hypocrisy complains:*

> I lie inconsolable on the ground
> Completely unworthy of the ass,
> Who in the past liked to hear my voice
> And did everything I taught him.
> He gently carried me about and lovingly nourished me.
> Thanks to him I became very rich
> And spent my life in comfort and peace.
> But now the ass has driven me away
> And bars me from his feed.

*Having been freed from religious exploitation, the common man now contemplates revolt against social and political injustice as well. Reason is portrayed as removing the veil from his eyes, so that he now at last sees his true situation. The tyrant astride his back argues that a life of labor and obedience to his masters is the peasant's destiny, while the merchant who is skinning him warns that any resistance will be met with greater force and only make his life worse. The poor ass laments,*

> There is no more miserable animal on earth
> Than I, who must work in rain and wind
> To grow what all the world consumes,
> While in return I barely get oat straw.
> Two evil children sit upon my back.
> The tyrant beats me about my head
> And digs his sharp spurs into my side,
> While the one behind skins me alive.
> Daily I bleed.
> O justice come quickly
> Before I go mad and strike out at them,
> Blinded by my misery.

*Legal justice, having been compromised by the powers of the world, sits impotent in the stocks and laments her inability to help. She refers the poor common man to divine justice or the Word of God, which now has the last word in the drama. A composite of biblical quotations admonishes the common man to accept his suffering and bear his cross patiently to the end, trusting in God alone for vengeance and justice.*

> Still today at this very hour
> God saves his poor people from the abyss
> Of tyrants, no matter how terrible,
> And from profiteering merchants,
> And makes them whole again,
> Just as he ended spiritual hypocrisy
> As soon as they believed his Word.
> For he remains true to his covenant.

Peter Flötner and Hans Sachs, in *Max Geisberg: The German Single-Leaf Woodcut, 1500–1550*, vol. 3, rev. and ed. Walter L. Strauss (New York: Hacker Art Books, 1974), p. 775.

As for the new social and political systems proposed by his competitors, Luther pronounced them all to be unworkable and undesirable, especially the theocracies of separatist Anabaptists and Spiritualists and the social utopias of revolutionary peasants. Nor can it be said that Luther ever "required" the princes of Germany to conduct the business of their offices as true Christians—something modern scholars admire Zwingli for attempting to do in Zurich. Luther would have found such criticism of his political philosophy laughable, both in terms of his own theology, which sharply distinguished civic virtue and Christian righteousness, and in light of the actual behavior of the politicians of the age, which, Luther believed, destined princes to be "rare birds" in heaven. To subject secular government to the Christian ethic of love and forgiveness and enlist it in the building of a New Jerusalem on earth was a dangerous misunderstanding of human nature and of government's limited role in human life. Rulers held a straightforward and workable divine mandate: protect the righteous who do their duty and obey the law and punish the wicked who do not. The good offices of government existed to serve simple civil order and justice, not to provide the nucleus of a theocracy presided over by fanatical Christians, to which Luther believed contemporary Anabaptists, Spiritualists, and even Zwinglians aspired. Historians who today confront Luther with the idealism of these groups, and treat the religious republics they envisioned as desired and realistic goals for early modern society, convey to their readers nothing so much as the power of modern socialist and Christian fantasies.

To accuse Luther's two-kingdoms doctrine of rendering temporal authority sacrosanct and unassailable simply distorts a clear public record. Though no ambitious social engineer, Luther did expect rulers to approximate standards of secular justice in accordance with the Word of God, which in practical terms meant the enforcement of the Ten Commandments. And when rulers failed to be just, Luther anticipated inescapable punishment, escalating from pastoral rebuke and lay civil disobedience to God-inspired rebellion on the part of oppressed subjects, or an invasion by a foreign power, if not both. Scripture and history, he liked to warn, taught that God's vengeance against hardened tyrants is always punishment in kind. If German rulers do not fear God, administer the law justly, and help the poor, "they will bring to rule a spirit of defiance and self-will among the sons of men that [will] transform Germany . . . into a *populus sine lege*, a lawless people."[32]

In Luther's time, democracy as we have come to know it today was entangled with utopianism. If Germans had embraced "democracy" as it was then envisioned by the leaders of communal theocratic movements, it would likely have done Germany far more harm than three centuries of autocratic rule by princes. Thomas Müntzer, for example, might well have brought Germany precociously into the twentieth century, but in ways all too familiar to us today. In July 1524, he won a much-coveted audience with the princes of Saxony, a golden opportunity to state in their presence his own views, in distinction from Luther's, on how Saxon society should be reformed. Müntzer chose as his text the second chapter of the book of Daniel. It served his purpose well, for the prophet Daniel had faced a similar challenge. His prince, King Nebuchadnezzar, had also been misled by false prophets, and to save the king Daniel had to demonstrate that he could interpret the king's dreams better than they, revealing a truer grasp of history's divine course. So Müntzer presented himself to the princes of Saxony as a new Daniel, while casting Luther, caricatured as "Brother Fattened Swine," as another false prophet like the wisemen who long ago misled King Nebuchadnezzar.

The princes, however, wanted none of Müntzer's sociospiritual egalitarianism and did not fall under his spell. Their flat rejection shattered Müntzer. "I censure senseless Christendom to its foundations," he wrote defiantly to Duke John on the day after. A few weeks later, he made it clear to his followers in the town of Sangerhausen that if he could not be a new Daniel to the reigning princes of the world, he would become their avenging angel. What the world now needed, he wrote, was a cleansing slaughter:

> I tell you truly that the time has come for bloodshed (*ein blutvorgyssen*) to fall upon this impenitent world for its unbelief. . . . Why do you want to let yourselves be led around by your noses any longer? One knows full well and can prove it with Scripture that lords and princes as they now present themselves are not Christians. Your priests and monks pray to the devil, and there are ever fewer Christians. All of your preachers are hypocrites and worshipers of man. Why do you want to hope in them any longer?[33]

Before a year was out, Müntzer had led peasant troops in battle at Frankenhausen. Defeated and captured, he lost his life as well as his cause, dying at the hand of the executioner on 27 May 1525.

To blame Luther for not encouraging "democracy" at this time is to ask him to have been a "winner" with distant generations by choosing to have no influence whatsoever over his own. It is also to expect him to have foreseen the future, when a democratic concept of government could be disentangled from the fantasies of spokesmen like Müntzer, who made democracy a danger to Luther's age, and prove itself as a viable political system.

## LUTHER'S GODLY COMMUNITY

It is the consensus of the scholars we have met in this chapter that the political thought of the younger Luther contradicts that of the older. Whereas the younger resisted the efforts of magistrates to rule over the soul and the conscience, the older is said to have eagerly delivered the franchise for reform into their hands. Urged on by Luther, the German princes used their role as agents of his reform to parlay themselves into absolute power within their respective territories. Unlike the Swiss reformers, who are said to have breathed the freer air of an independent confederacy and become astute politicians, Luther remained a naïve cleric in the political backwater of Wittenberg, his theological distinctions puny weapons against the totalitarian ambitions of the Saxon princes.[34] It is further argued that he undermined the salutary polarity he had created between church and state with his two-kingdoms doctrine by formulating another, competitive "doctrine of three orders" (*Stände*)—*oeconomia* (household and vocation), church, and state—each of which he portrayed as an autonomous sphere independently rooted in eternal law.[35]

Still another popular argument holds that rampant religious abuse, indifference, and indiscipline, discovered by official inspections of rural Saxon parishes in the late 1520s, brought about a fundamental change in Luther's approach to reform. Under this theory, a dismayed Luther concluded that proper standards in religion, morality, and education could only be maintained by coercion.[36] Scholars also debate whether the change that occurred in the older Luther's thinking derived from "monarchical" impulses that had been part of his political thinking from the start, as Blickle argues, or from other "monistic" and "absolutistic" tendencies in his thought. But few modern scholars question the basic premise.

Did such a fundamental change really take place in Luther's political thinking, and was he, or did he become, a champion of political absolutism? And is there a real connection between his Reformation and Germany's political development in the sixteenth and seventeenth centuries? Those who answer these questions affirmatively cite especially Luther's 1523 pamphlet in defense of communal spiritual autonomy, *A Christian Congregation or Community Has the Right and Power to Judge All Doctrine and Appoint and Depose Its Own Teachers*. Assertions of the proposition embodied in its title reappear in early 1525 as the first of the famous Twelve Articles of the Memmingen peasants published on the eve of their revolt. As an abstract political principle, it also reflects the participatory style of government one finds at the time in the free imperial cities and among the states of the Swiss Confederacy. Luther's 1523 pamphlet is said to be a recognition of the *political* maturity of villages and towns and not just a blessing of their spiritual autonomy; princely control of communal life is rejected—the very position the Reformation would later endorse and the Diet of Augsburg enshrine in the famous phrase, *cuius regio, eius religio*.[37]

Is the famous pamphlet of 1523 really such a major political statement? The pamphlet was addressed to the fledgling evangelical congregation in Leisnig, which had acted independently to appoint a congenial cleric to the parish church—an action repeated in other cities and towns during this period of transition from Catholic to evangelical regimes. When Luther approved such action, he did so on the basis of what he considered to be the peculiar nature of a "Christian congregation or community." Such a community, he claimed, had an inalienable right from Christ to judge true and false doctrine, because the sheep alone know their true shepherd (John 10) and can perceive a wolf who comes in sheep's clothing (Matt. 7:15).[38] Luther went on to distinguish such a Christian community from secular political communities, which, he believed, had necessarily to operate on completely different principles:

A Christian community acts in a manner totally different from that of a worldly community; for in the world lords command what they will and their subjects obey; "but among you," Christ says, "this shall not be." For among Christians each is the judge of the other and each is subject to the other.[39]

Luther further justified the action of the Leisnig congregation as a response to an emergency that had arisen in the town because of the absence of higher Christian (that is, higher evangelical) authority that should more properly have taken such action. The congregation thus became, so to speak, its own prince or bishop because no proper ecclesiopolitical authority was then in place in the new Protestant community:

> [In an emergency] a Christian, seeing the need of poor ailing souls, acts out of brotherly love and does not wait for an authorizing command or letter from some prince or bishop; for an emergency breaks all laws and has no law. [In such situations] love obligates the Christian to help where there is otherwise no one else who does or is appointed to do so.[40]

The purport, then, of the 1523 pamphlet was not at all to endorse a general principle of communal political sovereignty. It was rather the assertion of the right of evangelical Christians, whether individually or as a group (*jederman und allen Christen inn Gemein*), to take control of the church away from the "spiritual tyrants [of Rome], who have no more right to rule over Christian souls than do Turks and Jews."[41]

Luther had actually made the same argument earlier, in 1520, when he urged German noblemen to reform the church in the absence of episcopal willingness to do so. Heeding the warnings of Georg Spalatin, counselor to Elector Frederick the Wise and a good friend of the Reformation, that overt aggression by Luther's followers would prove counterproductive at the electoral court,[42] Luther consistently preached a moderate course of reform. Throughout the 1520s, however, he left little doubt that when the truth of doctrine and the salvation of souls hung in the balance, every Christian must become, so to speak, a "freedom fighter." So whether it was the Christian nobility in 1520, a local urban congregation in 1523, or the princes of Saxony and Hesse after 1526, Luther deemed the Christian laity to be "emergency bishops" with the right and the duty to act on behalf of the church wherever and whenever the times required.

Such a point of view was also consistent with the doctrine of the two kingdoms. In the context of temporal authority, this doctrine always had a dual purpose: to reassure rulers inclined to support the Reformation that it was no political revolt, and to keep rulers hostile to evangelical doctrine at arm's length from the new church. In the context of the new church, the goals of the doctrine were also twofold: to remind the faithful—especially the overzealous—of their responsibility to two worlds, one spiritual and one civic, and to console and encourage those who found themselves persecuted politically for espousing the new faith. The doctrine in no way refused political support from rulers friendly to the new church; indeed, all of the reformers actively sought such support, knowing that without it the new church would lack the administrative structure, financial resources, and external discipline needed to survive. From the start, the reformers' paramount goal was a reform in statute and institution, and that goal necessarily interwined church and state. Whether the princes who acted on the Reformation's behalf did so in their own minds anomalously as "Christian brothers," as Luther insisted they must, or simply as secular rulers with their own divine mandate to protect the righteous and punish the wicked, as the doctrine of the two kingdoms implied they might,[43] may be a distinction too fine for historical analysis. The important fact is that rulers and reformers worked together closely in Protestant communities, as realistically both knew they must in order for a successful reform to occur.

As long as the ruler in question was friendly to the Reformation, the political theory set forth in the famous pamphlet of 1523 would, of course, be consistent with the evolving principle of a ruler's determination of the religious confession of his land. By mid-century, this principle began to resolve, at least structurally, some of the enormous religious conflict generated in the empire by the Reformation. Luther never objected to any magistrate's suppression of the Mass or enforcement of an evangelical service of worship in its place (he viewed the use of such force as freeing conscience, not coercing it).[44] Nor did Luther ever defend the right of a community to choose a nonevangelical preacher, or, once evangelical, to revert freely to the Catholic fold. Luther denied outright any freedom of conscience for Anabaptists, an attitude characteristic of the age. Less characteristically, he wanted Saxon rulers to exile Jews to a land of their own in the early 1540s, viewing at that time Jewish legalism as a model for Rome's, and blaming both in the same breath for the failing fortunes of his reform. At no stage of its development did the Reformation give the slightest hint of supporting political egalitarianism or religious pluralism. The most radical notion it sanctioned was the right of a self-consciously Christian community to defy church tradition and proselytize evangelical principles. When, in 1525, Melanchthon condemned the first article of the Swabian peasants—the assertion of their right to choose their own preachers—he accused them of wishing only to appoint leaders who supported their material demands, a flagrant politicizing of the Gospel.[45]

Among Luther's contemporaries, Zwingli may have understood the great reformer's doctrine of the two kingdoms as well as any, for he too wrestled with the same practical problems brought on by the transition from Catholic to evangelical regimes. In the year that Luther defended the right of a Christian community to choose its own pastor, Zwingli offered his own version of a two-kingdoms doctrine in a sermon entitled *On Divine and Human Righteousness* (1523). As Luther had done in Saxony, so he assured Swiss magistrates of the nonrevolutionary character of his reform. And he pointedly reminded his followers, especially the growing, zealous Anabaptist congregation in Zurich, that the penultimate "human righteousness" expected of obedient citizens was as important to the kingdom of God as the "divine righteousness" that saved individual Christian souls.[46] In the same month (July), Zwingli published a set of guidelines, again similar to Luther's, for dealing with rulers "who attempt to govern unfaithfully and ignore the directives of Christ" (*untrülich und usser der Schnur Christi faren wurdind*), by whom he meant rulers who betray their divine mandate by favoring corrupt citizens and suppressing honest ones.[47] Against such rulers, he advised, in ascending order, the following actions: their orderly removal from office by those who had put them there; passive civic disobedience, if necessary unto death; and, as a last resort, patient expectation of a God-inspired revolt by a majority of suffering subjects (the ultimate providential relief).[48]

In 1529, in the Marburg castle of Landgrave Philip of Hesse, Zwingli debated with Luther (quite unsuccessfully) the nature of Christ's presence in the sacrament of the Eucharist. Shortly thereafter, while still licking his wounds, he made a revealing comment on the theory and practice of Luther's two-kingdoms doctrine in a letter to the Constance reformer Ambrosius Blarer (4 May 1529). Blarer had earlier shared with Zwingli the difficulties the magistrates of Constance were having as they attempted to enforce the Reformation on the populace at large, especially at the point of removing images from the churches and suppressing the Mass. Their use of force to that end offended some in Constance, who argued that the city's magistrates had no right to rule over conscience in this way, imposing beliefs and practices not accepted by all. Dissidents, apparently some Lutherans and Anabaptists in addition to those still loyal to the old church, appealed to a saying of Luther's that "the kingdom of Christ is not external." They appealed to this statement to buttress their claim that religious practice could not be imposed by force. Blarer was himself inclined to move slowly and cautiously in these matters; hence, his request for Zwingli's counsel.

In response, Zwingli invoked the example of Christ and the Apostles, who did not shrink from offending the consciences of their contemporaries and eventually persuaded them to do things they, too, had initially resisted. He dismissed as a "semierror derived from a paradoxical statement of Luther"[49] the argument that the kingdom of God is not external. It was a sentiment Zwingli also shared insofar as it counseled sympathy for those weak in the faith, but one he rejected outright to the extent that it delayed the suppression of the Mass and permitted the "idolatry of images" to continue in the churches of Constance. Magistrates, Zwingli declared, may with the consent of the church legislate and regulate religious matters that must be observed by all "even though not a few are offended by it . . . [and] the senate of Constance is not the church." Nothing seemed more fitting to the Swiss reformer than to have "honest and pious magistrates" undertake such "prudent, magnanimous, and merciful" action on behalf of the church[50]—a point of view he believed Luther fully shared.

The high point of the letter to Blarer and the magistrates of Constance came when Zwingli took Luther to task not for restricting Christianity to a private sphere of conscience, aloof from politics and society—a misinterpretation of Luther, he believed, by those who understood him poorly—but rather for being too quick to enlist the elector of Saxony, his protector, in the enforcement of religious belief as he, Luther, all too confidently defined it:

Let the senate [of Constance] judge with the Apostles and let the people there command in external matters [of religion] that are deemed essential, and simply ignore those who raise a tumult over externals and abuse the words of Luther ("the kingdom of Christ is not external"), either because they do not rightly understand them, or because they interpret them more widely than Luther himself does or the clear truth of the matter dictates. If Luther really thinks that it is unbefitting a magistrate to do anything that offends conscience, why does he force his own prince, the elector of Saxony, to enforce his own concepts and words in our dispute over the Eucharist? Why does he interdict our books and those of [the Basel reformer] Oecolampadius with water and fire? Is it because he believes that the greater part of the faithful think otherwise than we do? If that were the case, then the command of the prince would not be necessary. No, Luther fears a public airing of these issues, lest it anywhere become evident that he is in error. Hence, the violence and devices of [his ally, the Nuremberg humanist Willibald] Pirckheimer and his anxious letters which fear the light of day. By this rule, it is just as fitting for the pope to curse and damn what he hates or fears. Such is Luther in our judgment.[51]

Clearly, Zwinglian teaching had made no inroads into Saxony! But whatever negative characteristics he may have imputed to his great competitor, Zwingli never for a moment believed Luther to be a quietist bent on separating church and state, or withdrawing the Gospel as he understood it from social and political life. He saw Luther rather as enforcing his own (questionable) creed in too eager and uncompromising a manner.


## THE LESSER POLITICAL EVIL

German political history since the Reformation dwarfs Luther's doctrine of the two kingdoms, and this political theory hardly explains, much less can be blamed for, subsequent centuries of German political behavior. On the contrary, during Luther's lifetime, the doctrine of the two kingdoms arguably restrained the power of the German princes as much as it aided and abetted the political subservience of their subjects. Explanations that tie the course of German history to the doctrine of the two kingdoms ignore the full sweep of German political history before the Reformation—a history of fragmentation and division that is far more pertinent to explaining the rise of German absolutism than any conceivable Lutheran teaching. That both sides of the issue can be argued reflects the dual political legacy of the Reformation.

Luther's personal biography—not his politics or his theology—may provide a better clue to the origins of German political subservience. Despite his bold posturing as a theologian—in debate with Erasmus he once expressed his willingness to see the world "shattered in chaos and reduced to nothing" for the sake of the bondage of the will[52]—Luther was a man extremely fearful of social and political disorder. The subject comes up repeatedly in his writings with the strongest denunciation. Although he simultaneously believed that popular rebellion was an angry God's way of giving hardened tyrants their just deserts, he denounced rebellion as mere vengeance, serving no higher purpose: "it never brings about the desired results . . . generally harms the innocent more than the guilty . . . [and] always does more harm than good."

As early as 1522, Luther declared himself to be "always on the side of those against whom insurrection is directed, no matter how unjust their cause, and opposed to those who rise up in revolt, no matter how just their cause."[53] After the Peasants' Revolt, he confessed an inability even to imagine a situation in which an inferior might justifiably rebel against a superior, and he deemed it always the better course of action to suffer a theoretically "improvable" tyrant than to venture upon the sure chaos of mob rule. "There is hope," he pleaded, "that a tyrant may do better, allow himself to be instructed, learn, and follow advice." And was it not also the lesson of history that once rebellion and tyrannicide are accepted, "the thing grows and self-willed men call those tyrants who are not and kill whomever the mob takes a notion to?"[54]

Although Luther in 1530 joined Saxon jurists and other evangelical theologians in sanctioning princely resistance to the emperor, he never recognized popular political revolt as a legitimate redress of grievance. We find him scolding "lazy and worthless preachers who will not tell the princes and lords their sins," while at the same time expressing even greater distress over the private mutterings of laity and clergy against their rulers. In the secret hatred and cursing of rulers, which he observed going on in every corner of his world, he perceived a terrifying loss of social cohesion, "a secret fire, moving people to disobedience, rebellion, breach of the peace, and contempt for government."[55] When Luther rebutted arguments favoring revolt against tyrants in 1526, he stressed how precious peace and order were in the world:

God has cast us into the world under the power of the devil, so that we have here no paradise, but may every hour expect every kind of misfortune to befall body, wife, child, property, and honor. Should ten misfortunes not befall you in an hour, if you can simply live unassailed for just one hour, then you ought to say: "Oh, how great is the kindness that my God shows to me that in this hour every misfortune has not befallen me!"[56]

Behind such feeling lay neither theology nor political theory, but a personal cultural experience that made the risks associated with political control far preferable to those of political disorder. In a society where the specter of anarchy looms larger than that of tyranny, restricting freedom for the sake of achieving order will often be preferred to risking chaos in pursuit of dubious ideals, however attractive and desirable the latter may be in the abstract. Gradually improving tyrants seems, in general, a less risky course than forcibly retiring them. Modern political freedom and its institutions of justice function only in stable and secure societies, something the sixteenth century knew little of.

Luther's sensitivity to the chaos of his age was shared by a very great number of his contemporaries, and not just those who had a lot to lose. From prince to peasant, sixteenth-century Germany was not gripped by egalitarian ideals; contemporary conditions drove people in the opposite direction. To be free did not mean then what it means today; freedom was not equality of opportunity or the right to come and go as one pleased. To be free meant movement up the social ladder; those gaining freedom were those who found themselves in an increasingly secure niche within a universally recognized hierarchical society. In the literature of the era we find freedom tellingly associated with the ability to lord it over someone else. Georg Spalatin denounces rebelling peasants as "men who want to be lords themselves and free (*selbs Herrn und frei sein*)."[57] When Luther defined the supreme "freedom of a Christian," he described it first as being a "lord over all and subject to none."[58] Internally, village societies and urban guilds—the model communal units of the sixteenth century—operated according to their own very strict set of hierarchies. And, as among their betters, peasants in the countryside and artisans in the towns restricted effective rule within their organizations to the more well-to-do among them. Everywhere the strong dominated the weak.[59]

Nor were the free imperial cities shining examples of democratic corporations.[60] Zurich's adherence to Zwingli's theology, which was supposedly more socially enlightened than Luther's, and the city's membership in the Swiss Confederacy, supposedly more politically advanced than Saxon government, might lead one to expect Zurich to have been then a progressive model for the whole of early modern Europe. Yet during Zwingli's lifetime there was not a more controlled European city; there "big brother" always watched, and neighbors were encouraged by their government to spy on one another.[61] In this regard 1520s Zurich fully matched Calvin's Geneva of two decades later.

But none of this was unusual for the age. Even in the many imaginary literary utopias of the sixteenth century in which contemporaries depicted the ideal society, the authors invariably portray humankind, especially the masses, as weak and corrupt, requiring constant surveillance and coercion in the best of states. The utopian literature of the time indicates a clear preference for centralized authoritarian regimes in which no independent political entities or dissent are tolerated and obedience is the most valued and praised trait of the good citizen.[62] To Luther and his contemporaries, something more basic than political freedom and equality was at stake in the hierarchical ordering of home and society: the viability of life itself.

The association of viability with order may seem strange to people living in modern Western societies, which benefit from a level of material security unknown in the early modern world. But for people then such association was immediate, as it had been for people in preceding centuries, welling up from a level of conviction more elemental than theology and politics. Luther's age instinctively believed that society had to be regimented, with some ruling and some obeying, if it were to survive; if individuals did not cooperate and make sacrifices, none would advance. Such were the convictions that underlay the fondness of that age for patriarchy and hierarchy; and they were carried over immediately into marital relations, child rearing, and pedagogy.[63]

Both individual and official reactions to social and personal disorder display the deep emotional commitment at this time to law, order, and self-control. Consider, for example, contemporary denunciations of social rebellion and individual drunkenness—perorations on what no society should ever be and on what no individual should ever allow himself to become. Rebelling peasants are condemned as victims of their own animal self-indulgence, contemptuously breaking the social contract as they embrace courses of action both unnatural and unchristian. Contemporary historians and commentators variously denounce rebelling peasants as materialists and "mad dogs," "prideful fanatics" engaged in "gang violence,"[64] "wanton and uncharitable" people,[65] who "strive against nature and try to reverse it, as if the feet could rule the head."[66] In a popular pamphlet of 1525, the Lutheran pastor Johann Agricola scoffs at one Wolff Schwermer ("Mad Wolf"), a Müntzerite who has rebelled against his master, and wonders if the bestial side of the common man has now triumphed over him altogether.

> You say that you want to be "free," but by this you mean free to give nothing to anybody, for there is no obedience in you; free, indeed, to fall upon people and take from them by force what you claim to be your own; free no longer to work, so that you may degenerate in gluttony, drinking, gaming, and whoring, like wild, untamed animals.[67]

Even before the Peasants' Revolt broke out, Philipp Melanchthon joined the chorus of respondents to the articles of the Swabian peasants. He informed the peasants that the type or structure of a government was not as important as civil peace and order under it: "one divides property differently in Saxony than along the Rhine, but the Gospel nowhere requires governments anywhere to end serfdom." The great educator went on to express the opinion that the German masses needed more subjection and control, not less:

> A wild, untamed people like the Germans should not have as much freedom as they presently enjoy. . . . Germans are such an undisciplined, wanton, bloodthirsty people that they should always be harshly governed. . . . As Eccl. 33[:25] teaches; "As food, whip, and load befit an ass, so food, discipline, and work are the lot of a servant."[68]

The many sixteenth-century tracts on drunkenness and perceived related forms of personal self-destruction (dancing, whoring, and gambling) portray humankind as frivolous and undisciplined by nature, many internally near chaos, their very survival dependent on the degree to which they can break their innate habits, attain sobriety, and take control of their lives. "There is inborn in mankind by nature a lust to drink to excess," proclaims Jacob Schenck, the court preacher to the elector of Saxony; only an alteration of character by spiritual rebirth can counteract it.[69] In 1528, in a major tract on what he believed to be Germany's supreme social problem, the Spiritualist Sebastian Franck condemned pervasive drunkenness as the door to every individual and social vice: it weakens the body and shortens life, destroys honor and property, creates beggars, perverts judgment, blinds reason, excuses wrongdoing, inspires rebellion, encourages blasphemy, foolishness, ignorance, foolhardiness, promiscuity, and every form of disorderly life, makes people frivolous in word, work, and manner, spawns idolatry, and brings God's retaliatory wrath down upon society as a whole—altogether a certain sign of the Last Days.[70]

In 1531, Saxon rulers issued directives against morally disruptive forces in the land under the rubrics "blasphemy and drunkenness," the former the greatest sin against the first table of God's law, the latter that against the second. Describing blasphemers as "godless, disrespectful, wild, desperate, wanton people, who despise God," Saxon magistrates deemed drunkenness the supreme German vice: by "acting German" (*germanisieren*) people understand "getting drunk." Blasphemers and alcoholics are described as "subhuman species" (*wie das viehe leben*), laws unto themselves, defying both divine and human authority.[71] The Hessian reformer Melchior Ambach perceived the same socially catastrophic license in "uncontrolled, wanton dancing" (*uppigs/Sardanapalich tantzen*) which exposed the genitals; to Ambach's dismay, dancing was an increasingly popular and accepted pastime, occasioning "pretense, pride, wild spirits, hatred, frivolity, indiscipline, luxuriance, brawling, contentiousness, wounds, murder, adultery, whoring, among other sins and outrages." As an alternative amusement, more befitting creatures made in the image of God, Ambach recommended the "honorable and disciplined pleasure of chaste, pious dancing" in celebration of God's mercy after the example of David and Miriam in the Old Testament.[72]

As the political indiscipline of tyranny was believed to beget that of rebellion, and that of rebellion, renewed tyranny in a vicious cycle of providential punishment, so people associated the moral indiscipline of drunkenness with social and political expressions of divine wrath. Pamphleteers portrayed the Turkish invasions of western Europe as "God's whip" upon Germany's endemic gluttony and drunkenness and claimed that his lash would continue to fall upon German backs until Germany became again a land of "sober, rational, and disciplined people."[73] When, in 1546, a Lutheran pastor in Wertheim elaborated signs of Germany's moral corruption in explanation of the then apparent defeat of the Reformation by imperial armies, he pointed to the unprecedented pomp, excess, and indiscipline in dress, food, drink, and ambition, which had created widespread striving against the social order. "The heart of the problem," he concluded, "is that no one wants to be subordinate to another; everyone wants to have priority over others."[74]

The social experience of a great many Germans, then—not least those with something to lose and in a position to impose their will on others—inclined them to fear social disorder more than political tyranny. The Reformation directed its choicest condemnations at *spiritual* tyranny and *political* anarchy. Even the peasants, the great rebels of the age, whose basic grievances few doubted to be just, hesitated in the midst of their revolt, failing to strike decisively even when able to do so, because of uncertainty over the propriety of such action.[75] Surely such a set of priorities, so fundamentally different from those of Americans at the birth of their nation, had something to do with the sheer physical vulnerability of early modern Europe and the massive internal fragmentation that distinguished Germany, a land of more than three hundred autonomous political entities, from other European lands. Under the conditions of that age, strongman rule was less frightening and oppressive than tyranny is in today's world, and for most people then it was the lesser of two evils when the alternatives were contemplated.

If Luther's political thought was a conservative reaction to German fears of social and political disorder, it was also a constructive response to contemporary problems. A balanced assessment must conclude that the anti-authoritarian strains in Lutheran political philosophy and practice are as prominent as themes of political subservience, and that defiance of tyranny, both spiritual and political, is as manifest a part of the heritage of the Reformation as obedience to authority.[76] Luther's contemporaries saw him as both rebel and reactionary. If after the Peasants' Revolt and the Saxon visitations in the countryside, he bewailed common people as "pigs and cows," to cite the preface of his *Large Catechism* (1529), he also praised the common man's simplicity and honest work as a model for all Christians and recognized his spiritual equality according to the "priesthood of all believers" (Luther's teaching that each person in the end must believe for himself and not trust in another's words or ritual). If the Reformation gave the German states a new sense of their political sovereignty and ability to act on it, it also endowed them with a profound ethical and cultural mission, over which evangelical clergy were to stand a vigilant watch.[77] That centuries later German Christians and politicians in different social and political circumstances appealed to the conservative side of this heritage to support tyranny and racism is hardly something for which Luther and the Reformation can be made responsible. The sins of each age must also be its own. A truer legacy of the Reformation could as easily have been invoked with very different consequences, had the will to do so been there. If Lutheran political theory placed blinders on Lutheran churches when it came to mounting resistance against tyrants, the fault lay not with the teacher but with those taught.

What has given birth in the modern world to the "ugly German" seems to be not political conservatism and subservience at all, but rampant cultural romanticism and millenarianism. If anything can be said categorically about the German Reformation, it is that it was no friend to the "Third Reichs" of its age. Luther and his followers were the chief foes of the various theocratic experiments of the century, both spiritual and social, both mild and extreme, from the modest "theocracies" of Karlstadt and Zwingli, to the revolutionary spiritualism of Thomas Müntzer and the Anabaptist utopia in the city of Münster, where, in 1534, a regime of royal prophets briefly came to power. Finding themselves upon a sea of religious fervor, mainline Protestants admonished steadiness and sobriety, expecting only modest and difficult social progress—what Luther liked to call darning and patching the social fabric (*flicke und pletze dran*).[78] It would be difficult to find in any age another movement more devoted to unmasking the impossible dreams of the common man and saving him from his own gullibility. No small part of the Reformation's success can be traced to the reformers' dogged pragmatism, their grudging recognition of what was historically possible within their own age.

Historically, mass culture has been no haven of political freedom and social equality. Conversely, the proposition that elites are historically responsible for their denial is simplistic and reductive. The many have tyrannized the few as often as the few the many. The people of the past cannot reasonably be expected to have acted on options they either did not know they had or were incapable of implementing. The realistic option in Luther's age was for the dominant forms of government to become, by contemporary standards, more efficient in the exercise of their mandate and fairer in the treatment of their subjects. That is what Luther and his followers urged—patient, persistent improvement of government rather than its violent overthrow—and what, at least haltingly, began to occur on behalf of the common man in the wake of the Peasants' Revolt.[79] The recess of the Diet of Speyer in 1526 put it this way when local authority was reestablished in the wake of rebellion:

> Although the common man and our subject seriously forgot his place and acted crudely against his government in the recent revolt, in order that he may see that the grace and mercy of his rulers are greater and more forthcoming than his own irrational behavior, let every government be empowered, as opportunity and pleasure permit, to return to their previous place of honor all subjects who submit themselves unconditionally and have been punished for their actions, placing them again in office, requalifying and equipping them again to counsel, judge, give testimony, and hold office, so that they may at all times hear the concerns and grievances of others and render merciful and helpful decisions according to the nature of each case. Nor should [reappointed] magistrates, mayors, and other [of our] servants burden the people unreasonably, but leave those who obey the law alone.[80]

The Reformation did not aspire to great social and political change, nor did it create such change. Within established political regimes it made only modest promises of order and security, and it provided opportunities for greater charity and justice only to the extent that people and their leaders were willing to do their part. At its best the Reformation freed ordinary people from beliefs it deemed useless and harmful and from the passive acceptance of tradition that had rendered so many such easy prey to the *Menschensatzungen* of Rome and the pipe dreams of Germany's social prophets. To the extent that Luther's political thought was an integral part of that undertaking, it may be said to have served the spiritual and political maturation of ordinary Germans more constructively than did the impossible political ideals of the age.

# IV

# From Law to Life:

## The Reformation
## Embraced

# 7. Luther
# on Family Life

U nlike the old clergy, the new clergy married, virtually en masse. From the outset they demanded the right to marry; for both Saxon and Swiss reformers, clerical marriage was as prominent a tenet as justification by faith. In making it so, the reformers attempted to set an example of Christian life for the laity in domestic as well as in spiritual matters. Nothing caught the new clergy up more personally in the Reformation's transition from theory to real life than the institution of marriage. In the new families they created these clergy found an emotional warmth and intimacy that had escaped them in the cloisters and parishes of the old church. Possessed of wives and soon with children, Protestant clerics became self-styled marriage counselors and child psychologists, as freespoken and dogmatic in domestic matters as in divine. But marriage also put their religious thinking to a test celibate clergy had been able to avoid. Even a man as self-assured as Martin Luther discovered that life within a family had a way of rewriting theology.

When we think of Martin Luther, we understandably think first of the monk and theologian who wanted to reform the church, a great man of God seemingly obsessed with sin and the devil and lost in otherworldly pursuits.[1] But the monk and the theologian who wrote the Ninety-five Theses and threw an inkwell at the devil was also a husband and the father of six children. Problems of marriage and family life preoccupied Luther even before he married in 1525. While still a celibate priest, he wrote extensively on the subject. He portrayed marriage as an institution as much in crisis as the church and no less in need of reform. He describes marriage as "universally in awful disrepute," with peddlers everywhere selling "pagan books that treat of nothing but the depravity of womankind and the unhappiness of the estate of marriage"—a reference to misogynist and antimarriage sentiments popular among his contemporaries. Women and marriage were widely ridiculed in proverbs and jokes;[2] the biblical stories of the downfall of Adam, Samson, and David at the hands of women had gained popularity;[3] and the advocates of virginity and celibacy never missed an opportunity to remind the lovestricken of the sacrifices and suffering that marriage and parenthood entailed.[4]

It may seem surprising to learn that Martin Luther was a leading defender of the dignity of women and the goodness of marriage. He is perhaps too well known for his famous jesting comments on the meaning of woman's anatomy. "Women have narrow shoulders and wide hips," he quipped one evening at the table; "therefore they ought to be domestic; their very physique is a sign from their Creator that he intended them to limit their activity to the home."[5] Luther, however, also deserves to be known as the century's leading critic of Aristotle's depiction of women as botched males (Aristotle's theory assumed that a perfect generative act would always result in a male offspring).[6] Luther also criticized the church fathers (Jerome, Cyprian, Augustine, and Gregory) for "never having written anything good about marriage."[7]

Like the church fathers, the clergy of the Middle Ages were obsessed with chastity and sexual purity. Saint Augustine portrayed sexual intercourse in Paradise as occurring without lust and emotion, Adam and Eve calmly reflecting on God as their sexual organs chastely fulfilled the marital duty.[8] Approximation of such self-control, to the point of suppressing human sexual desire in imitation of Christ, had inspired the monastic life. The clergy not only attempted to live up to such ascetic ideals in their own lives, they also wanted to model the private sexual lives of the laity on them.

Consider, for example, a vernacular catechism from 1494, which elaborates the third deadly sin (impurity) under the title: "How the Laity Sin in the Marital Duty." According to the catechism, the laity sin sexually in marriage by (1) unnatural acts and positions, contraception, and masturbation; (2) desiring sex with another while performing it with one's spouse; (3) desiring sex with another while not performing it with one's spouse; (4) refusing the marital duty without an honest reason, thereby forcing a spouse to enter an illicit relationship to satisfy unfulfilled sexual need; (5) having sex in forbidden seasons (periods of penance, particularly Lent, during menstruation and the final weeks of pregnancy, and when a mother is lactating); (6) continuing to have sex with a known adulterous spouse; and (7) having sex for the sheer joy of it (*von wollusts wegen*) rather than for the reasons God has commanded, namely, to escape the sin of concupiscence and to populate the earth.[9]

Luther and the first generation of Protestant clerics rejected the patristic tradition of ascetic sexuality in both their theology and their personal lives. This rejection was as great a revolution in traditional church teaching and practice as their challenge of the church's dogmas on faith, works, and the sacraments. They literally transferred the accolades Christian tradition had since antiquity heaped on the religious in monasteries and nunneries to marriage and the home. When Saint Jerome, writing in the fourth century, compared virginity, widowhood, and marriage, he gave virginity a numerical value of one hundred, widowhood, sixty, and marriage, thirty.[10] "Faith, not virginity, fills paradise," the Wittenberg pastor Johannes Bugenhagen retorted in the 1520s. "Saint Jerome's unfortunate comment, 'Virginity fills heaven, marriage the earth,' must be corrected," agreed the Lutheran poet Erasmus Alberus; "let us rather say, '*Connubium replet coelum*, Marriage fills heaven.' "[11]

The first generation of Protestant clerics did not advocate equal rights for women in all walks of life, and none passes the stern tests posed today by modern feminist scholars, who depict the Reformation as having done women more harm than good, despite, or perhaps because of, the reformers' very positive evaluation of marriage. Idealizing women as wives and mothers, Protestants are accused of closing down wherever they could the contemporary institutions that allowed early modern women to have "an existence of their own in a more or less satisfying way"—namely, the cloister and the bordello. The claimed result: "an enormous impoverishment of previously provisioned women and the creation of a vast army of female beggars."[12]

This harsh judgment is made from the perspective of the most egalitarian segment of twentieth-century society. When the domestic policies of Protestants are viewed less anachronistically against the religious culture and domestic practice of the Middle Ages, they are seen to address issues of great relevance to the well-being of sixteenth-century women and to have assisted the efforts then under way to reform the institution of marriage.

## CELIBACY AND MARRIAGE

Luther and his followers regarded the cloister, with its glorification of virginity and celibacy, as the chief expression of the age's antifeminism and hostility to marriage. When Protestant towns and territories dissolved cloisters and nunneries, they did so in the sincere belief that they were freeing the women there from sexual repression, cultural deprivation, and domination by inferior and abusive male clergy and religious. Among the leaders of the Reformation, it was widely believed that in most cases women had been placed in cloisters against their will and without full understanding of the consequences. They also believed that nuns were more easily bullied by their superiors than monks, and had far greater difficulty breaking their vows and returning to the world when they chose to do so. The reformers had no concept whatsoever of the cloister as a special "woman's place," where women might gain a degree of freedom and authority denied them in the secular world, while at the same time escaping the drudgery of marriage, the domination of husbands, and the debilities of serial pregnancies and motherhood. Had such an argument been made to them, the reformers would surely have condemned it as an unnatural and unchristian attempt on the part of women to escape their God-given responsibilities in life. They would also surely have marveled at the spectacle of modern feminist scholars identifying with the cloistered women of the Middle Ages, to the sixteenth-century Protestant mind, their age's most sexually repressed group.

Luther rejected the cloister altogether as a proper solution to the problem of unmarried daughters, especially the younger daughters of noblemen and wealthy burghers. He insisted that fathers at every social rank had a responsibility to make proper marriages for all of their children and to avoid the mismatch of the cloister.[13] He actively encouraged fathers to remove their daughters from convents, and he tacitly approved the use of force to that end. In 1523, for example, he praised a Torgau burgher, Leonhard Koppe, who successfully plotted the escape of his daughter and eleven other nuns, among them Katherine von Bora, Luther's future wife, from the cloister at Nimbschen near Grimma. Koppe regularly delivered herring to the cloister and apparently smuggled the sisters out in empty herring barrels. Luther published a pamphlet account of the deed as an example for all parents with children in cloisters, comparing Koppe's freeing of the sisters with Moses' deliverance of the children of Israel from Egypt. He admonished parents to consider the plight of women placed in cloisters while they were still "young, foolish, and inexperienced." The great majority, he believed, discovered at puberty that they could not suppress their sexual desire and need for male companionship. In light of such facts, only "unmerciful" parents and "blind and mad" clergy could permit girls to suffer and waste away in cloisters: "a woman is not created to be a virgin, but to conceive and bear children."[14]

To document his charges against the cloister, Luther encouraged the publication of exposés by renegade nuns. One impressive example is Florentina of Ober Weimar, a noblewoman who had been placed in the cloister at age six. Discovering at fourteen that she lacked the aptitude for celibate vows, she so informed her superior, only thereafter to find herself forced to abide by the rules of the cloister and to endure ostracism, ridicule, imprisonment, and even thrashings whenever she again attempted to gain her release.[15]

As far as Luther was concerned, opportunities for marriage abounded; the rapid marriage of numbers of former monks and nuns in the 1520s was proof enough. Where the Reformation succeeded, new laws prohibited boys and girls from entering cloisters, and the majority of monks and nuns already there were either pensioned off or returned to their families, those among them wishing to marry receiving permission immediately to do so.

It was not the celibate ideal alone that Protestants believed threatening to the stability of contemporary marriage and family life. The marital legislation of the medieval church seemed to them equally menacing. Luther accused church law of encouraging immature and unhappy marriages by its recognition of so-called "secret" marriages. These were private unions entered into by youths of canonical age (at least twelve for girls and fourteen for boys) without the knowledge and consent of their parents and apart from any public witnesses. The medieval church sanctioned such unions grudgingly in an attempt to control premarital sex and to bring marriage, at its inception, under the moral authority of the church.

Luther also accused the medieval church of impeding mature marriages by defining numerous "impediments" to marriage within an exceedingly broad spectrum of biological, legal, and spiritual relationships. Traditionally the church had required a dispensation for a marriage to occur between couples related by blood or marriage as distantly as third cousins. Godparentage was treated as a "spiritual affinity" and prevented marriage between a godchild and a godparent and all of the siblings and children of the godparent. Adoption produced a similar impediment. Nor could a Christian marry a non-Christian (the impediment of "religious disparity"). Even defective eyesight and speech could prevent a valid marriage in medieval theology; a person who was blind and dumb had to obtain church dispensation to marry.[16]

For Lutherans, the secret marriages of youth indicated a cavalier approach to the most serious of life's decisions and the most important of human institutions. "When the honeymoon is over," warned the Eisenach reformer Jacob Strauss, "and one has to contend with the body of a sick mate, then we discover how lasting is the fidelity of a marriage based on lust."[17] Among both Lutherans and Zwinglians, new marriage laws required both parental consent and a public witnessing of the vows, normally in church, before a marriage could be deemed fully licit. As important as such measures were, they did not put an end to clandestine marriages. Confronted by youth in love who had sexually consummated their relationship and might even be expecting a child, Protestants found themselves recognizing marriages undertaken without parental consent as readily as Catholics had done.[18]

Although Luther opposed the private marriages of youth, he strongly defended the right of young people to marry whomever they pleased. Learning of parents who forced their children into unwanted marriages with unhappy consequences for all, he devoted a special tract to the subject in 1524. As the title indicates, he believed that marriage should be a family decision respecting the wishes of all family members, but especially of those most directly involved: *Parents Should Neither Compel nor Hinder the Marriage of Their Children and Children Should Not Marry Without the Consent of Their Parents.* He advised youth confronted with the "outrageous injustice" of a planned forced marriage to turn to their local magistrates for help when informal appeals through relatives, friends, or a sympathetic parent failed. Youth who found all such efforts frustrated were advised to flee to another land and there marry their chosen mate at will.[19]

As for parents confronted with a marriage they could neither willingly

Des wirdigen Herrn D. Joannis Bugenhagen
Pomerani / Pastoris der Kirchen zu Wittemberg / warhafftige
abcontrafectung / daselbs gemacht.

Wittenberg pastor Johannes Bugenhagen, ca. 1546; Lucas Cranach the Younger,
in *Max Geisberg: The German Single-Leaf Woodcut: 1500–1550*, vol. 2, rev. and ed.
Walter L. Strauss (New York: Hacker Art Books, 1974), p. 634.

accept nor easily prevent (or dissolve), Luther advised that they state their objections frankly, but permit the marriage to occur without their approval, thereby letting obstinate children learn by experience the wisdom of their parents.[20] As a husband and a parent, Luther appreciated both the difficulty of separating young lovers and the futility of forcing two people to live together against their will. If, as he believed, men and women were supposed to find in marriage "the things they naturally desire, namely, sex and offspring, a life together, and mutual trust,"[21] then to force two people together (or apart) against their will threatened both the purpose of marriage and social order beyond it.

As for the church's many impediments to marriage, Luther condemned them as "only snares for taking money," and he derided those who imposed them as "merchants selling vulvas and genitals."[22] He recognized as valid only those impediments of consanguinity and affinity set forth in Leviticus 18:6–18. This position made it possible for Lutherans to accept such previously forbidden marriages as those between first cousins, step-relations, and the siblings of deceased spouses and fiancées, and to deny altogether impediments based on contrived spiritual and legal grounds such as godparentage and adoption. According to Luther, "one may take as (one's) spouse whomsoever (one) pleases, whether it be godparent, godchild, or the daughter or sister of a sponsor (i.e., a godparent) . . . and disregard those artificial, money-seeking impediments."[23]

The politicians of the age were not as bold in domestic matters as the new theologians, and the laws and institutions of marriage did not in fact change as rapidly or as radically during the sixteenth century as the reformers had decreed they might in the 1520s and 1530s. The biblical impediments for the most part remained, and newly created marriage courts, which became predictably more conservative with age, rigidly supervised domestic morality. Still, it is a gross exaggeration to say that Luther removed the pope from the bedroom only to put the state there.[24] Foundations were laid in Protestant lands for both a more realistic and a more charitable treatment of marriage. On the one hand, new laws made immature marriages more difficult to contract, while, on the other, mature and disciplined marriages became less vulnerable to arbitrary spiritual harassment. The domestic surveillance encouraged by the Reformation had the stability of marriage and family, not impossible religious ideals, at heart.

## SPOUSES

Luther liked to turn traditional criticisms of women and marriage back onto the clerical critics themselves. He once described marriage, for example, as the only institution in which a chaste life *could* be maintained, and he insisted that "one cannot be *un*married without sin,"[25] arguments that could only have baffled the defenders of celibacy. Nothing seemed to Luther to be a more natural and necessary part of life than marriage. "Marriage pervades the whole of nature," he disarmingly points out; "for all creatures are divided into male and female; even trees marry; likewise, budding plants; there is also marriage between rocks and stones."[26] Living at a time in which most people married comparatively late (women in their early twenties, men in their mid- to late twenties), he praised the early marriages (at nineteen) and high fertility of the Israelites. He condemned women who shunned motherhood because children might diminish their leisure and pleasure.[27] "Our savior Christ did not despise motherhood," he reminded the advocates of the solitary life, "but took flesh from the womb of a woman."[28]

Luther had a high regard for the ability of women to shape society by molding its youth and civilizing its men through the institution of marriage. He joined the moralists of his age in praising women as mothers, for filling the earth with life, and as wives, for taming the beast within their husbands. "A companionable woman brings joy to life," he told his table companions one evening; "women attend to and rear the young, administer the household, and are inclined to compassion; God has made them compassionate by nature so that by their example men may be moved to compassion also."[29] Even when Luther seemed in jest to denigrate women, he could still bestow on them a high compliment. Once at table he declared, "Eloquence is not to be praised in women; it is more fitting that they stammer and babble." These unkind comments came after he had told a visiting Englishman (possibly the reformer Robert Barnes), who knew no German, that he should learn German from Luther's wife Katie because she was the more fluent, indeed, "the most eloquent speaker (*facundissima*) of the German language."[30] On more than one public occasion, Luther described Katie as his "lord": "I am an inferior lord," he would say, "she the superior; I am Aaron, she is my Moses."[31] He bore her outspoken criticism of his poor business instincts and misplaced charity with respect and good humor. Once he compared "household wrath," by which he meant a fight with his wife, with the wrath of God in politics, where war and death threaten, and in religion, where the soul and heaven are at stake, and drew the following conclusion: "If I can survive the wrath of the devil in my sinful conscience, I can withstand the anger of Katharine von Bora."[32] He also acknowledged his respect for her abilities in his last will and testament. Ignoring the traditional German practice of appointing a male trustee to administer a deceased husband's estate on behalf of his widow and children, he directly designated her "heir to everything."[33]

Katharine von Bora earned such respect from her husband, whom she surpassed in virtually all worldly matters. Modern feminist scholars who today praise the cloister as the ideal place for women in the Middle Ages may do so because the cloistered life seems at a distance to have been so much like the modern academic life of women—that is, a protected and privileged life, free from the cares of the real world, allowing educated women both power and the leisure to pursue their own thoughts. Katharine von Bora fled that life for one she believed held even greater opportunities for the women of her age. She became a model housewife and an accomplished businesswoman. To increase their income, she remodeled the old cloister in which she and Martin lived so that it would accommodate up to thirty students and guests. She also expanded the cloister garden and repaired the cloister brewery. She became locally famous as a herbalist, and her beer was so renowned that Luther once took samples to the electoral court. He dubbed her "the morning star of Wittenberg," as her day began at 4:00 A.M., much like that of the wife of a butcher or a merchant.[34] As the Luthers' example indicates, Protestant women could work outside the home as readily as women in previous centuries, despite increasing restrictions in the sixteenth century on women's vocational opportunities as a result of growing inflation and new state bureaucracy.

Luther obviously meant it when he said, "there is no bond on earth so sweet nor any separation so bitter as that which occurs in a good marriage."[35] His comments on marriage leave the impression of an experienced husband who had given the matter considerable thought. Take, for example, the following analysis: "In the beginning of a relationship love is glowing hot (*fervidus*); it intoxicates and blinds us, and we rush forth and embrace one another." But once married, we tend to grow tired of one another, confirming the saying of Ovid: "We hate the

Katharine von Bora, 1530; Hans Brosamer, in *Max Geisberg: The German Single-Leaf Woodcut: 1500–1550*, vol. 1, rev. and ed. Walter L. Strauss (New York: Hacker Art Books, 1974), p. 392.

things that are near us and we love those that are far away (*praesentia odimus, absentia amamus*)."[36]

> A wife is easily taken, but to have abiding love, that is the challenge. One who finds it in his marriage should thank the Lord God for it. Therefore, approach marriage earnestly and ask God to give you a good, pious girl, with whom you can spend your life in mutual love. For sex [alone] establishes nothing in this regard; there must also be agreement in values and character (*ut conveniant mores et ingenium*).[37]

Luther here expresses a point of view broadly shared by the moral authorities of his day, both Protestant and Catholic. Physical attraction may well play a role in the creation of a marriage, but it is no foundation for a lasting relationship. A mutual willingness to make sacrifices is what holds a marriage together over time. So when seeking a spouse, the most important question was always whether the object of one's desire was also a person worthy of respect and trust, that is, a person with companionable qualities and the ability to keep his or her word. According to Luther, both he and his wife to be had "begged God earnestly for grace and guidance" before they married.[38] They had in fact long been associated in Wittenberg between 1523 and 1525. Their relationship had engendered much gossip, as Luther was a constant visitor at the home of Lucas Cranach, where Katharine, a renegade nun under Luther's supervision, lodged. Luther twice attempted unsuccessfully to arrange other marriages for her. According to Catholic pamphleteers, they "lived together" in Wittenberg before they married.[39] Whatever the truth of this particular gossip, such practices were not uncommon among clergy at the time. Zwingli made public his secret marriage to a widow only a short time before the arrival of their child.[40]

Because of the importance attached to companionship in marriage, the reformers tolerated bigamous attachments as a solution to loveless marriages, particularly among powerful rulers, whose protection they needed and whose reckless behavior they could not curb anyway. They also endorsed for the first time in Western Christiandom genuine divorce and remarriage. Although the reformers viewed marriage as a spiritual bond transcending all other human relationships, it did not in their opinion create a permanent state. A marriage could definitively end this side of eternity and a new one begin for separated spouses. In his earliest writings on such matters, Luther expressed "great wonder" that the church forbade people to remarry who were irreconcilably separated and living apart because of one partner's adultery. "Christ," he pointed out, "permits divorce for adultery and compels none to remain unmarried [thereafter]; and Saint Paul would rather have us [re]marry than burn [now with lust and later in hell]."[41]

In the medieval church, divorce had meant only the separation of a couple from a common bed and table, not the dissolution of the marriage bond and the right to marry again. As long as both lived and the marriage was not annulled, a "divorced" couple remained man and wife in the eyes of the church and were so treated by law where the church prevailed. In practice, this situation meant that the turmoil of a failed marriage might never end for a couple.

Protestants, by contrast, generally permitted divorce and remarriage on five grounds: adultery, willful abandonment, chronic impotence, life-threatening hostility, and willful deceit (such as when a presumed virgin is discovered after marriage to have given birth previously to an illegitimate child or to be pregnant by another man). Most Protestant writers sympathized with the position of the Strasbourg reformer Martin Bucer, who declared no proper marriage to exist where affection was not regularly shared and all conversation had ceased.[42]

Luther personally preferred secret bigamy to divorce and remarriage, when a marriage had irretrievably broken down. He sanctioned such an arrangement for women with impotent husbands as early as 1521. If a woman in such a situation could not take her case to the divorce court out of fear of notoriety, he advised that she enter with her husband's consent a secret marriage with his brother or another male mutually agreed upon, and raise any children of this second union as if they were those of the impotent husband. Luther preferred such an arrangement to outright divorce because he believed it ensured continuing companionship and support for each spouse (in this case, psychological for the husband and financial for the wife), while at the same time it prevented whoring and adultery on the part of the healthy spouse (in this case, the wife), who gained from it a regular sexual outlet.

Bigamy obviously required exceptional tolerance on the part of the incapacitated person, and Luther knew that such charity of spirit would not always be readily forthcoming. If the incapacitated spouse refused to enter into such an arrangement, and the sexual desires of the healthy spouse remained overpowering, he instructed the healthy spouse to marry another and flee to a land where they might live together as man and wife without being prosecuted for bigamy.[43]

Protestant marriage courts did not permit divorce and remarriage to occur without first making every effort to reunite an estranged couple and revive the dead marriage. All concerned deemed reconciliation preferable to divorce in every case. Despite lip service to harsh biblical punishments, pastors actually discouraged extreme penalties for adultery, lest an estranged couple be driven even farther apart, as might happen when an adulterer was punished by exile or by fines that impoverished him. When a table companion once expressed to Luther the belief that adulterers should be summarily executed, Luther rebuked him with a local example of how harsh punishment had done more harm than good to a couple. A pious wife, who had borne her husband four children and had never been unfaithful, one day committed adultery. For the transgression, the enraged husband had her publicly flogged. Afterward, Luther, Pastor Bugenhagen, and Philipp Melanchthon tried to persuade the couple to reconcile. The husband was willing to take her back and let bygones be bygones, but the wife had been so humiliated by the flogging and the resulting scandal that she abandoned her husband and children and wandered away, never to be seen again. "Here," Luther comments, "one should have pursued reconciliation before punishment."[44] Chronic and willful public adultery, however, was treated harshly and without regret.

Both spiritually and socially, Lutheran theology held the community formed by a husband and a wife to be society's most fundamental. The marriage bond was too important to be allowed to stand when all conversation, affection, and respect between a husband and a wife had irretrievably broken down. And the same bond was also too important to allow a marriage to dissolve without a fight to save it. Protestants gained the right to divorce and remarry in the sixteenth century, but it remained a difficult one to exercise.

## CHILDREN

Luther prized fertility and seems to have been barely sensitive to the physically debilitating effects of multiple pregnancies on women. Overpopulation did not threaten his age, and both sexes then viewed

childbearing and child rearing as womankind's natural and divinely ordained vocation. Perceiving pregnant women to be both healthier and
happier than barren women, Luther urged wives to be constantly pregnant: "Even if women bear themselves weary or ultimately bear themselves out," he declared while still a bachelor (1522), "this is the purpose
for which they exist."[45] As an ex-monk who discovered the joys of marriage and parenthood late in life, at age forty-two, when he was financially
secure and internationally famous, he may be forgiven for scorning parents who did not view children as a blessing and for having so little appreciation for the economic burdens placed on less fortunate families by
too many children.[46] His role in domestic matters was always that of an
advocate for the family against the defenders of virginity and celibacy.
Believing that his age maligned marriage and parenthood, he exalted the
family in all its dimensions and utterly without qualification.

His comments on children and his behavior as a parent belie modern
critics who associate Protestantism with negative feelings about children
because of its teachings on original sin and the bondage of the will.[47]
Luther, who fondly referred to his newborn as "little heathens," praised
infancy as the most perfect state on earth. "The life of the infant is the
most blessed and best," he declared once at table. "Infants have no
temporal cares. . . . They do not . . . perceive the terror of death and hell,
but know only pure thoughts and happy speculations."[48] "(Whereas) we
old fools . . . argue over the Word of God, infants believe it in pure faith
without argument."[49] Observing his own children at play, arguing and
fighting with one another one minute but reconciled and embracing the
next, he comments, "How pleased God must be with the life and play
of children; all of their sins against one another are forgiven sins."[50]
Luther looked on children less than six years old as being especially
susceptible to moral education and religious virtue, something he attributed to the immaturity of their reasoning powers. By such a point of
view he did not intend to disparage reason so much as to recognize that
its advancement brought with it the entrenchment of self-will and the
cunning to plot against God.[51] Lutherans steeped their children in
catechetical and moral instruction, apparently skeptical of the possibility
of significantly shaping moral character after a child had reached puberty.[52] By age fourteen—in the moral life of a person, beginning
adulthood—the twig, for good or ill, was bent as the tree would
forevermore grow.

Education at home, in church, and at school was designed to suppress purely selfish behavior and encourage altruism and self-sacrifice in a child. The goal was not, as some modern scholars have argued, the creation of a child bereft of self-confidence and passively resigned to the will of his superiors. In the Lutheran home, a "disciplined child" was above all one capable of acting charitably for the sake of others, a courageous as well as a congenial child. In defense of a government's right and responsibility to maintain schools for the civic and religious instruction of all children, boys and girls alike, Luther informed parents that their children were "more God's than their own."[53] He meant that children were subject to "divine" rules and expectations in their rearing, which could not simply be left to parental whim. The creation of socially useful and responsible adults, able both to manage the world and to please God, was a communal responsibility shared equally by parents, teachers, and magistrates.

Luther had six children of his own (Hans, Elizabeth, Magdalene, Martin, Paul, and Margaretha), whom he subjected to high moral standards and strict discipline. "My greatest wish," he once confided at table, "is that none of my children become lawyers," a sentiment that expressed his association of the study of law with vanity and social inutility and lawyers, along with Jews and papists, with an acquisitive and self-justifying frame of mind that knew nothing of charity toward others or salvation by faith.[54]

Luther could be a stern father. Once he punished Hans, his eldest, for an unspecified but serious moral lapse by forbidding him to be in his father's presence for three days. At the end of this period, he required the boy to write a letter begging his father's forgiveness, to which letter the senior Luther replied that he would sooner have his son dead than ill-bred.[55] Nevertheless, Luther urged parents always to discipline their children with forethought and caution, taking into account the unique personality of each. Once he explained his entrance into the monastery as a cowardly act that had resulted from his parents' too strict discipline, which he believed had rendered him timid. He did not think the discipline wrong or the punishment undeserved, but he accused his parents of not taking sufficiently into account the effect of their punishment on him. They failed to adjust punishment to his particular temperament as a child. As a result, their discipline weakened rather than strengthened him.[56] A proper parental discipline, he concluded, should tailor punishment to a child's disposition and increase his self-confidence, while at the same time correcting his behavior.

If a parent's reaction to the death of a child may be taken as a commentary on parental character, Luther was a deeply loving father. When Elizabeth died at eight months, he commented on the personal devastation it brought: "I so lamented her death that I was exquisitely sick, my heart rendered soft and weak; never had I thought that a father's heart could be so broken for his children's sake."[57] Magdalene's death in 1542 at thirteen overwhelmed him to the point that his faith in God failed. He wrote of it to his friend Justus Jonas, pointing out that while he and his wife should be thanking God that Magdalene was now free of the flesh and the devil, neither could do so.

> The force of our natural love is so great that we are unable to do this without crying and grieving in our hearts . . . [and] experiencing death ourselves. . . . The features, the words, and the movement of our living and dying daughter, who was so very obedient and respectful, remain engraved in our hearts; even the death of Christ . . . is unable to take all this away as it should. You, therefore, please give thanks to God in our stead.[58]

As a theologian, Luther taught that death was no match for a Christian's faith. In 1531, as his mother lay dying, he consoled her with the words, "Should any thought of . . . death frighten us, let us . . . say . . . , 'Dear death . . . how is it that you are alive and terrifying me? Do you not know that you have been overcome [by Christ]? Do you not know that you, dear death, are quite dead?' "[59] Several months after Magdalene's death, he scolded her still sorrowing brother Hans for his inability to put his grief behind him and get on with his life as he must.[60] Yet, when Luther himself had to accept Magdalene's death, his theology and faith proved a poor consolation for the child he had lost. Returning home from her funeral, he tried to console himself by declaring that he had always been more merciful to girls than to boys, because girls needed more care and protection than boys, and that he now gladly gave Magdalene to God because he knew that God would provide her all the care and protection she needed, adding pitiably, "but in my human heart (*secundum carnem*), I would gladly have kept her here with me."[61] Later, in 1544, at the seemingly imminent death of his ten-year-old daughter Margaretha, he commented that, should she too die, he would "not be angry with God," as he obviously had been at the death of Magdalene.[62]

I know of no other occasion in Martin Luther's life on which his theology and faith were not a match for the enemies who threatened him. He defied the emperor, German princes, and several popes; he cursed and taunted the devil; and in the last years of his life he shouted down in the most unforgiving way what he perceived to be an international conspiracy of Jews, Turks, papists, and bad Christians, who plotted to undo his Reformation. His theology and faith truly failed him only at the death of a child. Some might find it disappointing that the great reformer could love a child more than he trusted God. Yet the theologian and man of faith was also a husband and a father who had taught that "no power on earth is so noble and so great as that of parents."[63] Marriage and parenthood were, arguably, the most satisfying parts of Martin Luther's tormented life, and the success of his Reformation was, arguably, most unambiguous in the domestic sphere. He could, then, be angry with a God who stripped him of his parental dignity by the death of a beloved child.

# 8. Turning Protestant: The Revolution Within

T he capture of a city council and the recitation of a new creed do not necessarily entail the conquest of people's hearts and minds. That truth is well documented by the history of the Reformation. When in 1539, after almost two decades of Protestant political success, Philipp Melanchthon defined the issues still separating evangelicals and "papists," his list was virtually identical to those of the pamphleteers of the early 1520s, right down to an article denouncing the familiar "fabrications" (*Menschensatzungen*) of the pope.[1] Despite official adoption of their creeds and their newly won control of churches and schools, the Protestant clergy continued to find traditional religious practices and folkloric beliefs very strong competitors.[2] People did not become evangelical either overnight or by the book.

But if legal change is not tantamount to behavioral change, neither are the two unrelated. Having begun with small groups of traditional clergy and laity convinced of the errors of the past and the need for reform, the Reformation became a movement capable of shaping history when magistrates and princes, for both pious and self-serving reasons, made evangelical teachings law within their respective towns and territories. Within these regimes new ordinances, curricula, and catechisms attempted to conform the beliefs of the masses to those of the devout few.

How did the revolution of the pamphleteers, secured by law and made routine by sermon and catechism, actually change the lives of people in Protestant lands? Can we gauge the impact of the Reformation on lay emotions and consciences? Was there also a "revolution within" parallel to that in public policy and official practice? Did the Reformation also find a place in people's hearts and affect the way they lived from day to day among their peers?

Historians who have tried to answer such questions have concentrated on indirect and very general indexes of religious belief and behavior, particularly the formulas and bequests of last wills and testaments and such information about religious devotion as one can glean from records of marriages, births, property transactions, and tax levies. Such sources, however valuable, necessarily only scratch the surface of the task of reconstructing daily reality. In these usually scant statistics, the people of the past speak to us across the centuries as mere ciphers in a register, the barest of human testimony.

Unhappy with such sources, other historians have focused instead on the church calendar and on public religiosity in an attempt to understand better the religious belief and practice of the past.[3] They look, for example, at traditional rituals, festivals, the cure of souls (sacramental and disciplinary), and court trials and inquisitions, both for clues to the true content of religious allegiance and as measures of the cultural impact of religion. How many people attend such events and services? What happens on a pilgrimage, at the celebration of the Eucharist, and during the interrogation of a suspected heretic? Are the laity passive, or do they assert themselves and bring their own beliefs and values to bear on established ritual? Were there clashes between the laity and clerical officials? How do elite and popular cultures interact?

What we can infer from the records of such public events and activities may, sadly, be all we shall ever know about the beliefs of most ordinary people, who have left behind few if any direct or personal records. Occasionally such sources will focus on a particular individual and cite his or her own words. Recently historians have brought a feisty Italian miller to life through the records of the Italian inquisition and a clever and beguiling country girl through those of the French courts.[4] But as a rule these sources are by their very nature broadly descriptive and rarely explanatory. And while we can learn from such records what the laity were exposed to as the church year unfolded or as they stood before church officials, we rarely learn anything about what the laity personally thought about such things or how they were affected by them in their private lives. We know the subjects' actions, words, thoughts, and feelings only indirectly as they are perceived and summarized by often indifferent, even unsympathetic officials writing in Latin or in an official vernacular the subjects themselves do not speak. In the end the best of such sources leave us without a direct contemporary voice and with largely impenetrable subjects who, the more they are studied and pondered, the more they seem to look and sound like ourselves.

This problem suggests that scholars of popular religious culture, contrary to their claims, are still dealing with religion as elite spectacle and special event, and not yet with it as an organic aspect of everyday life. In the end the study of lay belief through its set public forms appears to be just another official perspective on it, one not all that different from a contemporary government chronicle or theological tract as far as ordinary people's experience is concerned. But because of their limited nature and the lack of any direct personal testimony in such sources, they also allow the modern historian, aided by the modern social scientist, to substitute his own theories about human motivation and behavior for those of contemporary chroniclers, and theologians, which is fair enough, if one believes that people living centuries after an event can understand it better than those who actually lived through it. This more than anything else, I suspect, is what has made these sources so popular and anthropology and sociology the sine quibus non of the new history.

But what the laity may have made of religion on Sundays and holidays or in the presence of confessors, catechists, visitors, or inquisitors simply is not the most revealing perspective on the daily life of the era. On such occasions people found themselves upon a stage the clergy had set and followed a script the clergy had written. There is something to be learned here, but it does not go to the heart of the matter. If we are to describe the cultural impact of the Reformation on the laity, what we must know above all is what religion meant to them within their own workaday world, when they found themselves outside the corridors of the church and out of the gaze of the clergy, when "being a Christian" had meaning only as religious teaching either had or had not been taken to heart. What did religion mean to the laity in their space and on their time?

If we accept the fact that the sources do not exist for a fair and penetrating portrayal of ordinary life among people who leave behind no direct records of their personal thoughts and beliefs, then we face a decision if we still want to generalize about an age. Either we continue to stack the historical deck, as both contemporary and modern observers do by following their own pet theories and beliefs about mass behavior, or we base our generalizations on limited but contemporary sources that are direct, personal, and detailed. Perhaps we can get closer to depicting accurately the change from Catholic to Protestant belief by investigating the writings of literate laity. Detailed autobiographical sources begin to appear in significant numbers for the first time in the sixteenth century:

family chronicles, diaries, housebooks, and particularly letters.[5] In such sources the men and women of that century comment directly on their actions and their times, and in doing so they provide us personal records of the impact of Protestant polemic and propaganda, laws and catechisms. Such records are a superior measure of contemporary belief and behavior. Although they have been left behind by people in the literate, even learned, and therefore to some extent an "elite" class, they are testimony of an emotional life, and they record common human experiences. Being literate or illiterate, or having means or being poor, on many fundamental levels do not distinguish human beings in any age or culture, nor do they raise one or another group above the existential needs that religion universally serves. If we must generalize about the religious belief of the past, I believe we do so more securely from sources that directly convey a known contemporary voice than we do from sources that are removed from their subjects and can only occasion speculation about who is really speaking.

Autobiographical sources, of course, also have problems; they may be conventional, and individuals can portray themselves for posterity as persons they in fact are not. But at least in such sources, we encounter people who speak to us in their own words about events they actually lived through and pondered. We may, I believe, often learn more about what religion meant to an age from one well-documented life than from scores of general descriptions of mass behavior during Carnival and Lent, or from innumerable records of interrogations of laity by clerical tormentors and judges. Without the ability to make wider inference from more dependable biographical and autobiographical sources, our knowledge of the religious beliefs of the past must remain confined to impersonal patterns of group behavior, which leave ordinary people virtually silent about themselves as individuals with feelings and thoughts of their own.

In what follows I have selected two superbly documented examples of autobiographical comment on religion by laymen well versed in the subject. The first comes from Thomas Platter (1507?–1582), a Swiss who converted to the Reformation in the 1520s while a teenager in Zurich, and who lived into old age under a Protestant regime in Basel. The second commentator, Hermann Weinsberg (1518–1597), a Cologne burgher and lifelong Catholic, lived through both the Reformation and the Counterreformation in perhaps the most religiously traditional and conservative of German cities. Sensitive to the issues posed by both reform movements, Hermann comments freely on the changes they brought about in his world. His life also illustrates an important corollary to lay religious experience in the new Protestant regimes: just as living under a Protestant government did not necessarily ensure that one adopted the new Protestant faith, neither did the persistence of a strong Catholic regime prevent people's sympathizing with Protestant beliefs or maintaining traditional Catholic practices in defiance of the Jesuits and the Counterreformation.[6]

Both of our authors wrote after the fact. Platter composed his entire autobiography in 1572, at age sixty-five, working from memory and records he had kept over the years. In that year his wife, Anna, died after they had been married for forty years, and her death seems to have occasioned the composition of his autobiography. Within two months of her death, Thomas had actually married again. That may seem a bit precipitous from a modern point of view, but in the sixteenth century, marriages occurred for humane and pragmatic as well as for emotional reasons. At that time an old man could freeze or starve to death without a warm and friendly body nearby, and Thomas, at sixty-five, was very much in need of a helpmate. With such major changes in his life, he seems to have concluded that the time had come to tell his story for posterity.

Weinsberg began his great chronicle in 1560, when he was forty-two. It is the fullest autobiography by a German in the sixteenth century and reconstructs his life to that point from memory, living witnesses, and his own research in family records. After 1560, his chronicle became something of a daily diary, which he faithfully kept until his death in 1597. Both men, then, mold recollected earlier experience in accordance with a later, mature prespective on it. Neither account contains snapshots of actual moments, though Weinsberg's post-1560 entries are often same-day accounts. As is the nature of chronicles and diaries, each story is consciously framed from a different and settled religious point of view. And because each author interprets as well as recollects, his story leaves us with a clear and forceful moral. (In chapter 9, we will meet Protestants through a more spontaneous medium and a less processed source, the occasional letters of youth.)

It will be evident to the reader that Platter and Weinsberg were deeply devoted to their respective religious confessions. We would not, however, describe either as a bigot. Indeed, the reader may suspect by chapter's end that these two men were, for their century, every bit as enlightened about matters of faith as we are today. But, as we have also seen in earlier chapters, particularly among the new Protestant clergy, the Reformation also produced pharisees, men who do justice to the perjorative modern image of the "Protestant temperament" as obsessed, intolerant, unforgiving, and fully prepared to sacrifice life to dogma.[7] Still, we err and only indulge our sense of moral superiority over the past when we make such a temperament the defining trait of Protestants. As the subjects of this and the subsequent chapter demonstrate, the Protestant mind is a far more complex and interesting phenomenon.

## THOMAS PLATTER

Thomas Platter grew up in a traditional Swiss family and was expected to enter the priesthood. A coincidence of his birth foretold his vocation: he was born on a Shrove Sunday at the very moment the Mass bells rang out. The event gained a firm place in the family's collective memory, and Thomas grew up with constant reminders of it.

Thomas never knew his natural father, who died while Thomas was still an infant. Thomas grew up a sickly child, a circumstance he attributed to his mother's inability to nurse him. He claims to have survived during his first four years on cow's milk, something frowned on at the time because people then believed bovine milk inadequate to proper human nutrition and more likely to stimulate the development of the bestial side of human nature. But because Thomas's family did not have the means to hire a wet nurse, cow's milk was the only option. It clearly had no long-term ill effects on him, for he outlived all five of his siblings.

His family was never well off. Impoverished by his stepfather's indebtedness, the children had to contribute early to the family's welfare. Thomas's sisters went to work as servants as soon as they were able, and Thomas himself became a goatherd at age six, working first for his relatives and later for a wealthy peasant. At age nine or ten, he was sent to live with his uncle Anthony, a cantankerous old priest in the nearby village of Gasen. The plan was for the uncle to teach Thomas to read the Bible in Latin in preparation for formal schooling and a clerical career. But Uncle Anthony proved to be an "extremely angry man." He beat Thomas and occasionally lifted him up by his ears so that Thomas "screamed like a stuck goat," causing the neighbors to worry that he might be killed.

Thomas understandably did not stay long with his uncle. When the opportunity arose to depart Gasen with a visiting cousin (Paul Summermatter), he seized it. Thereafter, for almost a decade, Thomas wandered from place to place, working at odd jobs and diligently studying on his own.[8]

In the early 1520s, he enrolled in school in Zurich. Thomas recalls his student days as the time of the "dawning of the light of the Gospel," when the Mass and "idols" were still in the churches. Zurich did not remove images from its churches until 2 July 1524, and the Mass continued until 12 April 1525. During these turbulent years of transition from the old religion to the new, Thomas lived with his guardian and mentor, Oswald Myconius, who directed the church school (Fraumünsterschule) Thomas attended and was a leader of the Zurich reform movement. Having never had a true father, Thomas became very attached to Myconius and later referred to him as "father."

Because of his new evangelical beliefs, Myconius disliked having to perform some of the traditional Masses and requiems incumbent on his office. So he asked Thomas, as his *custos* or assistant, to perform some of these services in his place. At the time, Thomas still held traditional beliefs and, as he was preparing for the priesthood, he welcomed the opportunity to substitute for Myconius.

His compliance did not mean, however, that he was wholly naïve. Among his responsibilities was fetching wood and stoking the furnace in the church. Finding himself one morning without firewood, and Zwingli scheduled soon to preach, he remembered that "many idols" hung in the church. So he entered the empty church and removed a "Johannes" (that is, a painting of Saint John), which he substituted for the firewood. As he placed it in the furnace, he recalls having instructed it: "Little John, duck your head." Thomas reports that the missing painting disturbed the priests, who suspected that a covert Lutheran lurked in their midst. Thomas claims that the deed left him guilt-stricken. He kept it from his mentor for many years.

The example of Myconius and the preaching of Zwingli planted doubts about the old church in young Thomas's mind. He recalls thinking privately that the papacy was "pure mischief" (*bubenwerck*), just as Protestant pamphleteers were then alleging. But as an aspiring priest, he naturally resisted such thoughts. As his doubts grew, he clung all the more tenaciously to traditional piety. He says he prayed and fasted more than he really desired to do, and he cultivated new saintly patrons: the Virgin Mary, to intercede on his behalf with Jesus; Saint Catherine, to assist him with his studies; Saint Barbara, to ensure that he would not die without the sacrament; and Saint Peter, to hold open for him the gates of heaven.

Thomas also recorded his sins each day in a book, and on Thursdays and Saturdays, when free from school, he went into the church, sat alone in a pew, and enumerated them. On six separate occasions he joined pilgrims to the shrine in neighboring Einsiedeln. And he went frequently to confession. Once, after he had unthinkingly eaten cheese during a strict fast, a priest threw him into despair by refusing to absolve him without a prior penance. Apparently the penance was a demanding one, which Thomas could not quickly satisfy. The situation proved doubly painful to him because it left him ineligible to receive the sacrament with the other students and to attend a dinner that followed. Fortunately for Thomas, another priest, learning of his predicament, took pity on him and absolved him unconditionally.

The episode reveals his tender emotions at this time, when the old and the new religions warred with each other within him. In addition to such self-inflicted torment, Thomas found himself having to defend the old church against his irreverent peers, who advanced with much less uncertainty into Protestantism.[9]

A powerful sermon by Zwingli on John 10, "I am the good shepherd," finally broke down Thomas's defenses. When he heard Zwingli proclaim that God held shepherds responsible for their lost sheep, Thomas recalls feeling as if he'd been "yanked up by my hair." Thereafter he foreswore the priesthood, plunged into biblical studies, cultivated contacts with humanist scholars, and became openly evangelical in his religious outlook and practice.[10]

Conversion to the Reformation brought new personal difficulties almost immediately. He started to quarrel with his relatives, who considered Zurich a city of heretics—it being well known to them that Zwingli had criticized the pope, attacked the Mass, and rejected the use of images in church. Thomas says he endured "great poverty" in Zurich during these years because the people there, under the influence of the Reformation, refused to give alms for common use—a protest against years of abuse by mendicants and other professional beggars. To earn money and meals, Thomas performed menial chores. Many days he claims to have lived only on salted water, which he begged. When necessity forced him to "sing" on the street for his bread like a poor orphan (public begging by orphans was allowed by the reformers), passersby scorned him, partly because of his advanced age (he was now in his late teens), but mainly because begging had become so disreputable in Zurich in the wake of Protestant criticism. Thomas eventually found work as a courier for Zwingli and Myconius, shuttling messages back and forth between Zurich and Protestant sympathizers in still Catholic cantons.[11]

Having changed creeds, Thomas also took up a new vocation. The evangelical preachers of Zurich had constantly praised manual labor and decried the great number of clergy who did not follow the teaching of Saint Paul and earn their bread by the sweat of their own brows. So Thomas abandoned his clerical studies to learn a trade, something he says many others were also doing at the time because of hostility to clerical scholars created by the Reformation. He apprenticed himself to a master ropemaker, a Lucerner named Rudolf Ambuel, who had himself earlier interrupted a planned clerical career to take up a trade and to marry, also under the influence of his Zurich mentors. To purchase the hemp required for his apprenticeship, Thomas spent his modest maternal inheritance.[12]

After his apprentice year, Thomas moved to Basel and there began to practice his new trade. He could not, however, bring himself to abandon his first love, books, particularly the classics, which he perused at night and on holidays, and even on the job. Once he hid a Plautus given him by scholar-printer Andreas Cratander among his hemp, to read on the sly when his master was away. His contacts with humanists also grew; he met the eminent German Beatus Rhenanus, whose students he had gotten to know well, and also the great Erasmus. For a brief period, Thomas took some time off from his work to teach schoolboys elementary Hebrew, which he had earlier learned in Zurich from the Hebraist Theodore Bibliander, one of Myconius's regular table companions. Thomas taught the boys for only an hour a day in the parish school of Saint Leonhard's Church, reading with them through the book of

Jonah, an arrangement worked out by the school's learned master, Johannes Oporinus.[13]

In 1529, Thomas married his mentor's maid, a woman a few years older than he, whom he had known since his student days in Zurich. The Myconius family seems initially to have been more interested in the match than Thomas. Not only did they encourage it, they also promised to make the couple their heirs. In the beginning, the marriage lacked passion. It went unconsummated for six weeks and was only then fulfilled at Myconius's urging. Learning that Thomas and Anna had not yet slept together, Myconius instructed them in their spousal duties. Thomas writes that he and Anna had been "ashamed to lie down with each other," although they knew that it was "something that must happen at some time," as indeed it did.[14]

Right after the marriage, Thomas and Anna visited his hometown of Wallis, where they found a tepid reception because, as Thomas reports it, "[my family] had hoped I would become a priest." His abusive uncle Anthony, the priest, confronted him one day in the Church of Saint Martin in neighboring Visp and asked if it were true that he had brought home a wife. When Thomas acknowledged that he had, his uncle responded that it would have been better for him to have brought home a whore—which Thomas might conceivably have done, had he become a priest. Whereupon Thomas pointedly informed his uncle: "Sir, you will not find it written in the Bible that it is better to have a whore than a wife"—a comment he says that struck at his uncle's self-esteem, because he fancied himself an expert on Holy Scripture. "He spent a lot of time reading the Bible," Thomas comments, "though he understood little of it." The episode left the two men estranged.[15]

Thomas and Anna lived and worked in Visp, she spinning wool, he making rope and teaching (thirty students in winter, "barely six" in summer, according to Thomas). Although family relationships improved, Thomas's "Lutheranism" (*Lutherey*), as all dissent at this time was branded, alienated him from the local clergy, despite their efforts to be friendly with him. He recalls how burdensome going to church and singing the Mass became for him, "because it was against my conscience to assist idolatry and not to be able at all times to say freely what was in my heart." Commanded by conscience and advised by Myconius, Thomas and Anna decided to move back to Basel.

Their departure was delayed, however, by the birth of their first child, which provided another occasion for the assertion of their new evangelical beliefs. As Anna's labor began, the midwives placed a wooden rosary around her in the name of Saint Margaret, the patron saint of women in labor; and they urged her to have a Mass said on her behalf. But Anna declined the Mass and appealed beyond all such aids: "Oh, I trust in the true God to help me through this," she assured the midwives. Thomas attended the birth, as was customary for fathers in his home-town. The father's presence was required, first, to bond husband and wife closer together. But the midwives also wanted fathers present so that they might see firsthand that everything humanly possible had been done to ensure a successful birth. Midwifery was a high-risk business, and the midwives' association with death and injury to mothers and children often made them objects of hatred and abuse.

Anna successfully delivered a daughter, who was baptized "little Margaret," but died within a year. Several days after her birth, Thomas learned from town gossip that some of his relatives had smugly expected Anna to die in childbirth, as a divine punishment for his having turned his back on the priesthood. So outraged was Thomas by such sentiment that he bluntly informed his relatives that he would sooner become a gravedigger or a hangman than be the priest they wanted him to be.[16]

After moving to Basel, Thomas worked first as an assistant to Opori-nus, who taught him something about the printing business. Subse-quently, Thomas moved to the town of Brunnentrutt, where he assisted a physician and briefly contemplated a medical career. Slowly winding his way toward what would become his life's vocation, he applied for the position of schoolmaster in the Catholic village of Sitten. His applica-tion failed, however, because a competitor, more unworthy than he, slandered him before the bishop there. He described Thomas as one who readily broke fasts, called members of the old faith "idolaters," and refused to associate or to work with them. In other words, he portrayed Thomas as a bigoted Protestant, whose schoolmastership would only be contentious and disruptive.[17]

All was not lost for Thomas, however. In Basel, he mastered the printing trade and later established his own very successful shop. His success in turn won the admiration of city officials, who persuaded him to become Basel's schoolmaster, a post he was to hold for thirty-one years and one in which he distinguished himself as guardian of the school's independence from the local university, which had oversight of the school. Thomas especially resisted efforts by the university's Arts Faculty to modify the school's curriculum so that students would not advance so far in the arts, particularly in dialectics. Under Thomas's direction, the school prepared students so well in the arts that they matriculated in fewer arts courses when they reached the university.[18] As one who had cast aside both childhood ambition and family expectations for religion's sake, Thomas might have been expected to stand his ground also against those who would have him compromise his educational principles. Neither in the schoolroom nor in his own conscience was he a person who would allow himself to be bullied.

Readiness to follow conscience against both familial and public authority characterized the lives of Thomas and Anna Platter. In the heady days of the Reformation's ascent, their evangelical beliefs encouraged this trait in them.[19] Both personally and religiously they welcomed the changes then going on in the world around them. Where a matter of religious principle or their own happiness was at stake, they did not hesitate to break with tradition and embrace what seemed to them to be the truer point of view and the more effective course of action. They rejected the faith of their parents, which for Thomas meant major vocational change. He describes the most important decisions of his life as acts of conscience against perceived idolatry and spiritual coercion. In his autobiography, we can see the Reformation that had been propagated by theologians and pamphleteers and enacted into law by magistrates and princes actually taking form in ordinary human lives.

Although he was no trained theologian, Thomas had his own clear religious perspective on life. Looking back over his life in middle and old age, he repeatedly calls attention to the role of divine providence in it, the one recurring piece of theology in what remains a very secular chronicle. He believed that from his days as a goatherd, the hand of God had protected him from danger and on three occasions had directly intervened to save him from certain death. He also saw God foiling attempts on Zwingli's life so that the great Swiss reformer "might die in the open . . . a shepherd with his flock."[20] The intervention of divine providence also explained for Thomas how he and Anna, neither of whom had any inherited wealth, had been able nonetheless by hard work alone to own at one time no fewer than four houses in Basel. And again, he believed it to be the work of providence that one so lowly born as he could be the schoolmaster of Basel's children for three decades. "How is it that I still live, stand, and walk?" he asks himself near the end of his journal, as he recounts for his son Felix his many perilous travels and adventures. "It is," he concludes, "because God has protected me through his angels."[21] Thomas's new religious faith had given him the inner confidence and courage to take risks in the world.

## HERMANN WEINSBERG

The Reformation also touched the lives of laity in Catholic lands whose governments never officially recognized it or gave it free concourse.[22] A striking example is the slightly eccentric sometime lawyer, fourteen term councilman, and petty wine merchant of Cologne, Hermann Weinsberg (1518–1597).[23] In his multi-volume chronicle, an unusually frank and intimate source written between 1555 and 1596, we meet a man deeply divided between tradition and change. On the one hand, he is a timid and reclusive man, who apart from his youthful years in school and occasional retreats to neighboring villages during plague, lived his entire life within the family compound in Cologne. He was also a mainstay in the middle echelons of the city government. His conservatism stemmed in part from a youthful hernia that afflicted him throughout his life. His mother believed he had brought it on himself by binging on cold fatty soup, while his father traced the injury to beatings he had received in school, or perhaps from too strenuous running and jumping at play.[24]

At the same time, Hermann remained a controversial figure within his own household and hometown. An outspoken anticleric, he openly admired Erasmus and shared a number of Protestant criticisms of the church and proposals for reform. He also supported the right of Protestants to serve in Cologne's city council, and from time to time, he associated with Calvinist ministers, whose numbers grew in Westphalia in the second half of the century.

Protestantism had a real presence in Cologne, but, according to Hermann, the outcry against it from high clerical and political authorities exceeded its actual threat.[25] In the autumn of 1578, he reports warnings from the archbishop of Cologne against the heresy (*verdamte leren*) then being preached in the city's private homes and on its streets as well as purveyed in pamphlets. Sharper surveillance of Cologne's presses had been ordered by the city council in September. In December, the city

Die Sechs furtreflichen geistlichen gaben

# THE SIX SPIRITUAL GIFTS OF FAITH

This illustration, prepared especially for women, portrays in seven panels the Protestant ethic as contemporaries knew it. It is said to consist of faith, love, hope, discretion, righteousness, moderation, and endurance, by which the faithful triumph over sin, death, and the devil (final panel). The panels illustrate a poem by the Nuremberg layman, Hans Sachs, which concludes as follows:

> These seven spiritual gifts
> Give us a completely Christian life.
> They can be briefly summarized:
> True faith is the root
> That makes us entirely God's.

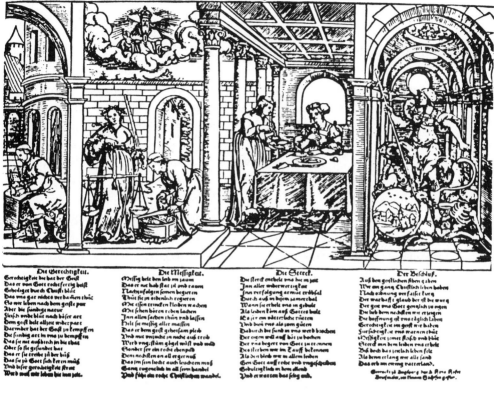

We show our neighbor love,
We live each day in hope,
We are righteous through the Spirit.
Discretion keeps us vigilant,
Moderation tames our flesh and blood,
Endurance helps us through our suffering
Until this life is done
And we inherit together
An eternal Fatherland.

Erhard Schoen and Hans Sachs, in *Max Geisberg: The German Single-Leaf Woodcut: 1500–1550*, vol. 3, rev. and ed. Walter L. Strauss (New York: Hacker Art Books, 1974), pp. 1082–83.

council discussed warnings about Protestants received from Emperor Rudolf II and the elector of Mainz. Believing that "many in Cologne were more inclined to the new religion than to the Catholic," they had written to urge the magistrates to take measures against private Protestant preaching before it caused "unrest and harm."[26]

The Reformation did indeed create problems for Cologne's citizens and clergy. Hermann reports, for example, the case of a young licentiate, apparently a lawyer, newly elected to the city council, whose interfaith marriages threatened the loss of his seat in the council. The man in question had buried a non-Catholic first wife outside of Cologne and was on the verge of taking a second wife, also non-Catholic. Fearing that the new marriage would spark opposition within the council, he turned for support to the lawyer's guild, which Hermann served as banneret. In the end he did take his seat in the council, but only after he had sworn an oath of allegiance to the old faith and promised that he would not lobby for religious innovations (*kein neuerong inzuforen*).[27]

In January 1579, police rounded up suspected Cologne Protestants after torturing an evangelical tailor into naming people he had seen at private Protestant gatherings. According to Hermann, many burghers were involved, including several council members. The magistrates accused them all of "conducting or attending secret meetings, sermons, and religious devotions (*exercitia*)" in their own home or another's. Among them was a man who had officiated at the wedding of Hermann's nephew. According to Hermann, he was charged in addition with having taken a wife "in a non-Catholic manner," by which apparently was meant that he had married outside the church without benefit of an ordained priest. Those among the arrested who refused to recant the Augsburg Confession—the official Lutheran creed—and pay the fine for failing to baptize their children in the official churches went to jail. Hermann reports great concern both in the council and among the clergy over "the discovery of people who had no interest whatsoever in coming into the churches, but who wanted to perform their own private services of worship instead."[28]

Hermann's family had long stood fast by the traditional faith. They built and endowed a Franciscan cloister, Maria of Bethlehem, which became home to Hermann's sisters and to his only child, an illegitimate daughter, Anna, who entered at age twenty and eventually became the abbess. Hermann actively supported the convent until his death.

Temperamentally conservative, he professed a code of moderation in all things, including religion. "Middling" or "moderate" (*mittelmeissich*) remained a favorite self-description; "blessed are those who stick to the mean (*medium tenuere beati*)" his motto.[29]

Hermann's piety could be naïve and credulous as well as enlightened and critical. As a young man, he prayed to Saint Appollonia for relief from recurring pain in his mouth, the result of a childhood infection that had required the surgical removal of some teeth and gum tissue.[30] When his sister Agnes, a nun in the family cloister, died of plague, Hermann reported her successful arrival in glory. According to his account, the sisters of the convent had agreed among themselves that as each died she would send the others a signal to indicate her arrival in heaven (*das sei selich were*). Shortly after Agnes's death the sisters beheld a blinking star, which they and Hermann took to be that sign.[31] Hermann also regularly commemorated the deaths of his two wives, Weisgin and Drutgin, in traditional ways. He once spent the sizable sum of 126 gulden to provide Drutgin with vigils, Masses, candles, and beguines at graveside, among other personnel and services.[32] And he composed his last will and testament with the assistance of a priest and left it on deposit in Saint James's Church.[33]

Hermann's traditional piety also manifests itself in the things that make him feel guilty and ashamed. When he recalls his affair with his family's maid, Greitgin, the mother of his daughter, Anna, he describes himself as "the devil's weed."[34] With the passage of years, he attended confession less frequently, apparently never more than twice a year. As a youth, he considered the sacrament a distressing experience. Of his first confession, at age seven, he recalls that at the time he "would rather have gone through fire." But as confession became a regular habit, and the penances imposed on him proved light (only a few rosaries and other prayers), the sacrament lost its sting and Hermann came to look on it as a good thing.[35] We find him in 1574, at fifty-six years of age, declaring that he is not at all ashamed to confess his sins any longer, for he knows that no one is without sin. So at ease with his penance had he by then become that he shares with posterity an open confession of both his failings (hastening to point out qualifying circumstances) and his many inward graces. For the sixteenth century, the statement is a unique display of spiritual frankness.

First, his failings. Hermann describes himself as arrogant, desirous of glory and "uncommon honors," taking little pride in his dress, preoccupied with his family's reputation, penny-pinching (but more out of thriftiness and lack of income than greed), and stubbornly protective of his own and his friends' interests when "great matters" are involved (and far more likely to relent when treated kindly than when dealt with in a high-handed fashion). He confesses a fondness for "well-proportioned, beautiful women," all the while knowing that evil desire is worse than the deed itself. By contrast, he is ill-disposed toward strangers. Devoted to food and drink, he will not leave a table until he is full, and he is quite unhappy when he has to fast, though he can do so when he must. He likes to go to church and hear the sermon, but he is reluctant to pray and read Scripture; worldly things interest him more than spiritual things. He is merciful and sympathetic to others, but he doesn't much like to act on such feelings. While he loves talk and gossip, he prefers not to speak up in council meetings unless it's an emergency. Shy by nature, he is bold and aggressive when provoked.

On the more unambiguously positive side, Hermann describes himself as a helpful counselor and a peacemaker. Neither depression nor sorrow overwhelm him. He also views himself as impervious to flattery and begging ("I do not desire much from any man, nor do I give much to any man . . . I gladly preserve what is mine and never burden another") and resentful of wastefulness ("I like to preserve what is mine and ask nothing of anyone"). He tends to let matters lie and doesn't hold grudges or seek revenge. Seldom will he curse, insult, or degrade anyone, unless angered. He is keen on decorum, order, and custom, and quick to reprove anyone who is not; and he cannot tolerate a lie. Though an honorable man who usually acts justly, he admits that he can be swayed by self-interest (*parteilicheit*). He supports the clergy, but their "abuses, cunning, greed, and pride" outrage him. And while he is fond of common people (*arbeiter*), he deals very cautiously with them.

In sum, Hermann by his own words is a man who "desires only to lead a quiet and peaceful life."[36] His sentiments are those of a man who prefers patience and continuity to conflict and change in virtually everything; as long as the world around him did not profoundly disturb his peace, he was prepared to accommodate it.

Despite his traditional piety, Hermann, as he readily admits, often clashed with the clergy and had a reputation among family and friends (falsely and unfairly, he believed) for anticlericalism and covert evangelical sentiment.[37] His outbursts do exceed what the modern reader might expect from a Catholic layperson at this time; often they seem worthy of a Protestant pamphleteer. In the spring of 1575, for example, after a successful court suit in which the city's Chapter of Saint George forced the resignation of the popular schoolmaster of Saint James's Church, Hermann concludes his account of the incident with the comment, "It bothers me that the clergy meet, declare what is right, and dispose of matters by their own laws, while the laity must endure it until God comes to their aid."[38] Three years later we find Hermann complaining about the "cunning, greed, stratagems, and power of the clergy, against which one has hitherto been unable to speak without being accused of heresy or revolution." He believed it fortunate that laymen like himself could now "see through their schemes" and that the clergy were under tighter secular control and no longer able to amass property and wealth as easily as they did before.[39]

In 1579, at the height of the religious wars in the Netherlands, Hermann saw Protestant dissent growing, while churches were being destroyed in Holland, Zealand, Flanders, and Brabant. These developments led him to ponder whether it was better to endow new churches and cloisters or to invest his inheritance in the Weinsberg family house and his own posterity, concluding that the times argued for looking after one's own. There are a great many securely beneficed "spiritual housefathers," he reasons, but few natural housefathers who are as well off; the clergy have done better at securing their future through lay endowments than the laity by their investments. Does not Cologne now bulge with endowed churches, cloisters, and chapels and with privileged clergy and religious, many of whom treat laypeople as second-class Christians? "At one place the canon law compares the prophet Balaam to the spiritual estate and the ass on which he sits to the worldly estate; such an opinion I can now certainly appreciate." To prove his point, Hermann appended to these ruminations a detailed accounting of the many clerical properties in Cologne.[40]

In June 1591, Hermann singled out Cologne's religious orders for criticism—Augustinians, Franciscans, Dominicans, Carmelites, and others that had long prospered in the city. "No emperor has as many palaces and castles as these orders have handsome, well-built cloisters," he complains. Their numbers are "unbelievable," their incomes from rents "inestimable." He further accuses Cologne's religious of alternately flat-

tering and frightening the laity into giving them what they themselves
will not work to gain.

> What ancient custom and righteousness forbade the pastors of old
> from taking in lieu of their labor, the monks today get under the
> appearance of poverty by begging alms from good people. On the one
> hand, they flatter them; on the other, they terrorize them. For the
> sake of their own gain, they make hell out to be so very horrifying—
> and not only hell, but purgatory as well.[41]

Hermann blamed a great part of the conflict in his world on the
clergy's "stratagems of greed" (*practiken der geirheit*). He drew this conclusion in the summer of 1578 after he and his brother had failed in their
efforts to place a relative in a local convent. The negotiations had broken
down because the beguines in charge demanded that the candidate
surrender her entire inheritance as a condition of entrance. The episode
enraged Hermann, who saw in it another example of the harsh treatment
accorded the laity by the spiritual estate, contrary to its every precept.

> Having entered the monasteries in order to give themselves to God,
> the religious have come in time to possess almost half of the world,
> for whatever is once given to them remains with them. Their strat-
> agems of greed are perhaps not the least cause of the present great
> conflicts in Christendom. As the Catholics took great power and
> possessions by means of the old religion, their opponents (*die widderpar-
> tien*) now do so by means of the new.... What the religious took
> [gradually over centuries] by cunning and cajolery, their opponents
> now want to take back by force and the sword, as one sees happening
> today in many lands and cities.[42]

As for his personal spiritual life, Hermann made a private peace with
his church. He accepted its imperfections philosophically along with the
good he still believed it capable of. His devotion to his church, though
earnest, was tinged with resignation. Early in 1588, he went to the
Augustinian cloister to make his confession, an annual habit of forty-
five years standing. On this particular day, he found a young monk in
the place of his regular confessor. The youth asked him such questions as
whether he had ever killed anyone or been party to a killing, committed
adultery, or been in the company of people who had spoken or acted
against the Catholic religion. Hermann observed that his youthful inter-

rogator read these questions from a tablet in his hand (apparently an abridged confessional manual). Hermann assured him, not quite truthfully, that he knew in his heart by God's grace that he was free of such great sins, and that had he ever knowingly committed them, he would have confessed them often and long ago.

The encounter irritated Hermann. At its conclusion, the monk asked him for a fee (*ein stewr*), pleading poverty and the need to buy many books. Hermann ignored his entreaty, but after the monk absolved him he relented and gave him six albus. His private remarks reveal both his ambivalence about official religious practice in Cologne and his continuing, if chastened, devotion to it.

> What one asks about and investigates in confession, also what one contrives there, can be curious indeed. I have certainly heard strange things there. But should one say too much about this, he will be accused of being un-Catholic. At this time the people of Cologne are prepared for all kinds of things in religion and church. For the sake of goodwill and peace, I forego scrutinizing them as long as other important matters are not also involved. One cannot deny that in all holy and good things there are abuses, and so it may also happen here that, as what is good remains good, what is bad will also remain bad until there is a change for the better.[43]

Despite his discontent with the clergy of Cologne, Hermann believed he lived in an age of spiritual enlightenment—and not just because the clergy had come under tighter lay control. Once in his room two candles fell to the floor and a bell pealed simultaneously, seemingly of their own accord. Hermann thought about how in the past such occurrences had always occasioned conversations about supernatural forces.

> They often led to talk of spirits, souls, elves, cunning women, and magic (*geisten, seelen, twergen, wissenfrawen, und zaubereien*). Many claimed to have seen something. But now, praise God, one does not need such things to explain such an occurrence. It is said that so much arguing has occurred over religion and faith that some wish to avoid these topics altogether. In the past some [clergy] used deception and trickery to terrify the people for their own gain. I leave it to God to straighten all of this out and I hold no opinion about it. The theologians may know best from their knowledge of Scripture; but perhaps they

also err. I notice that they are not agreed among themselves, that the old theologians have different views about it from the new. Some say that apparitions are a deception of the devil (*Teufelsdroch*), others that they are an optical illusion (*kankelei der augen*). Those who are immature and believe easily are soon convinced of such prophecies [of devilish deception]. The Old and New Testaments contain several examples by which one attempts to prove their occurrence. Personally, I do not know [what these examples prove], nor can I say that those who so argue have rightly understood and interpreted [Scripture].[44]

Three sources appear to have informed Hermann's skepticism about the supernatural world and his criticism of clerical abuse. One was a commonsense folk tradition with biblical overtones stressing self-respect and self-reliance. Among the proverbs by which Hermann claimed three generations of Weinsbergs had lived were these: "Never borrow from those who command you to hold your hat in your hand." "Without hard work, one is unworthy of his bread." And Hermann's favorite may have been, "Always reach for a golden wagon; if it escapes you, you may still get a [gold] harnessing pole pin (*spannagel*)." Hermann believed he had done this himself when he gained a secure place in the city council after aspiring to the top post of burgomaster.[45]

A second major intellectual force in Hermann's life was Erasmus, whom Hermann heard lecture twice in Emmerich, in 1532 and 1533, and whose birthplace in Rotterdam he visited in 1569. Hermann owned many of the great humanist's books, and he claims to have read them. His chronicle entry upon learning of Erasmus's death in 1536 states in Latin, "Now has the most learned and eloquent light of the world gone out." When Hermann looked back over the sixteenth century in the year before his own death (1596), he thought Erasmus had been "the most learned man of the time in all the arts, in both secular and religious letters."[46] He must have perceived in Erasmus's ability to be both loyal to the church and sharply critical of it a congenial personal model.

Finally, there was the Reformation itself, whose impact within and beyond Cologne, in ways both large and small, always interested Hermann. He reports in 1567 the success of a Calvinist field preacher, who drew more than a thousand auditors from Cologne, despite (or perhaps because of) the growing presence of Jesuits in the city and official prohibitions against attending such sermons.[47] In 1579, Hermann entertained a Calvinist preacher at dinner, requesting in advance that he refrain from theological discussion at table for the sake of Hermann's sister-in-law and niece, apparently a nun, whom Hermann described as "good Jesuits," a phrase that meant for him opinionated and dogmatic about religion.[48] According to Hermann, the preacher had a difficult time containing himself, while his niece, knowing something of his religion, had also been eager to debate him. Still, they got through the evening rather well.

On 2 March 1548, Hermann recorded his personal reflections on what he calls "the many changes that have occurred during my age," turning first to those brought about in religion by Martin Luther.

> There have been many different beliefs (*opiniones*), sects, uprisings, and wars that have led to the destruction of churches, cloisters, and chapels in the kingdoms of Germany, England, Scotland, Denmark, Sweden, France, and many other principalities; and ceremonies and customs common in sermons, Masses, the hours, pilgrimages, and processions as I first knew them are now no longer held.[49]

Of Luther himself, Hermann wrote with a certain neutrality: "Whether in the end the harm or the good of his Reformation will be the greater, only God knows," hastening to add that he, like all his ancestors, remained loyal to the church. He also took note of the passing in 1531 of the Basel humanist and Protestant reformer Johann Oecolampadius, acknowledging his great learning and expressing the wish that he had remained within the church. In an entry on Mary Tudor, drawn largely from the work of the Protestant historian Johannes Sleidanus, Hermann described the Protestants who fled her reign as adherents of the "purer religion" (*Lauterscher religion*).[50]

Thus did Hermann Weinsberg at the end of the sixteenth century, within one of northern Europe's most traditional cities, acknowledge the revolutionary success of the Reformation. Time, place, and temperament did not encourage in him the personal and religious experimentation that had characterized the lives of Thomas and Anna Platter. His world was a less mobile one than theirs, and his world view less open to novelty. He was also more patient with the imperfections of the world around him. Willful contradiction of his family's wishes or rejection of the basic doctrinal teaching of his church probably never entered his mind. Yet he found resources within his own religious tradition to unmask as perceptively as could any 1520s Protestant pamphleteer the church's self-aggrandizement and exploitation of credulous laity. He also supported the legal reforms of Cologne's magistrates designed to curtail the church's power and privilege within the city. Though not a particularly courageous man, much less a revolutionary, in his own way he too refused to allow either his priest or his private piety to tyrannize him.

As Hermann's life demonstrates, the Reformation was not the only source of reform sentiment in the sixteenth century. Still, the Reformation succeeded among the laity largely because it laid claim to such sentiment as had no other religious movement before it. Protestants popularized the notion that purely historical traditions, no matter how old and how sacred, could be broken at will whenever they became spiritually and financially onerous; God had not become man to afflict people. By inculcating deep and lasting suspicions about the claims of the clergy to authority and the fidelity of tradition to Holy Scripture, the Reformation—though not always the reformers—encouraged the laity, guided by their own reading of Scripture, to believe and think for themselves in matters of religion. This newfound independence of mind, fostered, not impeded, by the new Scriptural mandate, eventually worked as much against the new clergy—some of whom wanted to impose their own brand of religious conformity—as it did against Roman Catholicism. Ironically, the new lay self-confidence in religion, originally encouraged by the Reformation, rendered the Reformation something of a Pyrrhic victory in the minds of many of its clergy, including Martin Luther.

But by the very nature of the Reformation's original inspiration, the very last place one would expect to find evidence of its success is among laity who mechanically recite its catechisms and passively obey its laws. That may have become a clerical goal, but it was never the layman's Reformation, nor the Reformation's actual achievement as a historical movement. Disobedience and discord show a religion's vitality and growth as well as revealing its divisions and dogmatism. The revolutionary legacy of the Reformation, whether in the sixteenth century or in the twentieth, lives on in ordinary people who have the courage to express doubts about the sanctity of tradition, to challenge institutions that falsely claim a greater than human sanction, and to defy laws that would trample individual conscience in the name of God.

# 9. The Religious Beliefs of Teenagers

One might expect Western youth in any premodern century to reflect their culture. The adolescents of the Reformation grew up in a world far more culturally unified than that of their modern counterparts. True, there were things that youth did and things that adults did. Transient student organizations peculiar to youth, both official and unofficial, existed at school (student associations) and in the professions (journeyman unions). And youth then as now knew how to hide their true feelings. In both urban and village societies, parents struggled as they do today to inculcate their values in their children. But the adult world was not confronted in the past with an independent and competitive culture of youth, as it is today. Parents, children, and public institutions were in basic agreement over right and wrong and how people made the best use of their lives. Harsh conditions kept youth dependent on their parents, guardians, and masters well into their twenties. And youth too recognized that conformity and obedience best served their prospects for success and happiness. Because the reigning social code was as vital to their own well-being as to that of their elders, youth organizations reinforced rather than challenged it. In the countryside, youth conducted noisy serenades (charivari) for newlyweds and childless couples, rudely publicizing community standards and ex-pectations. In the cities, journeyman unions ran the guild festivals and enforced the guild laws.[1] The young, in a word, could also be bastions of conservatism.

It is only in very recent times that the language, dress, entertainment, and wisdom of the young have ceased to be those of their elders; and virtually unheard of in early modern society were adults who envied and aped the lifestyles of the young. Youth also previously shared the religious and moral values of their parents more trustingly. Only one viable culture existed for young and old alike; the independence and privilege after which all strove were found in the adult world.

Such consensus made possible a more rapid maturation of the young.

By age fourteen or fifteen, the youth of early modern Europe had many useful and productive skills; by comparison with their counterparts today, they were mature. True, that maturity came at the cost of forcing the young to enter adulthood vocationally, while emotionally they were still children and adolescents. And at the same time, the same youth were denied the independence and privileges of adulthood. Yet the forced combination of precocious vocational maturity and delayed adult status did not create deep and bitter generational strife, despite the resentment of protracted dependency on the part of young people. The early acquisition of true vocational skills rather worked to stabilize the young and to engender patience and cooperation, steadfastness and persistence, on the part of children and parents alike. In early modern Europe the young knew their talents as well as their place.

By contrast, a sizable portion of the Western world today bestows adult status on children still emotionally in their teens, before they are able to do any useful and productive work. Whereas the early modern parent believed that emotional happiness followed vocational compe-tence (hence, early service and apprenticeship for children), the modern parent has become convinced that emotional maturity must precede vocational success, that a child must first "find" himself before he can "define" himself. Today, a parent is more likely to recommend a therapist than a shovel to a teenager.

The youth of early modern Europe thus reflected well the world around them. This was not only because of the greater cultural unity of that world, but also because young people in every age tend to conduct themselves in a less guarded fashion than adults. Youth are both more impressionable and more reactionary; they embrace a culture uncondi-tionally when it befriends them, and they mock it fiercely when they think it betrays them. Tender age renders them trusting and eager, while dependency makes them skeptical and cautious. But either positively or negatively, the young in every age have a talent for dramatizing the issues at stake in a culture.

In early modern Europe, the burden of dependence on the adult world also forced the young to be precociously calculating, lest their actions unintentionally alienate essential support in an age that gave youth few second chances. So while we find youth at that time saying what they felt with a spontaneity comparatively rare in the contemporary adult world, they also knew equally well what they needed to say in order to please and sway the many authorities in their lives.

The subjects of this chapter, with a few exceptions, are four Nuremberg boys between the ages of fifteen and twenty-five.[2] They come from two separate branches and three generations of an important Nuremberg family, the Behaims, and taken together their lives cover more than a century, from roughly 1525 to 1640, the full evolutionary span of the Reformation. Each was away from home for long periods of time, during which he wrote scores of letters to family and friends. In these letters the boys describe new experiences and share personal thoughts and feelings on a great many subjects, not the least of which is religion.

The first boy, Michael (1510–64), the youngest of three siblings, left home at the age of twelve for merchant apprenticeships in Milan and Breslau. He returned eighteen years later, a successful merchant with a business of his own. The second youth, Paul (1557–1621), an eldest son and the most privileged of the four, left home at fifteen for six years of schooling in Leipzig and Padua. By his forties he had become arguably Nuremberg's most powerful politician. His younger brother Friederich (1563–1613) followed in his footsteps at age fourteen, studying first in nearby Altdorf before then going on to Padua. He became a village magistrate (*Pfleger*) in his late twenties. Finally, there is Stephan Carl (1612–38), who at fifteen departed Nuremberg for study, service at a nobleman's court, and ultimately soldiering in the New World. An emotionally disturbed youth who succeeded at nothing he undertook, he died an early death, at twenty-six, while serving with the Dutch West India Company in Brazil.[3]

By contemporary standards the families of the four boys were upper middle class. The personal worth of each, measured in shared property and paternal inheritance, ranged between one thousand and three thousand gulden. (By comparison, Nuremberg's city physician and schoolmaster received between fifty and sixty gulden per annum, while the city's chief legal counsel averaged four hundred.[4]) But the boys' wealth was strictly a paper sum. Throughout their youth, it was not at their disposal, but tightly controlled by guardians and family members. Also, as each boy was fatherless before his teens, his family's consumption remained grossly disproportionate to its income, so that each grew up with constant reminders to be abstemious and thrifty and lived with a sense of impending economic crisis. During his ten-year apprenticeship, Michael lived virtually as a working-class person; and Stephan Carl experienced all of the terrible deprivations of war, being captured and wounded on separate occasions during the Thirty Years War and dying an impoverished musketeer in the New World.

The religious comments and behavior of the Behaim boys fall under four headings. There is, first of all, the piety they share with their age, more or less common to Protestant, Catholic, Jew, and unchurched alike. Then there are anti-Catholic polemics, both conscious and subliminal, which years of Nuremberg sermons and catechism classes fixed deep within their minds. Next there is a patently self-serving rhetorical Lutheranism reflective of the self-preoccupation and narcissism of youth. Finally, the Behaims, children and parents alike, exemplify in their lives classic Lutheran teaching about the forgiveness of sin and moral reconciliation with both God and man.

## PIETY AND PROVIDENCE

During the sixteenth century people of all religious persuasions regarded unusual happenings in nature and the heavens as divine portents. The birth of a deformed animal or human, the growth of an abnormal plant, the passage of a comet, the display of the northern lights, the appearance of sun dogs (parhelions)—any or all such things might be read as signs of impending divine judgment. The smallest irregularity could become instant prophecy, as happened in 1560 when "bearded grapes" were discovered growing in a vineyard near Prague.

The Behaims were as credulous as any when it came to such things. Each boy saw God's hand not only in nature and history, but also in his own personal and professional life. In March 1529, Michael wrote to his cousin and guardian, Friederich VII Behaim, paternal grandfather of our Friederich (VIII), about a "terrifying sign" that had appeared in the sky over Breslau. An armored man, bearing a bloody sword, bowed down to a great star and then proceeded to hack to death an old woman sitting nearby. Michael also reported sightings of multitudes of such soldiers about the same time in the sky over Liegnitz. What this portended, he concluded, "one must leave to God," although, for his part, he associated such spectacles with divinely inspired Turkish invasions of western Europe in just punishment of Western sins. After hearing reports of Turkish victories in Romania, Michael wondered if God had chosen to "blind the German nation [to its sins] and leave it to such punishment [as Turkish domination]."[5]

In 1580, young Friederich Behaim reported the appearance of three suns and four rainbows over Altdorf, which he believed to be a portent of impending violent storms and conflict among the princes.[6] In nearby Nuremberg,[7] where the same spectacle had also been seen, a contemporary artist depicted and explained the spectacle as a warning of rebellion against the city's magistrates and clergy. Although Stephan Carl reported no such sightings, he held a similar faith in God's providence. After deserting the Swedish army in 1635, he wrote of his wish that God might become "Regent and Housekeeper" in Germany, driving all foreigners from the fatherland and preserving the "true, soul-saving religion" there.[8]

The Behaim boys give particular attention to divine intervention in their own lives. When in April 1634, imperial Croatian soldiers took Stephan Carl captive, he attributed his misfortune most assuredly to "God's special will and destiny," claiming that God had wanted him to suffer "extreme punishment and chastisement" for his many sins and deceptions.[9] By contrast, he believed that God had guided him safely down the Rhine to Amsterdam in the summer of 1535, saving his life from rioting peasants, treacherous waters, and marauding soldiers on more than a hundred occasions.[10]

None of the boys had a deeper sense of providential oversight of his life than did Michael. During his years in Milan in the 1520s before he turned Protestant, he had been a devout teenager, devoted particularly to the Virgin Mary. His surviving letters from Milan and Breslau during these years bear the salutation "Praise be to God and Mary." During the great Milan plague of 1525, he prayed fervently to the Virgin of Loreto, and he believed that it was she who had saved him from certain death, in gratitude for which he vowed to make a pilgrimage to her shrine, which lay about twenty-five miles north of Rome.[11]

With the new year 1528, the Virgin vanished altogether from Michael's letters. Henceforth, they bear a terse new evangelical greeting: "Praise be to our Lord Jesus Christ," which Michael within weeks simplified still further to "Praise be always to God."[12] Whether the change resulted at the time from deeply altered religious belief or simply reflected conformity to Nuremberg's post-Reformation epistolary convention, after age twenty Michael never again petitioned the deity so demonstrably for his personal safety in time of need. Thereafter, he seems even to have been surprised when God favored him. In May 1532, for example, he suffered a serious injury "by God's decree," as he describes it, one that threatened to leave his right hand permanently impaired. Recounting the incident to his guardian, he expressed pleasure that God had healed him so quickly, yet at the same time he confides that he hadn't thought God would be so gracious to him in his recovery.[13]

After 1528, Mary's place as intercessor and miracle worker was taken in Michael's spiritual life by a Christ who simply worked salvation and by a God who afflicted and healed people freely, and mysteriously, at will. In Michael's new Protestant faith, as in that of the other boys, God became more a force to be reckoned with than a person on whom one might confidently rely. He was, to be sure, a mighty fortress, as Luther's great hymn described him, but his cannons now seemed to roll about loose. In the classic Protestant traditions, both Lutheran and Reformed, as distinct from the reigning Thomist tradition of the late Middle Ages, God's freedom and sovereignty were seen to transcend his goodness and

---

### BEARDED GRAPES

*In the sixteenth century, people routinely interpreted changes in nature as warnings from God to repent and reform their lives morally. Such portents might be found anywhere in the heavens or on earth. The extreme to which such sensitivity might go is illustrated by the discovery of bearded grapes growing in a vineyard near a cloister in Prague. From two grape clusters were seen to hang strange long beards, a part of which was yellow-gray in color, like the beard of an old, degenerate man, while the remainder was thick and red. According to the accompanying interpretation, the red beard is a sure sign of God's wrath at the pervasive alcoholism (indicated by the yellow-gray beard) said to be currently afflicting both young and old alike. From this vice springs every human calamity, from premature senility to violent death. Without prompt penance and turning to God, the author warns, there can be no escape from it.*

Hans Glaser, in *The German Single-Leaf Woodcut, 1550–1600: A Pictorial Catalogue,* vol. 1, ed. Walter L. Strauss (New York: Abaris Books, 1975), p. 361.

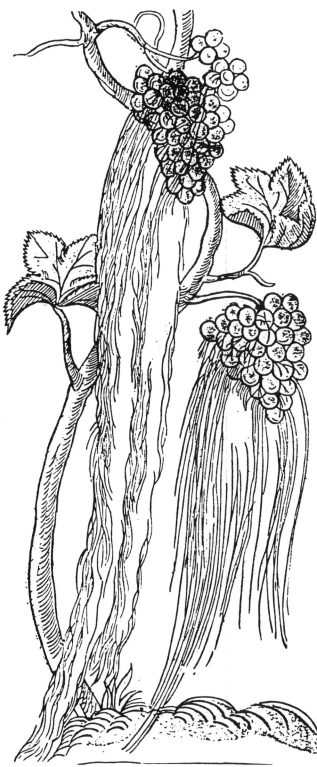

# Ein Wunderbarliches

Gewechs/ etlicher Weyntrauben/ so
mit seltzamen Bärten/ in nechst verschinem Sep
tember/ sein gefunden worden zu Prag im
Beham/ in einem Weingarten Bey einem Closter zur Newstat da-
selbst/ Anno 1560.

Ann Gott der Almechtig die Gotlose böse welt/ hat wöllen straffen
so lieff er gemeinklich vorher gehen
wunderbarliche zeychen/ beyde am
Himel vnnd an Erden/ Dardurch
er endlich das Gotlose volck/ widerumb zu jhme
möcht bekeren/ vnd zur buß bewegen/ Wie dann
hin vnd wider in der heyligen Göttlichen schrifft
solchs steht geschriben. Also haben wir warlich
Götliches zorns/ auch seiner grossen güte nit wenig der selben zeychen vnd wunderwerck/ in kur-
tzen jarn gesehen vnd ersarn/ Do gewißlich Gott
der HERr zu dieser vnser letzten zeyt/ vns trew-
lich wil warnen vor künfftiger straffe/ vnnd ver-
manen zur busse. Vnter welchen sonderlich wol
zu betrachten vnd war zu nemen ist/ Ein Wun-
derbarlichs Gewächs/ etlicher Weintrauben so
in nechst vergangnem September dises 50. jars
sein gesehen vnd erfunden worden/ zu Prag in
Behamen/ in einem lustigen Weinberge bey einé
Closter/ zur Newstat daselbs gewachsen/ Do
nemblich ein yetzlicher derselben Weintrauben
hat von sich gelassen/ vnd abhangend gehabt/ ein
seltzamen langen Bart/ Jnn der erst etwas gelb-
lich/ vnd grawhärig durch einander/ Wie an eynem alten Man anzusehen/ biß zur Erden lan-
gend/ Hernach aber verändert er sich vnd ward
an der gestaldt/ gleich wie ein dicker Rot farber
Mans Bart/ zwey mal so lang als der schwartz
strich hie vnden verzeychnet.

Dieses vnd dergleichen wunderbarliche zey-
chen/ was sie vns gutes sollen mit bringen/ Jst in
Heimligkeyt Gottes/ Verstendige leut aber/ deu-
ten dise Rot bärtige Weintrauben/ auff den grossen zoren Gottes/ vber das grewliche vnnd ver-
dammliche laster der Trunckenheyt/ So leyder
schier in allen Landen/ beyde bey jungen vnd alten Personen/ seer vberhand genommen/ Dardurch denn aller vnrath (wie vor augen) thut
entspringen/ Als nemblich/ Ein hessliches blödes
alter vor der rechten zeyt/ Ja auch endlich ein je-
bes erschröcklichs ende mit todschlagen/ zu todt
fallen/ vnd Achtung Gottes gewalts/ vnnd dergleichen. Wie dessen viel Exempel/ auch zu vnse-
ren zeiten/ möchten angezeygt werden aber kürtz
halben dißmals alhie vnderlassen. GOtt gebe/
das wir Buß thun/ vnnd vns one allen vertzug/
endlich zu Gott bekehren. AMEN.

Bey Hans Glaser/ Brieffma-
ler zu Nürnberg.

love, though Protestants believed that the latter were also very real. One approached such a God not with the offerings of good works expecting fairness, but in simple faith and trust hoping for mercy. Such a perspective on religion, with roots in late medieval Augustinianism and Ockhamism, made the nature of God a far more burning question for Protestants than the quality of an individual's moral life. Everything in religion hinged on *God's* keeping his word and proving to be as good as the Bible portrayed him. What if God turns out to be a liar? What if he is neither as powerful nor as true as his Word proclaims? What if the seeming contradictions in his nature that people experience on earth prove true also in eternity? The question that drove Martin Luther to near despair was not whether he himself was a sheep or a goat, but whether in the end God was carnivorous or herbivorous. Until the latter question was resolved, the former remained meaningless.

---

## PARHELIA (SUNDOGS) IN THE SKY OVER ALTDORF AND NUREMBERG

*On 12 January 1580, between 1:00 P.M. and sunset, many people beheld strange occurrences in the sky over Altdorf and Nuremberg, among them Friederich Behaim. According to the authors of this broadsheet, who appear to have been clergy, two shining smaller suns (actually luminous spots or parhelia) appeared on each side of the sun. Above all three was a bright rainbow, and above it a second rainbow, gleaming white. A third rainbow appeared above these, and still a fourth was seen above them and to the right. Under this last rainbow shone a great white cross, a portion of which touched two of the rainbows.*

*According to the authors, the appearance of many suns in the sky portends changes in government and division in the church. The sun signifies key personnel in church and state, while the smaller suns on either side represent those without authority who aspire to take power. In this particular example, the news for incumbents is good. As on this day the sun remained firm in the sky and the smaller ones disappeared, so too will the challenge to established power fade away. These heavenly signs are thus a divine warning to unrepentant, godless people, while the faithful may take them as a consolation and promise that their salvation is near.*

Hans Mack, in *The German Single-Leaf Woodcut, 1550–1600: A Pictorial Catalogue*, ed. Walter L. Strauss (New York: Abaris Books, 1975), p. 656.

# Warhaffte Contrafactur / derer jüngst erschienen grossen Wunderzeichen dreyer Sonnen vier Regenbogen, vnd darinn zweyer Liechter klarheyten, auch grossen weissen Creutzes am Himel, an vilen orten gesehen werden, als folgende Figur fidelich außweiset.

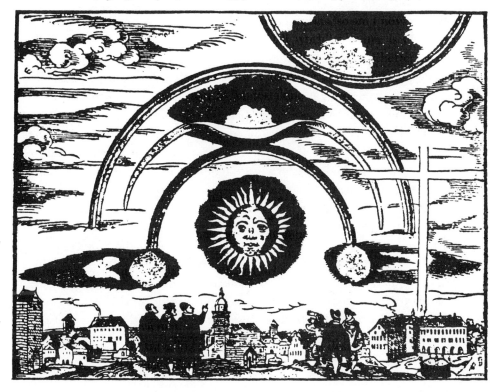

En 12. Januarij dises lauffenden M. D. LXXX. Jares, ist an vilen orten vmb Nürnberg, sonderlich aber im Sebalder Walt, drey mal trage von Nürnberg von 7. der klaren Vhr, das ist ein stund nach mittag biß zur Sonnen vntergang dise wunderzeichen gesehen worden. Nemlich zu beyden seyten der Sonnen zwey helle liechter vnd neben Sonnen, welliche frey glantz vnd ziralen von der Sonn gewendet vber disen dreyen Sonnen ist ein gar heller schöner Regenbogen gestanden, darauff ein anderer weisser flammender Regenbogen, welliches oberhalb gebogen, vnd doch bede örterweder herunterwerts geschmidt sich ereraat.

Der dritte Regenbogen gantz schön leuchtend hat sich vber disen beyden ereraet. Der vierde, ist aber dem dritten grossen Regenbogen gestanden etwaßner als die andern drey, doch röttlich vnd zur seyten gerund in mitlichter mitte, eine schöne helle klarheyt zesehen worden, auff der seyten aber ist ein lang vnd grosses weiß Creutz, wie solches alles dise Contrafactur außweist, erschienen, welliches mit dem einen zwerchstück die beyden Regenbogen berüret, vnd gleichsam einen durchzug gemacht hat, solliches alles ist von vilen fürnemen vnd glaubwirdigen personen gesehen worden.

Was aber solliche wunderzeichen bedeuten vnd mit sich bringen möchte, ist als klein Gott bekant nit, welches die jeten geben, ist auch ingezweiffelt war das auff solliche vilen Sonnen erscheinung, änderung in den Regimenten, vnd waltungen in der Kirchen sich bedten. Die Sonne bedeutet die Regimente regieren, vnd für nembsten Lehrer in der Kirchen die neben Sonnen sind die so sich in die Regiment vnd Kirchen wöllen eindrangen, vnd deß gewalts enterpfleiben, denen doch die verwaltung nit zugehörig ist, vnd gleich wie die Sonne bleibt vnd die neben Sonnen verschwinden, also bestehen auch die jenigen welliche zu verrichtung grosser sachen von Gott beruffen vnd erfodert, die andern aber welliche deß Scheinischeins sich anmassen verlieren sich gegen darüber zu scheitern. Kurz vor Künig Ludwigs in Ungern sind drey Sonnen gesehen worden, darauff nach seinem tödlichen abgang drey Herren sich vmb das Königreich haben angenommen. Solcher Exempel könden vil auß alten vnd neuen Hystorien angezogen werden so es die gelegenheit geben wolte. Wir sollen aber damit brauchtet sein daß wir auß den leyten vnd treuen warnungen vnsers HErrn Jesu Christi bericht haben, wann disz vnd dergleichen zeichen am Himel sich werden ereraen, daß die Sonne der Oberträgheret vmer welliche studin wie Malacha am 4. spricht heyt ist nun nicht mehr lang wird aussen bleiben, sondern auffgehen in der Himels welchen kommen, vnd sein gericht auff dem Regenbogen mit grosser krafft vnd Herrlichret halten vnd vollziehen. Die zeichen am Himel dienen den vnbussertigen Gottlosen, vnd verkündigen inen Gottes ernstliche straffen. Den Gottsfürchtigen aber, vnd auserwehlten seind sie zum trost für argselig daß sie ihr Erlöser empfangen erleben, vnd sich herzlich freuen sollen darumb daß sich ihr erlösung herzu nahet Luce am 21. Sicherheyt vnd eine schwere sünde sollen doch Christliche herzen in dem krummen zorn zerathen die zeichen der welt bedecken, sich zum Creutz von dem lieben Gott uns für augen stellt schicken vnd zu herzen führen daß die liebe Gott vns zur warnung zeichen teyl erscheinen.

Wir sollen auch Gott von herzen bitten, er wolle vnsere herzen mit dem liecht seiner klarheyt regieren, auff daß wir nicht wandeln in der Finsternisz, sondern im Glauben durch den HErrn JEsum Christum das warhafftige Liecht, vnd den heyligen Geist, erleuchtet auß dem Rath der finsternisz in das Reich des liechts gebracht werden eben ende künnen bleiben vnd wie die lieben Sterne am Himel mögen leuchten immer vnd ewiglich AMEN.

## Zu Nürnberg / bey Hans Mack Brieffmaler, wonhafft ins Ayrers Hof.

As a Protestant, Michael became a cautiously hopeful person when he thought about God and was no longer the naïvely dependent one of his Catholic youth. In part it was simply maturation; but it also reflected his altered religious beliefs. Still, when something good happened in his life, he never doubted its source or the proper response: "Praise be to God!"

Despite the Behaim boys' appreciation of God's absolute sovereignty over nature, history, and their own destinies, they and their parents also believed that their physical well-being and worldly success had a definite connection with their piety. When parents and guardians invoke religion in their letters to the boys, they have uppermost in mind its utilitarian qualities. They believed that a devout child was a more secure and a more promising child, safer from the temptations that might leave him with syphilis or place him on the gallows, and also less likely to end up in an obscure occupation or unemployed.

After the great merchant Andreas Imhoff became guardian to Paul Behaim, Sr. (1519–68)—the father of our Paul and at the time (1534) a novice apprentice in Kraków—he exhorted the then fifteen-year-old Paul to be helpful, honorable, and conscientious in all his dealings with his masters, but above all else to be "God-fearing." "This is the chief thing," he writes; "if you have this, you have everything."[14] Andreas knew that a God-fearing Paul would be better disciplined, maintain an immaculate reputation, make steadier progress in his apprenticeship, and in the end have a surer future as a merchant. A century later, Stephan Carl's guardians assured him that if he lived by God's commandments, he would without doubt enjoy good fortune and success.[15] The same belief in the basic, generic prophylactic quality of religion led Frau Magdalena Behaim, a devout Lutheran, to urge her son Friederich, during his first year of law school in Padua (1581), to nurture his "Christian devotion" by going regularly to Italian (Catholic) religious services.[16]

None of the boys associated his own vocational success more emphatically with divine providence than did Michael. The reason may have been that the odds against his succeeding had been so much greater and his success, when it came, proved well beyond his own expectations. As an unhappy apprentice in Breslau in the 1530s, Michael repeatedly expressed the hope that God would not forsake him, but by his grace help him become a "respected man" (*zu eehren kommen*), by which he meant a merchant with his own successful business. It was God, Michael believed, who bestowed on him a Breslau woman of substance to be his wife—and not only a woman of substance but also one he truly liked and loved. At the comparatively young age of twenty-three, Michael became engaged to Margaretha Emmerich, the daughter of a Breslau merchant. Actually, the betrothal was secret; Michael undertook it strictly on his own, without consulting his Nuremberg relatives or seeking his guardian's consent—something very much against the custom of the time and most upsetting to his family. By Nuremberg law, a son who married without parental consent might be disinherited as late as age thirty.[17]

Not one of Michael's relatives attended the wedding in Breslau. They had expected to play a role in the choice of his wife, and the possibility that she would not be a Nuremberg woman had never crossed their minds. When Michael later apologized abjectly to his guardian for having acted without his counsel, he blamed the marriage entirely on the irresistible providence of God, declaring the union to be more the result of God's willfulness than of his own.

In this way, God enabled Michael to do what Nuremberg law and his family together would not readily have allowed: to enter a marriage independently at his own initiative and with a foreigner.

Many a Catholic lad also found himself in a similar situation. But one may doubt that any ever explained such a marriage in quite the way that Michael did, when he defended his action to his chagrined family. This is how he put it:

> She [Margaretha] caught my eye and I caught hers and we were joined together by God. He ordained that it happen this way by his divine will. I thank him for giving me a good, respectable girl, whom none of my family need be ashamed of. If I may speak frankly, he might have punished me with a loose whore with lots of money who is the talk of the town.[18]

As the latter comment makes clear, Michael had a keen sense of the unpredictable will of God within an individual life as well as within the larger course of history. God could distort or enhance a personal life as easily as he could rearrange nature or the heavens. All of the boys believed that God acted frequently, so to speak, out of character, and they accepted such behavior as simply part of the nature of a sovereign Lord. When it came to dispensing worldly success and fortune, God did not strictly abide by either the biblical rule of just deserts or the biblical promise of undeserved mercy. As Michael observed in the lives of his own masters, a lazy, incompetent man might succeed in the world, while an honest, hard-working man is kept down.[19] Regardless of what one might read in the Bible or hear in a sermon, God did not necessarily do his best by his creatures after they had done theirs by him.

One clear consequence of this perception of deity was a tendency to take God and religion with a grain of salt. God was real and powerful and he would do what he would do—of that the Behaim boys had no doubt. But they also never showed any sign of having lost sleep over God's sovereignty; nor did they ever petition God obsessively. They gratefully took what God gave them when it was good, and they made the best of it when it was not. Otherwise, they simply proceeded on their own course. In Michael's case, the result of God's special attention proved to be a happy one; God permitted him to follow his own heart, which he was doing anyway, and to gain new wealth and independence in the process.

## ANTI-CATHOLIC POLEMICS

Michael's cousin twice removed, Paul Behaim, Jr., was the most self-consciously Lutheran of the four boys. Like Michael, he too had been stricken by plague while in Italy, and he suffered in addition the loss of some of his possessions. He accepted these misfortunes as God's just judgment on his sins. Still, he believed that God had favored him in more important ways. For example, he had protected Michael's soul so that his faith in God's Word remained strong while he lived in a land that clearly abused it.[20] One hears in Paul's letters the anti-Catholic polemics of the Lutheran pamphleteers of the 1520s, which Nuremberg sermons and catechisms kept alive long after the Reformation. On 8 June 1576, he concludes a letter to his mother with the following comment on the feast day of the Paduan patron saint, Anthony (1195–1231):

> 8 June, on which day a feast was held in Padua for one Anthony, the likes of which is not seen here at any other time of the year. This is not the Anthony with the pig [the Egyptian anchorite] nor the other [presumably local] saint, who people there [in Nuremberg] know

something about. This is the patron saint of the city, who is supposed to have done many marvelous things, along with many other lies contrived [about him] to deceive simple people.[21]

While in Padua, Paul conducted private religious services of his own. He asked his mother to send him a copy of the Neuber edition of Luther's hymnal and other Lutheran devotional books, assuring her that he could safely read such books in private, if he did not make a point of showing them to others.[22] Nuremberg's reputation as a major Protestant center made its merchants suspected couriers of propaganda south, so at this time one did have to take care. Two years earlier, in 1574, the clergy of Lucca had harassed Paul's future brother-in-law, Balthasar Paumgartner, Jr., and other Nuremberg merchants by insisting that they observe local religious holidays and fasts. In the 1590s, the Luccan Inquisition placed visiting Nuremberg merchants under surveillance— something Balthasar and his colleagues protested to the Nuremberg city council.[23]

In marked contrast to Paul, brother Friederich readily accommodated himself to Italian religious custom. After his mother had written urging him not to neglect his Christian devotion while in Padua, he agreed to attend public religious services there. "I will act on [your exhortation] as far as possible," he assured her, "for I can also receive [Christian] teaching [*lehr*] from the Italian sermon, and it is useful as well for learning Italian; along with vespers, it is not so bad."[24] In the first draft of his letter, he even went so far as to say he "liked" it!

Such behavior indicates that Lutheran teaching did not automatically turn its lay devotees into bigots. Even a highly self-conscious Protestant youth like Paul Behaim gained from his faith such inner confidence and sense of superiority over "Italian religion" that he could readily conform to Catholic religious practice, when Italian law or business demanded it. It was sufficient for one to be internally immune from its errors.


## RHETORICAL LUTHERANISM

Once inside the heart and mind of an individual, a particular religious teaching not only may not be influential, it may itself become captive to the character of the person it would otherwise transform. Such seems to have been the case with Stephan Carl, by every contemporary measure an incorrigible youth. He regularly spent money beyond his means; he flunked out of the Altdorf Academy after his first year, the first member of his family to fail at school; and he proved to be so inept when he began service at court that his master restricted him to waiting on tables.

His family recognized his moral failings early. "I lie awake many a night," his mother writes, "because I cannot conclude otherwise than that your letters, with their citations of God's word, are pure hypocrisy"—this after Stephan Carl attempted to explain away his debauchery and thievery at school.[25] With the termination of his academic career, his elder half-brother and guardian, Lucas Friederich, recalled that he had stolen sweets as a child and dismissed him as a bad seed. He believed such a youth required a master unafraid to starve and beat him out of his self-indulgence.[26]

Stephan Carl routinely invoked religion in defense of his wrongful deeds and whenever he wanted to gain the many material things he desired. He seems to have known instinctively what had to be said to convince those in authority around him of his sincerity and resolve, and thus keep money coming his way. He became, in short, a master of pious protestation and feigned conversion.

As a spokesman for early modern religiosity, he is obviously eccentric, and we read his letters three and a half centuries later no surer than his family that his words convey his true personal feelings. But precisely because he is so patently self-serving, his espoused religious beliefs tell us something about the religious values of those around him, for he carefully tells all what he is sure they want to hear. His letters play so shamelessly to his audience that they perhaps convey the religious mind of the contemporary lay public better than they do his own.

A case in point is his correspondence with his mother in the spring of 1629. Stephan Carl burned his last bridge to her when she caught him selling a schoolbook for cash to finance his bad habits. At first, he lied to her about the book, claiming that it belonged to a poor student for whom he merely performed the services of a middleman. Frau Behaim had previously accused her son of lies and hypocrisy; this time she added to his sins that of pride. The new accusation unleashed in the seventeen-year-old Stephan Carl a torrential recitation of seemingly everything he had ever heard about this most deadly of sins as he scrambled to gloss over the incident. Here is a brief sample of his comments, which in their entirety fill a whole manuscript page.

Almighty God commands humility from us on almost every page of Holy Scripture, and he sternly warns that there is nothing in us he opposes more than pride. These are some of the sayings that are known to you . . . "God resists the prideful, but he gives his grace to the humble"; "he who raises himself up will be put down, and he who lowers himself will be raised up. . . ."

How hostile God is to pride is easily deduced: he can tolerate it neither in heaven nor on earth. Why was the devil cast out of heaven and into hell? Because he began to be prideful and to hate his [angelic] companions. Why were our first parents thrown out of Paradise? Because of their pride and desire to be like God. Pharaoh, who was truly prideful, declared war on almighty God and discovered to his great loss, that what is said is true: "The vengeance of God runs down the proud." The earth swallowed alive Korah, Dathan, Abiram, and the rabble that joined them when they wantonly revolted against Moses and the princes of Israel [Numbers 16].

I could bring forth many more examples of this vice, but my paper, and particularly my time, are now running out. Especially [to be mentioned here are] the fruits of pride, such as its ability to render creatures faithless, estrange them from their Creator, and bring God's wrath down upon their necks. No evil is less easily borne than the wrath of God. It is terrifying to fall into the hands of God, unbearable to lose the grace of the Highest. Who, then, would not curse pride as the very gates of hell and tremble before it as before a poison deadly to both body and soul?

From these words, you [dear Mother], not I, may now conclude whether or not I am guilty. But would you, for sure, for sure, let me know [which you think it is]?[27]

Stephan Carl's dissertation on pride hardly addressed the moral issue at hand, and it left his mother more convinced than ever of her son's flawed moral character. One thing it makes clear to the modern reader is that youth at this time had their heads full of catechetical instruction and could readily quote the Bible, even when, as in Stephan Carl's case, little of it actually penetrated their hearts or had any effect on their behavior. Stephan Carl believed that his recitation of biblical condemnations of pride would so impress his mother that he might thereby regain her favor. But his mother knew as well as we that knowledge of a catechism was no acid test of a Christian frame of mind; nor is it any proof of the Reformation's success.

Belief in the devil and witches was another tenet of the boys' religious faith, which they were prepared to invoke against anyone who got in their way. That is exactly what Stephan Carl and his cousin Georg Wilhelm Pömer did after the wife of their Altdorf tutor told their parents about their degenerate behavior at school. When the boys discovered her whistle-blowing, they demonized her before any who would listen. Stephan Carl wrote to his mother,

> If one looks at a few calendars, one will see that it is written there for this week: "the devil will rage and be set loose [calendars then bore weekly biblical verses]." There is also a common saying that when the devil does not go in person [to do his dirty work], he sends an old woman in his place. The devil has always been a liar and he tells nothing but lies, and now one [of his own] has told considerable lies about me solely to ingratiate herself [with you].[28]

Later Stephan Carl decried the same woman to his guardians as a "foul and heedless beast," who deserved to be poisoned.[29] For his part, cousin Georg Wilhelm not only declared the woman a witch, he even contemplated killing her. "If only it did not put the soul as well as the body at risk," he confides to Stephan Carl, "how gladly would I practice what the poet [Juvenal] writes: 'Vengeance is more pleasing than life itself' [*Satires*, 13.180]. But when I think about the future, I cannot let anger rule me; for wrath belongs to God."[30]

A final example of Stephan Carl's rhetorical use of religion appears in his correspondence from Amsterdam in the spring of 1635. Having gone there to escape the war in Bavaria in which he had served as a cavalier, he planned eventually to take passage to the West Indies and begin a new life there in the employ of the Dutch West India Company. Five difficult years had passed since he left school. With his every failure, he had vowed to become financially independent of his mother and to bring her more joy than sorrow before her death. Finding himself again in need, he reiterated that promise. This time he wanted twenty thaler (thirty gulden) so that he could buy trinkets in Amsterdam to sell at great profit to natives in the New World, and thereby gain what he called some "easy traveling money." He portrayed himself as being truly penitent and resolved at last to amend his life. And he describes the anticipated voyage to the New World as the best way a sinner as great as he can do penance; it is, he tells his mother, tantamount to entering a cloister.

The comparison must have given his pious Lutheran mother a momentary start, even though it was clear that Stephan Carl's cloister was not that of the church fathers or of Christian tradition. Stephan Carl put it this way:

> I very sincerely ask Mother mercifully to forgive me and to forget all that has happened up to now in Germany. As a great evildoer and sinner can do nothing better than betake himself to a cloister, there to make amends for his evil works, serve God by doing good works, and surrender all his worldly desires and actions, so am I now entering the best cloister of godliness. There all worldly luxury is forgotten and one recognizes his greatest need, so that no one is better served than God. I know of no better way to make amends for all that has happened in the past than by undertaking this voyage.[31]

Perhaps Catholic youths departing Amsterdam for the East or West Indies also construed the sacrifices of the voyage and their tenure in a primitive new world as a metaphor for a religious vocation. For a youth from Lutheran Nuremberg, the "best cloister of godliness" could only have been service to God and man in a secular calling. But Stephan Carl's comment also makes clear that a century of Protestant polemic against the religious life and the dissolution of cloisters in Protestant lands had not destroyed the power of this traditional religious image among the Lutheran laity. Stephan Carl recast the image, emptying it of its traditional content, yet it still held a spiritual significance for him and his family. For their faith too held self-denial and self-sacrifice to be God-pleasing virtues.

As for the easy traveling money this image was designed to elicit from his mother, Stephan Carl's eloquence failed. During the months in Amsterdam, he ran up expenses in the hundreds of gulden through an Amsterdam middleman authorized by his family to look after his needs. When his guardians discovered this extravagance, they refused for a long time to reimburse the middleman, whose oversight of Stephan Carl, or rather lack thereof, had pleased them none too well. Soon isolated in Brazil and fearing his unpaid Amsterdam debts would end his access to credit everywhere, Stephan Carl pleaded with his family to pay his creditors immediately. Meanwhile, ever resourceful, he found a new creditor in Recife—a fellow Nuremberger, who knew of Stephan Carl's family, but, fortunately for Stephan Carl, had no knowledge of his alienation from them or of his indebtedness in Amsterdam.

## TRUST AND FORGIVENESS

The Behaims lived in a world shot through with dependent relationships, and for no group more so than for parents. When parents sent their children off to school, put them in apprenticeships, or arranged for them to enter court or military service, they depended utterly on the goodwill of intermediaries and foreign masters for their children's care and well-being. In such an interdependent society, few personal traits were more desired and admired in a person than a reputation for trustworthiness. Duties done and kindnesses rendered held the fragile civilized world together and created lifelong obligations on the part of the recipients. The Behaims believed that such deeds would be fully repaid by God in eternity, if not by grateful family members in this life. After Paul's father died, for example, Michael's sister wrote to remind him that he still had his mother and many good friends to rely on. She encouraged him in his new circumstances to entrust himself and his siblings to the care of their new guardian, Andreas Imhoff. "Assure him [Imhoff]," she writes, "that what it is not possible for you and your siblings to repay him [for his services to you], you will ask the Lord God to give him a thousandfold."[32] When Stephan Carl's academic career ended, his half-brother arranged a position for him at the princely court in Altenburg, thanks to the assistance of an old friend there. "For this great kindness," he wrote to his friend, "God, who rewards all good deeds, will surely not let my lord and his most dear family go unrewarded; the unceasing and impassioned prayer of our beloved and worried mother will see to that."[33]

In the world of the Behaims, trust secured human relationships in much the same way that faith made uncertainty about God's nature tolerable. In both relationships, that with God and those with strangers, one had to rely mainly on words and promises and because of the great distances involved—both with God, who was everywhere, yet nowhere, and with masters and intermediaries, who were often lands apart—one had only as much security as one could believe.

Even Stephan Carl, in his perverse way, deemed trustworthiness the test of Christian character. After six months of outrageous profligacy in Amsterdam, he wrapped himself around the cross in an attempt to convince his guardians that such expenditures had been made with great regret and were out of character for him: "Had I [as my guardians charge] run up such incalculable bills gladly and intentionally, I would not be a Christian . . . and because of the unspeakable grief such would cause my mother, God would punish me in soul and body here on earth and even more so in eternity!"[34]

If trustworthiness was important in a person, even more so was the ability to forgive others and to make peace with one's enemies. It made no sense in a society that left one vulnerable in so many ways to have enemies either human or divine, when friendship was a feasible alternative. So the Behaims constantly urge one another to repent and be reconciled with those they have wronged and to forgive and extend charity to those who have wronged them, so that in the end they may be estranged from no one.

When Stephan Carl's carousing and stealing at school were first exposed, his mother's immediate reaction was to remind him of God's mercy and his need for penance. "You can easily imagine what I am thinking," she writes,

> that God may have mercy [on you]. You tell me that the water fountain is now your greatest joy [that is, in place of the beer tap], also when you hear it said in church, "Give," which is as it should be for a true Christian. However, you [in fact] much prefer [to take] a little money [for yourself]. By such thoughts and actions, you are steering a course [straight] to the gallows and hellfire. . . .
>
> But because I have learned that . . . you will receive the holy sacrament on Good Friday, I will pray again for you and your soul's salvation. . . . So humble yourself before God from the depths of your heart. Acknowledge and confess to him your great and weighty sin

in true penance . . . [and] seek his forgiveness for the sake of the merit of Jesus Christ. . . . Then may the angels who have for so long been saddened by your many sins rejoice over you as over a penitent sinner.[35]

As schoolboys, Stephan Carl and his cousin Georg Wilhelm, as we have seen, had felt victimized by their tutor's wife when she reported their misdeeds to their parents. Although both boys initially demonized her and even contemplated her death, Georg Wilhelm in the end admonished Stephan Carl to forgive her. Learning of Stephan Carl's plans to take the sacrament, he wrote to him urging that he make peace with the woman as part of his penance:

> I ask you to contemplate carefully the words of the fifth petition [of the Lord's Prayer], "As we forgive our debtors," and to forgive your hostess. [Admittedly] she has poisoned the truth and made [failings] not so terrible in themselves out to be much worse than they are. Still, if you want God to forgive you, you must also forgive her, even though it is a bitter pill.[36]

The Behaims subjected interfamily relationships to the very same code of conduct. While a law student in Padua, Paul Behaim had argued violently with his mother over a reduction of his annual stipend. Very angry words were exchanged between mother and son. Contrite and regretful in the aftermath, Paul wrote to confess his wrong to her and to beg her forgiveness. His words, doubtless chosen with care, suggest again the degree to which intimate relationships were approached with religious presuppositions and moral values in mind. They convey a layman's version of the religious and ethical teaching instilled in the boys by the culture of Lutheran Nuremberg.

> After God, who has given me you, it is you I cannot thank enough [for all that I have]. I now see and experience for the first time what kind of mother I have, and I am horrified and lament within myself when I think of the many ways I have insulted and angered you over the past six weeks, allowing the vexatious devil to provoke me against you. I have been unworthy to have you look on me as your son. My every trust now is that you will no longer hold this sin and misdeed against me, but will forgive and pardon me as one who has been foolish and gone much too far.[37]

The difficulty with attempts to connect a particular religious confession with a particular form of moral behavior lies in the fact that life is never as clear as doctrine. Religion as it is creedally defined and religion as it is actually lived exist at different ends of a very long spectrum, along the length of which many nonreligious considerations and elemental emotional needs constantly intervene, affecting the behavior of most people as much as what they profess the gospel to be. In this regard, religious behavior may be compared to behavior within a family, where the relations between a husband and a wife and, in turn, between parents and children have an internal logic and force of their own quite apart from reigning professional theories about manhood and womanhood, and about parenthood and child care. We know, for example, that in actual family life in Renaissance and Reformation Europe wives were treated with far greater respect and shared far more authority within the burgher household, and children were shown far greater love and more frequently indulged by their parents, than much contemporary comment on gender and family—not to mention the modern literature on these subjects—would lead a reader to believe.

It may well be, then, that one can find religious commentary and behavior similar to what we have found among the Behaim boys also among contemporary Catholic youth, who also believed in divine providence, made anticlerical comments, and were taught by their church to forgive others as God had presumably forgiven them. That possibility does not diminish, however, the importance of Protestant teaching in the formation of such behavior on the part of the Behaims. Had they not been steeped in the religious culture of their Lutheran city, they would have conceptualized themselves and their world differently and made many of life's decisions otherwise than they did. So while prudent historians should not presume today to tie theology and culture together as assuredly as did the historians of only a generation or two ago, if we are exacting in our research, we can still say a great deal about the spiritual pedigree of lay moral behavior in early modern Europe.

Of course, how one defines the intent of a movement has everything to do with how one finally evaluates it. If we believe that the original goal of the Reformation was the creation of a more pious kind of Christian in the towns and backwoods of Europe, and by that we mean a person who is able to recite from memory the doctrines and creeds of the new faith, overcome common moral failings like drunkenness and fornication, and passively accept new clerical and political authority as they are imposed on him from above, then we prepare ourselves in advance to find a shallow and failed Reformation. The Reformation was a far more complex affair and deserves a more sensitive interpretation.

The original intent of the reformers and pamphleteers who invented the Reformation was not to create docilely devout Christians, but to raise less credulous ones. The religiously gullible and greedy layperson was as loathsome to Protestants as the pope in Rome and as much the subject of their pamphlets, sermons, catechisms, and moral ordinances. The evangelical preachers of the 1520s exhorted the laity to be less accepting of tradition, to see through indulgences, relics, pilgrimages, Masses for the dead, papal authority, and clerical privilege—an enormous world of popular religious belief and practice allegedly without much biblical basis or honest pastoral intent, at least within the contested German territories. In the revolutionary literature that defined the Reformation at its inception, the image of the good Christian was preeminently that of a Bible-savvy layperson internally in control of his or her own spiritual life, immune to spiritual manipulation, uncoercable in conscience, able to see through Christian utopias and sociopolitical pipe dreams, and, while respectful of tradition, never one to trust in it uncritically.

If the Behaims may be taken as lay end-products of the Reformation's evolution over a century, they suggest that the Reformation that survived among the laity was more akin to that of the pamphleteers of the 1520s than to that of the visitors and catechists who became prominent in later decades. The Behaims were literate in their faith, but hardly doctrinaire, and certainly never obsessed. Conceptually and existentially, they put their own clear stamp on what they believed, and they shaped their religion according to their own needs. They had their own lay version of that complex of religious belief and practice which Martin Luther summarized with the phrase, "justification by faith"; and it guided and disciplined, emboldened and consoled them in both ordinary and extraordinary times. Luther had understood that famous phrase to mean that one could do absolutely nothing for one's salvation except trust in God's Word as it was known in Holy Scripture. For ordinary people like the Behaims, it came to mean that one's spiritual energies should never be diffused and spent on things one could neither fathom nor control.

# Conclusion

The modern world likes to think it has put religious bias and competition behind itself, and one who would critically compare religious confessions, past or present, openly courts controversy. As the offspring of a Roman Catholic mother and a Protestant father, I would like to think that I have undertaken such a comparison with at least a genetic predisposition for fairness.

Protestantism is a religion that has won battles, but never the war. It has not become the majority religion of Europeans, much less of people around the world. That this would be the case was already clear in the sixteenth century. A majority of Europeans then preferred traditional Catholic piety and accustomed folkloric beliefs to the new Protestant faith, and that preference has stood the test of time. Today, even secular historians of culture, who have no particular religious allegiance and for whom religion is only a window onto more basic social reality, find traditional religious practice intrinsically more engaging than Protestantism.

The limited appeal of Protestantism, existentially and intellectually, is not difficult to explain and should have been expected. Traditional Catholic piety and folk beliefs are far older and richer religious systems. They are arguably more emotionally involving for their adherents. They also accommodate human frailty and folly more conscientiously and with greater enterprise than their Protestant counterparts. The devotion to the continuity of the world of the living with that of the dead, the predictable cycle of sin and forgiveness, the breathtaking shrines and sparkling festivals, the sensuous, tangible piety—all of these things make traditional religion more enticing for the devout layperson and curious ethnographer alike. Protestant faith by comparison has seemed all too simple and austere a religion, the spiritual equivalent of a sobering cold bath.

The aspirations of Protestants have also tended to exceed their abilities. For all their inveighing against *Menschensatzungen* and lay credulity,

sixteenth-century Protestants also had their specters and flights of religious fancy, not least of which were witches' sabbaths and Jewish
cabals. Though fewer in number and less materialistic in nature, defining
Protestant beliefs and practices were no less gripping for the faithful,
who also feared the power of sin, death, and the devil and anxiously
sought in their religion a surer defense. And the new Protestant clergy
proved to be less loath to bully their congregations than their earlier
denunciations of papal tyranny might have led one to expect. But because
there is no inherent spiritual superiority of the clergy over the laity in
Protestantism, these same clergy have had far more difficulty exalting
themselves in the presence of their congregations than have their Catholic counterparts. As members of a religion in which each biblically
informed conscience is believed to speak *ex cathedra*, Protestants have
had little taste for spectacle or patience with hierarchy. Experience and
tradition have taught them instinctively to associate both with sham and
tyranny.

By comparison with traditional practice, the Reformation radically
simplified religious life—a change still strikingly visible today, as a visit
to a Catholic Mass and a Protestant service will immediately attest. Many
people found themselves relieved of much burdensome conventional
piety. But the Reformation also posed a new and different spiritual
threat for the laity. Although Protestantism had simpler religious rituals,
each had suddenly become absolute, its importance enhanced by the
reduction of religion to a claimed vital core. This raised the stakes
spiritually for devout believers. The slack had gone out of religion, but
with it went also, as the passage of time confirmed, some of the familiarity
and comfort. The reformers in the end created a version of what they
had originally vehemently opposed: an elite religion. But it was elite only
spiritually, not in a social sense, and it placed the laity and the clergy
on an equal footing in the eyes of God. It was a religion for any and all
who could forego the sweet deceits of traditional piety.

The new test of Scripture gave Protestants a powerful weapon against
arbitrary spiritual authority. Who on earth could ever again instruct the
minds or oppress the consciences of a people who had successfully
defeated the proclaimed vicar of Christ? Few countries have in their
history an example of such bold and successful defiance of established
sacred and secular authority as Germany in the age of Reformation. A
tremendous inner pride and a sense of spiritual superiority sprang from

such national will, as appealing to German Catholics as to German Protestants. Amid their centuries-old territorial divisions and their new confessional alignments, the Reformation gave all Germans a new awareness of their unity as a people.

But here, too, for some, the Reformation had again sown the wind. The layman's ready access to Scripture and the catechetical armoring of the young in Protestant lands created a powerful new religious authority within. Sensitive laity now faced potentially a different kind of spiritual bully, one who occupied their own consciences and who, unlike a priest, bishop, or the pope in Rome, could not so easily be argued with. And the demands of this new authority always rang clear and true and without pause.

Because religion is intrinsically social and cultural, it informs and shapes a people's moral behavior as profoundly, or as negligibly, as it does their spiritual belief. Religious doctrine and liturgy are propositions; they become reality only as people apply them to their everyday lives. The Reformation left a moral imprint on German society, one that is visible in the public institutions of Protestant lands and in the behavior of the people who passed through them. Its boldest proposition was a declaration of independence from the excesses of traditional Christianity and popular religious culture. The reformers raised spiritual skepticism and moral criticism to new levels. Living in what Erasmus eulogized as an "age of folly," Luther and his followers proclaimed that they would no longer be party to it, but would instead lead sober and enlightened lives, beyond such dependence and self-deception, secure in God's clear Word and simple truth. In the process of attempting to do so, they left for all Germans a dual legacy of pride in themselves as a people and the inner resources to resist the fantasies of religious and national chauvinism. To people of all nationalities the first Protestants bequeathed in spite of themselves a heritage of spiritual freedom and equality, the consequences of which are still working themselves out in the world today.

# Appendix: A Digest of Theories about the Reformation

W as the Reformation a true revolution? Did it really change people's behavior and affect reigning institutions? These questions have long preoccupied scholars, and never more so than today. How they are finally answered will determine whether the religious revolution of the sixteenth century continues to hold its traditional place of importance in the history of Western civilization.

The range of opinion on the Reformation is enormous. One scholar describes it as a political revolt in the classic sense of the term: one ruling elite displaced another in Protestant cities and lands as secular rulers overturned traditional episcopal authority and brought the organization of society by the medieval church to an end.[1] Other scholars point to French Calvinism and English Puritanism as the beginnings of modern ideological revolution. By this they mean revolutions in which commitment to a cause becomes so total that everything else in life is rendered secondary to it.[2]

By contrast, a long tradition of scholarship has argued that the most revolutionary features of the Reformation were unconscious and unintended. This is particularly true of scholars who follow the nineteenth-century sociologist Max Weber. According to Weber, the Reformation taught its followers to resolve religious anxiety by being successful at their work. The pursuit of worldly success, he believed, inadvertently created a congenial "ethic" for the development of methodical capitalist enterprise, thereby making the Reformation appear to be more revolutionary and modern than it actually was.[3] Along these same lines, some scholars associate the Reformation with the rise of a self-absorbed secular culture increasingly independent of all religion.[4]

Still others maintain that the Reformation actually strengthened what it set out to destroy. Having successfully undermined traditional Catholic belief and ritual in the minds of many laypeople, it unintentionally stampeded many of them into the far worse superstitions of folk magic and witchcraft. According to this argument, the great witch panics of the sixteenth and seventeenth centuries were actually efforts to resolve the new fears and anxieties created by the successful ecclesiastical revolution.[5] According to yet another scholar, the Reformation "broke the crust of [European] religious unity" only to release a subterranean oral religious culture, "the silent voice of Europe's common man," which Protestants then persecuted as pagan and heretical.[6]

Alternatively, a majority of scholars today view the Reformation as a very modest spiritual movement, both self-limiting and easily manipulated by secular political power; and, when compared with the social and political revolts of the century, a very minor event in its history.[7] It did not, they believe, break radically with the past in any social or political sense. A similar point of view is expressed by scholars who doubt that the Reformation ever cherished any great social ambitions or held a true political agenda. In this portrayal, the Reformation emerges as a conservative campaign on the part of elite Christian clergy to subdue a surrounding native culture that had always been and preferred to remain semipagan. What distinguished Protestant from Catholic clergy in this undertaking, it is claimed, was only greater Protestant discipline and zeal.[8] In a similar vein, the Reformation has been described as an overly ambitious attempt to impose on uneducated and reluctant men and women a Christian way of life utterly foreign to their own cultural experience and very much against their own desires.[9] Still other scholars today pronounce the Reformation intrinsically reactionary and view it as bound from the start to a world view that impeded the rise of a new cosmology and science and sanctioned Europe's sociopolitical status quo—the last hurrah of the Middle Ages, not the beginning of the modern world.[10]

# Notes

INTRODUCTION

1. Quoted by Koppel S. Pinson, *Modern Germany: Its History and Civilization* (New York, 1954), p. 8.

2. Ibid., p. 9. A more complex version of this thesis is Lionel Rothkrug, *Religious Practices and Collective Perceptions: Hidden Homologies in the Renaissance and Reformation*, a special issue of *Reflexions historiques* 7 (1980).

3. Karl Holl, "Die Kulturbedeutung der Reformation," in *Gesammelte Aufsätze zur Kirchengeschichte*, vol. 1: *Luther* (Tübingen, 1948), pp. 468–543; English: *The Cultural Significance of the Reformation*, trans. K. Hertz, B. Hertz, and J. H. Lichtblau (Cleveland, 1962).

4. *Sermon on the Sum of a Christian Life*, in *Luther's Works*, ed. J. Pelikan and H. Lehman, 51 (St. Louis, 1957), p. 284.

1. TURNING THE WORLD UPSIDE DOWN

Portions of this chapter appeared in the *Lutheran Theological Seminary Bulletin* 70 (1990): 3–12; several paragraphs from this version open and close chapter 11 of Donald Kagan et al., *The Western Heritage*, 4th ed. (New York, 1990).

1. See the Appendix.

2. *Deutsche Reichstagsakten, Jüngere Reihe*, 2 (Gotha, 1896), pp. 670–704. Partially translated by Gerald Strauss, *Manifestations of Discontent in Germany on the Eve of the Reformation* (Bloomington, Ind., 1971), pp. 53–63. I draw on both sources for the discussion that follows.

3. Anton Störmann, *Die städtischen Gravamina gegen den Klerus am Ausgange des Mittelalters und in der Reformationszeit* (Münster in Westfalen, 1912), pp. 12, 18–19.

4. Johannes Schildhauer, *Sociale, politische und religiöse Auseinandersetzungen in den Hansestädten Stralsund, Rostock und Wismar im ersten Deittel des 16. Jahrhunderts* (Weimar, 1959), pp. 69–79; Axel Vorberg, *Die Einführung der Reformation in Rostock* (Halle, 1897), p. 26.

5. Karlheinz Blaschke, *Sachsen im Zeitalter der Reformation* (Gütersloh, 1970), pp. 104–8, 116.

6. Heide Stratenwerth, *Die Reformation in der Stadt Osnabrück* (Wiesbaden, 1971),

pp. 19–21; Konrad Hofmann, *Die engere Immunität in deutschen Bischofsstädten im Mittelalter* (Paderborn, 1914), pp. 14–15, 29.

7. Rolf Kiessling, *Bürgerliche Gesellschaft und Kirche in Augsburg im Spätmittelalter. Ein Beitrag zur Strukturanalyse der oberdeutschen Reichsstadt* (Augsburg, 1971), pp. 294–98; 355–59.

8. Gerhard Pfeiffer, "Das Verhältnis von politischer und kirchlicher Gemeinde in den deutschen Reichsstädten," in *Staat und Kirche im Wandel der Jahrhunderte*, ed. W. P. Fuchs (Stuttgart, 1966), pp. 86–87.

9. The example is taken from David Rosenberg, "Social Experience and Religious Choice: A Case Study, the Protestant Weavers and Woolcombers of Amiens in the Sixteenth Century," Ph.D. diss., Yale University, 1978.

10. The importance of political experience in determining religious preference in Germany and Switzerland is the subject of Bernd Moeller's now classic little book, *Reichsstadt und Reformation* (Gütersloh, 1962), which has inspired a generation of scholars.

11. Peter Blickle, *Die Revolution von 1525* (Munich, 1981 [English: *The Revolution of 1525*, trans. Thomas A. Brady, Jr., and H. C. Erik Midelfort (Baltimore, 1982)]; Thomas A. Brady, Jr., *Turning Swiss: Cities and Empire, 1450–1550* (Cambridge, 1985).

12. See Günther Franz, *Der deutsche Bauernkrieg* (Darmstadt, 1952).

13. See the twelve articles of the Memmingen peasants, in Günther Franz, ed., *Quellen zur Geschichte des Bauernkrieges* (Darmstadt, 1963), pp. 175–79.

14. The following discussion draws on these studies: Klaus Leder, *Kirche und Jugend in Nürnberg und seinem Landgebiet 1400 bis 1800* (Neustadt an der Aisch, 1973); Lorna Jane Abray, *The People's Reformation: Magistrates, Clergy, and Commons in Strasbourg, 1500–1598* (Ithaca, N.Y., 1985); Fritz Büsser, *Würzeln der Reformation in Zürich* (Leiden, 1985); Miriam Chrisman, *Strasbourg and the Reform* (New Haven, 1967); Rudolf Endres, "Zur Einwohnerzahl und Bevölkerungsstruktur Nürnbergs im 15./16. Jahrhundert," *Mitteilungen des Vereins für Geschichte der Stadt Nürnberg* [henceforth *MVGN*] 57 (1970): 242–72; Irmgard Höss, "Das religiös-geistige Leben in Nürnberg am Ende des 15. und am Ausgang des 16. Jahrhunderts," *Miscellanea historiae ecclesiasticae*, vol. 2: *Congrès de Vienne, Aout–Septembre, 1965* (Louvain, 1967), pp. 17–36; Robert M. Kingdon, "Was the Protestant Reformation a Revolution? The Case of Geneva," in *Transition and Revolution: Problems and Issues of European Renaissance and Reformation*, ed. Robert M. Kingdon (Minneapolis, 1973), pp. 53–76; and Charles Garside, *Zwingli and the Arts* (New Haven, 1966).

15. Steven Ozment, *The Reformation in the Cities: The Appeal of Protestantism to Sixteenth-Century Germany and Switzerland* (New Haven, 1975), p. 139.

16. Hans Bernitt, *Zur Geschichte der Stadt Rostock* (Rostock, 1956), p. 151.

17. H. C. Erik Midelfort, "Protestant Monastery? A Reformation Hospital in Hesse," in *Reformation Principle and Practice: Essays in Honour of A. G. Dickens*, ed. Peter N. Brooks (London, 1980), pp. 71–94.

18. Cf. Richard Gawthrop and Gerald Strauss, "Protestantism and Literacy in Early Modern Germany," *Past and Present* 104 (1984): 33–42.

19. August Franzen, *Zölibat und Priesterehe in der Auseinandersetzung der Reformationszeit und der katholischen Reform des 16. Jahrhunderts* (Münster, 1969); Steven Ozment, *The Age of Reform, 1250–1550: An Intellectual and Religious History of Late Medieval and Reformation Europe* (New Haven, 1981), chap. 12.

20. Geoffrey Parker, *Europe in Crisis, 1598–1648* (Ithaca, N.Y., 1979), p. 50.

21. James M. Kittelson, "Successes and Failures" (see the Appendix); Steven Ozment, "Die Reformation als Intellektuelle Revolution," in *Zwingli und Europa*, ed. Peter Blickle (Zurich, 1985), pp. 27–46; and Chapters 8 and 9 below.

22. Robert W. Scribner, *"For the Sake of the Simple Folk": Popular Propaganda for the German Reformation* (Cambridge, 1981); Peter Blickle, *Deutsche Untertanen. Ein Widerspruch?* (Munich, 1981); idem, *Reformation im Reich* (Stuttgart, 1982); Gerald Strauss, *Law, Resistance, and the State: The Opposition to Roman Law in Reformation Germany* (Princeton, 1986); Brady, *Turning Swiss*.

23. See Chapter 4.

24. Paula Sutter Fichtner, *Protestantism and Primogeniture in Early Modern Germany* (New Haven, 1989).

25. Bernd Moeller, "Probleme der Reformationsgeschichtsforschung," *Zeitschrift für Kirchengeschichte* 14 (1965): 246–57.

26. See Chapter 6.


## 2. Religious Origins and Social Consequences

1. Joseph Lortz, "Zur Problematik der kirchlichen Missstände im Spätmittelalter," *Trierer theologische Zeitschrift* 58 (1949): 5. The many obstacles to reform of the late medieval clergy are among the subjects of Francis Rapp's *Réformes et Réformation à Strasbourg . . . (1450–1525) (Paris, 1974)*.

2. Francis Oakley, *The Western Church in the Late Middle Ages* (Ithaca, N.Y., 1979), pp. 123–24, 215–16. See also Lawrence G. Duggan, "The Unresponsiveness of the Late Medieval Church: A Reconsideration," *The Sixteenth Century Journal* 9 (1978): 3–26.

3. Johan Huizinga, *The Waning of the Middle Ages: A Study of the Forms of Life, Thought, and Art in France and the Netherlands in the Dawn of the Renaissance*, trans. F. Hopman (Garden City, N.Y., 1954), pp. 50–51, 67, 151–58, 161–63, 167–68.

4. This thesis is also elaborated in regard to late medieval scholastic thought

by the late Etienne Gilson, *Reason and Revelation in the Middle Ages* (New York, 1938).

5. "The Origins of the French Reformation: A Badly-Put Question?" in *A New Kind of History and Other Essays: Lucien Febvre*, ed. Peter Burke, trans. K. Folca (New York, 1973), pp. 60–65.

6. Jean Delumeau, *Catholicism Between Luther and Voltaire: A New View of the Counter Reformation* (New York, 1977), p. 176. See the critique of this thesis by John van Engen, "The Christian Middle Ages as an Historiographical Problem," *American Historical Review* 91 (1986): 519–52.

7. "[The term Reformation] goes all too easily with the notion that a bad form of Christianity was being replaced with a good one. . . . It is too high-flown [a concept] to cope with actual social behavior and not high-flown enough to deal sensitively with thought, feeling, and culture" (John Bossy, *Christendom in the West: 1400–1700* [New York, 1985], p. 91).

8. Ibid., pp. 35, 46–47, 57–58.

9. Ibid., pp. 92, 95, 120, 135.

10. Ibid., p. 97.

11. Bernd Moeller, "Piety in Germany Around 1500," in *The Reformation in Medieval Perspective*, ed. Steven Ozment (Chicago, 1971), pp. 50–75; Steven Ozment, *The Reformation in the Cities: The Appeal of Protestantism to Sixteenth-Century Germany and Switzerland* (New Haven, 1975), chap. 2.

12. Delumeau, *Catholicism Between Luther and Voltaire*, p. 158.

13. Jacques LeGoff, *Hérésies et sociétés dans l'Europe pré-industrielle 11e–18e siècles* (Paris, 1958); Steven Ozment, *The Age of Reform, 1250–1550: An Intellectual and Religious History of Late Medieval and Reformation Europe* (New Haven, 1981), chap. 3.

14. Gerald Strauss gently scolded this pervasive practice in his address to the Association of Modern Historians during the December 1989 meeting of the American Historical Association: Gerald Strauss, "Viewpoint: The Dilemma of Popular History," *Past and Present* 132 (1991): 130–49.

### 3. THE REVOLUTION OF THE PAMPHLETEERS

A condensed version of this chapter has appeared in *Forme e destinazione del messaggio religioso: Aspetti della propaganda religiosa nel cinquecento*, ed. Antonio Rotondo (Florence, 1991), pp. 1–18.

1. "History and Psychology," in *A New Kind of History and Other Essays: Lucien Febvre*, ed. Peter Burke, trans. K. Folca (New York, 1973), p. 7.

2. Wieland Schmidt, "Vom Lesen und Schreiben im späten Mittelalter," in *Festschrift für I. Schröbler zum 65. Geburtstag*, ed. O. Schmidtke et al. (Tübingen,

1973), pp. 309–27; Rudolf Hirsch, *Printing, Selling and Reading, 1450–1550* (Wiesbaden, 1974), pp. 10–23; A. L. Gabriel, "The College System in Fourteenth-Century Universities," in *The Forward Movement of the Fourteenth Century*, ed. F. L. Utley (Columbus, Oh., 1961), pp. 97–99.

3. *Der deutsche Buchhandel. Wesen, Gestalt, Aufgabe*, ed. Helmut Hiller and Wolfgang Strauss (Hamburg, 1975), p. 23.

4. Steven Ozment, "Pamphlet Literature of the German Reformation," in *Reformation Europe: A Guide to Research*, ed. Steven Ozment (St. Louis, 1982), pp. 85–106; *Flugschriften als Massenmedium der Reformationszeit*, ed. Hans-Joachim Köhler (Stuttgart, 1981).

5. Bernd Moeller, "Stadt und Buch. Bemerkungen zur Struktur der reformatorischen Bewegungen in Deutschland," in *Stadtbürgertum und Adel in der Reformation*, ed. W. J. Mommsen (Stuttgart, 1979), pp. 29–39; Elizabeth Eisenstein, *The Printing Press as an Agent of Change*, 1 (Cambridge, 1978). See the skeptical reaction of Robert W. Scribner, "Oral Culture and the Diffusion of Reformation Ideas," *History of European Ideas* 5 (1984): 237–56.

6. *Lectures on the Epistle to the Hebrews* (1517–18), in *Luther: Early Theological Works*, ed. and trans. James Atkinson (Philadelphia, 1962), pp. 194–95.

7. The new scriptural mandate is attested literally by the appearance of pamphlets consisting entirely of biblical verses, for example, an anonymous string of fifty against indulgences: *On Aplas von Rom kan man wol selig werden durch anzaigung der götlichen hailigen geschryfft* (n.p. [early 1520s], Oxford, Bodleian Library (henceforth OX-BOD), Vet.D 1 e.75 (1). The Strasbourg gardener Clement Ziegler published a collection of biblical verses against venerating images and saints: *Ain kurtz Register und Ausszug der Bible in wölchem man findet was Abgöterey sey unnd wo man jedes suchen soll* ([Strasbourg], 1524), OX-BOD, Tracts Lutheran (henceforth T.L.) 39.188.

8. "Auch spricht Christus Jo. 14: Ich bin die warhait; er spricht nicht: Ich bin gewonhait": *Ein nützliche Predig zu allen christen/Von dem vasten, und feyren/geprediget worden* [Augsburg 1522], in *Flugschriften aus den ersten Jahren der Reformation*, ed. Otto Clemen, 2 (Nieuwkoop, 1967), pp. 21–22; henceforth Clemen.

9. Kettenbach reports ten arguments made by Catholic apologists in defense of the authority of tradition: (1) the Spirit guides the pope and councils in their rulings; (2) where two or three are gathered together in Christ's name, Christ is present; (3) the Apostles altered the Gospel and those who stand in their place may also do so; (4) Christ permitted many changes to be made in God's law to Moses (for example, in regard to circumcision, eating pork, and observing the Sabbath); (5) Parisian schoolmen have long drawn conclusions that are not literally in Scripture; (6) Scripture was written down by men—it too is "menschen leer"; (7) St. Augustine has taught; "I would not have believed the gospel had the power

and authority of the church not forced me"; (8) Protestants themselves preach lessons from history and nature that one cannot find in the Bible; (9) if Protestants can deny the whole of canon law, Duns Scotus, Thomas Aquinas, and other such authorities, then Scripture too can be denied; and (10) the Christian church has for a long time altered the Gospel by withholding the Eucharistic cup from the laity: *Ein Sermon wider des pabsts kuchenprediger zu Ulm*, ([Augsburg], 1523), pp. 36, 38–39, 40–41, 44–46, 47–49.

10. *Ein Sermon . . . zu der loblichen statt Ulm zu eynem valete* (Bamberg, 1523), in Clemen 2. 109–10.

11. In another of his sermons, a defense of Luther, Kettenbach elaborated fifteen abuses of the sacrament of penance: *Ein new Apologia unnd verantworttung Martini Luthers wyder der Papisten Mortgeschrey* ([Bamberg], 1523), in Clemen 2.160–64.

12. *Ein Sermon . . . zu der loblichen statt Ulm zy eynem valete*, pp. 111–18.

13. Two prominent examples are Lucas Cranach the Elder's *Passional Christi und Antichristi* (1521) and Judas Nazarei (pseud.), *Das Wolffgesang* (early 1520s). Cf. Robert W. Scribner, *For the Sake of Simple Folk: Popular Propaganda for the German Reformation* (Cambridge, 1981), 148–89.

14. *Verglychung des aller heiligsten herrn und vatter des Bapsts, gegen dem seltzem fremden gast in der Christenheyt genant Jesus*, in Clemen 2.146–47.

15. "Denn das wort gots leret auch gehorsam leysten der öberkeit, bringt eynigkeit und fryd, aber menschen leer und wort brengen unfryd, ungehorsam, jamer und leide," *Ein Practica practiciert* ([Bamberg], 1523), in Clemen 2.188, 192. I will quote the original in the notes when the passage in question strikes me as being exceptionally pithy, rich, or striking, or possesses nuances no translation can fully do justice to.

16 *Ein nützliche Predig . . . von dem vasten*, pp. 14–15, 21–23.

17. *Ein Sermon wider des pabsts kuchenprediger zu Ulm*, p. 36.

18. Ibid., p. 38. According to Kettenbach, the world had been in error about the truth for the greater part of its history—fully five thousand years before God made the first covenant with Abraham, then among the Jews themselves for fifteen hundred years (the period during which they denied Christ), and finally among the Saracens and Muslims for eight hundred years, that is, since the appearance of Muhammad. Christians, too, are said to have been falsely led for three or four hundred years, since the papacy gained worldly prominence and scholasticism captured the universities and monasteries in the twelfth and thirteenth centuries: *Ain Sermon oder predig von der Christlichen kirchen* ([Augsburg], 1522), in Clemen 2.92.

19. Ibid., p. 100.

20. Ibid., p. 101.

21. Ibid., pp. 101–2.

22. On the role of laughter in ideological change, see Julio Caro Baroja's comments on its role in the decline of witchcraft: *The World of the Witches*, trans. O. N. V. Glendinning (Chicago, 1965), p. 218.

23. *Mich wundert das kein gelt ihm land ist* (n.p., 1524), in *Johann Eberlin von Günzburg, Sämtliche Schriften*, 3, ed. Ludwig Enders (Halle, 1902), pp. 171–72.

24. Ibid., p. 174.

25. Ibid., pp. 175–78.

26. "Wir haben ein got, der thut uns nichts guts, er verderbt uns gar am gut, wie du gehort hast, auch am leib, so er uns gebeut vil vasten, verbeut uns eier, butter, fleisch zu essen, offt mussen wir von seinentwegen im krieg sterben, zu letzt umb einen groschen thut ehr uns in ban und verdampt uns ewiglich. Eintweder ist gar kein got, oder unser got ist nit der recht got. Ein got ist, der seinen dienern guts thut, beschirmet und selig macht": ibid., p. 178.

27. Ibid., p. 180.

28. Hans Sachs, *Disputation zwischen ainem Chorherren und Schuchmacher* (n.p., 1524), Yale, Beineke Library, pp. A 4 b–B 1 a.

29. "Gewonnhait ist vergencklich": ibid., pp. B 2 b–4 a.

30. This work brought the first charges of Lutheranism against Zwingli, who protested that he taught St. Paul's gospel, not Martin Luther's; *Huldreich Zwinglis sämtliche Werke*, ed. E. Egli et al. (Leipzig and Berlin, 1905–), 2.147.

31. *Antwort eins Schwyzer Burens über die geschrift Jeronimi Gebwilers* (Zurich, 1524), in *Flugschriften des frühen 16. Jahrhunderts. Microfiche Serie 1978*, ed. Hans-Joachim Köhler (Zug, 1978–), henceforth Tü fiche, 241–42/960, pp. A 2 a–b.

32. *Ain Schoner Dialogus oder Gesprech/von aynem Münch und Becken/wolcher die Oster ayer Samlen wollt* (Augsburg, 1524), Tü fiche 4/n. 17, pp. B 3 b–4 a.

33. *Ayn freüntlichs gesprech/zwischen eynem Parfusser münch/auss der Provintz Osterreich/ der Observantz/und einem Löffelmachern/mit namen Hans Stösser* (n.d., n.p.), OX-BOD T.L. 84.20, pp. A 2 b, A 3 b, A 4 a–b.

34. "Pfaffen und Münch haben mit der hell/feegfeüwr, beycht/buss/und menschen gesetzten daz arm volck erschreckt/gleich wie die ältern jre kinder erschrecken mit dem pöpel hinnder der thür/auff das sy dester leychtter gelt über kommenn," *Klag an königkliche Maiestat Ungern und Behem wider ainen Lutherischen münch prediger ordens über viertzig artickel von jm geprediget zu Tetzschen in Behemerland* ([Wittenberg], 1522), OX-BOD T.L. 31.184, Tü fiche 724/1841, p. A 3 b.

35. *Eyn Brüderliche und Christenliche Heyliger geschrifft gegrundte ermanung/von einem unterthon und schefflin/Seynen Pastor oder pfarrhern zu geschickt/yn dem er jn seins pastor ampts erynnert/und seine schefflin mit dem wort gots zu weyden/und keyn taglöner an sein stadt zu stellen* (n.p., 1524), OX-BOD T.L. 37.142, pp. A 3 a–b.

36. *Ain new gesprech von Zwayen gesellen/die an ir arbait gangen sein* (n.p., 1524), OX-BOD T.L. 38.163; Tü fiche 627/1628.

37. Johann Schevan, *Ein Sendbrieff darinne er anzeigt aufs der Bibel und schryfft/warumb er Barfusser orden des er etwan ym kloster zu Basell gewest verlassen* (Wittenberg, 1523), OX-BOD T.L. 28.121; *Grund und Ursach auss Göttlichem Rechten/Warumb Prior und Convent in Sant. Annen Closter zu Augsburg ihren Standt verandert haben* (1526; Kempten, 1611), Simmlerische Sammlung, Center for Reformation Research, St. Louis, henceforth CRR; *Ain Geschichte wie Got ainer Erbarn closter Junckfrawen [Florentina of Ober Weimar] aussgeholffen hatt* (Wittenberg, 1524), OX-BOD T.L. 96.10. In *Ein Sendbrief von einem jungen Studenten zu Wittenberg an seine Eltern im Schwabenland von wegen der Lutherischen Lehre zugeschrieben* (n.p., 1523), a son politely urges his mother to stop believing in "fantasey," "zauwberey," "ketzerey," "Teüffels gespennszt," and "Aberglawben": Clemen 1.16–17. See also *Ein Dialogus oder Gespräch zwischen einem Vater und Sohn die Lehre Martini Luthers . . . belangend* (n.p., 1523), Clemen 1.25–50.

38. *Eyn newer Dialogus oder gespräch zwischen ainem verprenten/vertribnem Edelman und ainem Münch* (n.p., n.d.), OX-BOD T.L. 83.19, Tü fiche 171/467, p. A 3 a–4 b. The dialogue portrays a monk's deceitful use of "pure fantasy" to win sacrifices from the laity as a greater act of thievery than a nobleman's becoming a highway-man; ibid., p. A 4 b.

39. "In Christo ist kein absünderung/kein zeychen/sonder so vil unser getaufft seint/haben Christum anzogen. . . . Bedorffen die rechten Christen kein zeychen dann das sie jr creütz tragen/und dem herzen nachkommen/das stehet nit in eusserlichen creutzen/die man on die kleydung . . . henckt/sondern in dem geyst." *Das Blatten/Kutten/Kappen/Schern/Schmern/Saltz/Schmaltz/und alles dergleichen/Gott ab-schewlich seindt finstu grundliche Anzeygung der Geschrifft* (Woims, 1524), OX-BOD T.L. 82.22b, pp. C 3 b, D 2 a. Urbanus Rhegius may be the author.

40. Ambrosius Blarer, *Ir gwalt is veracht/ir kunst wirt verlacht/Irs liegens nit gacht/gschwecht ist ir bracht/Recht ist wiess Gott macht* (n.p., 1524).

41. Eberlin von Günzburg, *Mich wundert*, p. 163.

42. "Hilff lieber Gott, wie manchen iamer hab ich gesehen, das der gemeine man doch so gar nichts weis von der Christlichen lere, sonderlich auff den dörfen, und leider viel Pfarherr fast ungeschickt und untüchtig sind zu leren, Und sollen doch alle Christen heissen, getaufft sein und der heiligen Sacrament geniessen, können widder Vater Unser noch den Glauben odder Zehen gebot, leben dahin wie das liebe vihe und unvernünfftige sewe, Und nun das Evangelion komen ist, dennoch fein gelernt haben aller freiheit meisterlich zu missebrauchen," *Luthers Kleiner Katechismus*, ed. J. Meyer (Bonn, 1912), p. 4.

43. Johannes Bugenhagen, *Der Erbarn Stadt Braunschwyg Christenliche Ordenung* (Nuremberg, 1531), pp. A 2 b–4 b, = CRR, *Die evangelischen Kirchenordnungen des*

*16. Jahrhunderts*, 1, ed. A. L. Richter (Leipzig, 1971), pp. 106–20; Johannes Brenz, *Kirchen Ordnung. In meiner genedigen Herrn der Margraven zu Brandenburg* (Nuremberg, 1533), p. A 3 a, = CRR, Richter 1. 176–211.

44. *Bekandtnuss der Evangelischen Leer/in Zehen Hauptarticulen* (Augsburg, 1546), pp. A 2 b–3 b. This is the 1530 original, reissued in 1546 as a safeguard against error and to encourage church attendance.

45. Ibid., p. A 4 a.

46. Steven Ozment, *When Fathers Ruled: Family Life in Reformation Europe* (Cambridge, Mass., 1983), p. 47.

47. *Ein kleglich gesprech Bapsts Leonis/und Bapsts Clementen/mit jrem Kemmerer/ Cardinaln Spinola/in der Helle gehalten/den jetzigen Kirchenstand belangend* (n.p., 1538), OX-BOD T.L. 66.19, pp. A 4 a–b; B 2 b.

48. *Ein gesprech eines Evangelischen Christen/mit einem Lutherischenn/darynn der Ergerlich wandel etlicher/die sich Lutherisch nennen/angezeygt/und brüderlich gestrafft wirt* (Eylenburg, 1524), Yale, Beineke Library, pp. A 4 b, B 2 a–b.

49. *Grund und ursach ausz der hailigen schrifft wie und warumb/die Eerwirdigen herrn/ baider Pfarrkirchen S. Sebalt und sant Laurentzen Pröbst zu Nüremberg/die missbreüch bey der hailigen Messz/Jartag/Geweicht Saltz/und Wasser/sampt etlichen andern Ceremonien abgestelt und erlassen und geendert haben* (Nuremberg, 1524), OX-BOD T.L. 36.106, pp. C 3 a–b, F 4 b; G 3 a, G 4 a, H 1 a, J 1 a–b.

50. Ibid., p. B 1 a.

51. *Ein Ratschlag/Den etliche Christenliche Pfarherrn/Prediger/unnd andere/Götlicher schrifft verstendige/Einem Fürsten/welcher yetzigen stritigen leer halb/auff den abschied/jüngst gehaltens Reichstags zu Nürnberg/Christlicher warhait underricht begert/gemacht haben* (Nuremberg, 1525), OX-BOD Vet. Die.138.

52. *Verantwortung unnd auflösung etlicher vermeintter Argument und ursachen So zu Widerstandt unnd verdruckung des wortt Gottes und heiligen Evangelions Vonn denenn die nitt Christen sein und sich doch Christen namenns rumen täglich gepraucht werden* ([Augsburg], 1524), Clemen 2.352–53, 364, 368, 371, 385, 390. The pamphlet was once attributed to Christoph Schappeler, coauthor of the famous *Twelve Articles* that summarized the grievances of the Schwabian peasantry on the eve of the revolt of 1525. On Spengler's authorship, see Martin Brecht, "Der theologische Hintergrund der 12 Artikel der Bauernschaft in Schwaben von 1525," *Zeitschrift für Kirchengeschichte* 85 (1974): 41–44, with reference to Hans von Schubert, *Lazarus Spengler* (Leipzig, 1934), pp. 401–6.

53. "Christus sagt, das man vatter unnd muter vereern, in sy aber nit vertrawen oder glaubenn soll, sonder welicher in jne (nit auff indert einen menschen) vertrawe, der werd allein selig"; *Verantwortung*, pp. 354, 362–63.

54. Ibid., p. 365.

55. Ibid., pp. 368, 390.

56. "Aber mit dem gewissen, welches allein auff das wort gottes gerichtet seyn soll, ist ein mensch allein und on alles mitel got unnd nyemandt anderem unterworffen"; ibid., pp. 370, 374.

57. Ibid., pp. 374–76, 383–84.

58. Ibid., p. 388.

### 4. Evangelizing the Real World

Portions of this chapter appeared under the title, "The Social History of the Reformation: What Can We Learn From Pamphlets?" in *Flugschriften als Massenmedium der Reformationszeit*, ed. Hans-Joachim Köhler (Tübingen, 1981), pp. 67–97.

1. *Eyn gesprech bruder Hainrichs von Kettenbach mit aim frommen altmüterlin von Ulm von etlichen zufeln und anfechtung des altmütterlin/auff welche antwort gegeben von bruder Hainrich* (n.p., 1523), OX-BOD T.L. 26.75, p. A 2 b. Another version appears in Clemen 2.52–75.

2. *Eyn gesprech bruder Hainrichs*, p. A 4 b.

3. Ibid., p. B 1 b.

4. Ibid., pp. B 2 a–b, C 4 a.

5. Ibid., p. C 1 a. In the preface to the German translation of his Latin attack on the sacrament of Penance (1521), Oecolampadius had eloquently defended vernacular translations of the Bible and other religious books for the laity. Such translations, he points out, have traditionally been compared to casting pearls before swine, a point of view that demeans the laity: "Sein die ainfeltigen nit auch menschen: sein sie nit auch Christen: sein sie nit auch durch den tauf gerainigt/ und werden unser mitbürger und miterben Christi: Soll man jnen on warhayt sagen/unnd die warhait verhalten?" *Ain sunderliche leer und bewerung/dass die Beicht ainem Christen menschen nit bürdlich oder schwär sei* (n.p., 1521), Edinburgh University Archives, p. A 3 b.

6. *Eyn gesprech bruder Hainrichs*, p. C 4 a.

7. A popular argument in Protestant propaganda held that the so-called "old religion" of the medieval church was in fact a fabricated "new religion," while the alleged "new religion" of the Reformation was actually the ancient religion of Scripture. This argument is also prominent in Kettenbach's pamphlet, which describes the "old doctrine or lies" served up by the universities and canon law as the product of the previous four hundred years, "new doctrine and fantasy," whereas the gospel preached by the reformers "has existed for more than a thousand years," from the first Christians until the fall of the church to the papacy in the eleventh century (ibid., p. C 2 a). The most popular version of this theme

in the 1520s was a great anonymous pamphlet entitled *Vom alten und newen Gott, Glauben und Ler* (1521). See Hans-Georg Hofacker, "Vom alten und nüen Gott, Glauben und Ler," in *Kontinuität und Umbruch. Theologie und Frömmigkeit in Flugschriften und Kleinliteratur an der Wende vom 15. zum 16. Jahrhundert*, ed. Josef Nolte et al. (Stuttgart, 1978), pp. 145–77. *Vom alten und newen Gott* appeared in English translation in 1522 ("The Old God and the New") and enjoyed wide circulation in subsequent decades, no doubt because this theme was a central one in the developing Anglican church.

8. *Eyn gesprech bruder Hainrichs*, pp. C 3 a–b.

9. "Christus ist unser gerechtmachung/sein gerechtigkait stet vor unser sund/ so wir jm getrawen/warumb suchen wir gerechtmachung/oder frum zu werden durch unns selber/durch ubergülte ölgötzen/höltzen hailigen/wallen/opffern den bildern/den heiligenn," ibid., pp. A 4 b, C 3 b.

10. It has been estimated that every well-to-do family in Strasbourg had endowed Masses in one or more of the city's churches; Thomas A. Brady, Jr., *Ruling Class, Regime and Reformation at Strasbourg, 1520–1555* (Leiden, 1978), p. 228.

11. There appears to have been an affinity between the egalitarian strains in Protestant theology and the social mobility of both rising urban elites and impoverished working people, both of whom had something to gain from change and joined the Reformation in disproportionate numbers; Natalie Zemon Davis, "Strikes and Salvation at Lyons," *Archiv für Reformationsgeschichte* 56 (1965): 54, and idem, "The Rites of Violence: Religious Riot in Sixteenth-Century France," *Past and Present* 59 (1973): 80–81; Norman Birnbaum, "The Zwinglian Reformation in Zurich," *Past and Present* 15 (1959): 39; Brady, *Ruling Class*, pp. 229–30, 238–39.

12. Compare Robert W. Scribner, "Is There a Social History of the Reformation?" *Social History* 4 (1977): 483–505, and Keith Thomas, *Religion and the Decline of Magic: Studies in Popular Beliefs in Sixteenth-and Seventeenth-Century England* (London, 1971), pp. 493–97.

13. Steven Ozment, *The Age of Reform: An Intellectual and Religious History of Late Medieval and Reformation History* (New Haven, 1980), pp. 381–96; idem, *When Fathers Ruled: Family Life in Reformation Europe* (Cambridge, Mass., 1983).

14. *Ein Christlich bedenckenn W. Linken Ecclesiasten zu Aldenburge. Von den Testamenten der sterbenden Menschen. Wie die geschehen unnd voltzogen werden sollen nach götlichen gesetz* (Zwickau, 1524), British Museum, pp. B 1 b–3 b.

15. Ibid., pp. C 1 b, C 3 b–4 b.

16. Ibid., pp. C 3 a–b. Compare Thomas Starkey's very similar arguments in justification of the total dissolution of English monasteries; G. R. Elton, *Reform and Reformation: England 1509–1558* (Cambridge, Mass., 1978), p. 238.

17. *Von Arbeyt und Betteln/wie man solle der faulheyt vorkommen/und yederman zu*

*Arbeyt ziehen* (Zwickau, 1523), British Museum, pp. A 3 b–4 b. Linck summarizes: "Dann wo einem ein ding beschwerlich ist/suchet er davon erlediget zu werden/ wer in diesem leben arbeyt und schmertz fület/der begeret eins anndern lebens/ wer betrübt ist der suchet trost/also gibt arbeyt ursachen das der mensch ruwe und trost bey God suche," ibid., p. B 1 a.

18. "Von arbeyt leyden/und allen gemeynen bürden der menschen freyhen/ wöllen gar exempt sein/von zollen/schossen/wachen/reysen etc. . . . one gesetz . . . dass heyst in gemeyner menschen arbeyt nit sein/und straffe der menschen nit tragen," ibid., p. B 3 a.

19. Ibid., p. B 3 b.

20. Ibid., pp. C 3 b–4 a. At his most condemnatory, Linck rages against begging as "ein grundtsuppe/und versamblunge aller Uebertrettung der gotes ordnungen und gebot/Ein anfang aller laster/Ein deckel des geytzes/welcher ein abgotterey ist/entgegen/des nechsten liebe," ibid., p. C 4 b.

21. Ibid., p. E 2 a. Anticipating a problem Protestants were creating for their own clergy by condemning clerical idleness and greed, Linck hastened to justify community support of clergy who performed "true spiritual work": "Die gröste entschuldigunge steet auf dem das sie dem worte dess Evangeln dienen/und yn götlicher schrifft tag und nacht sich üben darmit die andern arbeitende leüt so nit geleret/oder andern zeitlichen sachen obligen müssen bey inen genugsam unterricht irer gewissen suchen und finden mügen," ibid., p. E 3 a.

22. Ibid., pp. C 3 a–4 b.

23. "Die ordenlich lieb an jr selber anfahet/nit an seiner eygnen personen/ sondern an seinen mitglidmassen und genossen," ibid., pp. C 4 a–b. By its very nature love wants to help everyone, "er sey frembt oder heymisch," but limited resources force on it an order of priorities.

24. Ibid., p. D 1 b.

25. The 1522 Nuremberg ordinance simply turned away itinerant beggars ("frembden herkommenen bettlern/so nit burger oder burgerin hie seindt"); any discovered in the city, if truly destitute, received minimal aid, but their names were taken and they were warned that a repeat appearance would bring a stern punishment: *New Ordenung der betthler halben/In der Stadt Nurmberg/hoch von nöthon beschehen* (Leipzig, 1522), OX-BOD T.L. 93.4, esp. pp. A 2 b–3 b, A 4 a–5 a. Other early Protestant welfare ordinances are discussed by Carter Lindberg, "There Should Be No Beggars Among Christians: Karlstadt, Luther, and the Origins of Protestant Poor Relief," *Church History* 46 (1977): 313–34.

26. Jacob Strauss, *Haubtstuck und Artickel Christenlicher leer wider den unchristlichen wucher/darumb etlich pfaffen zu Eysnach so gar unrüwig und bemüet seind* (n.p., 1523), OX-BOD T.L. 27.94. The accusation of encouraging the common man not to pay

his debts is reported in Strauss's second treatise on the subject: *Das Wucher zu nemen und geben, unserm Christlichem glauben und bruderlicher lieb (als zu ewiger verdamniss reichent) entgegen ist, unuberwintlich leer und geschrifft* (n.p., 1524), OX-BOD T.L. 36.93, p. E 7 a.

27. *Quellen zur Geschichte des Bauernkrieges*, ed. Günther Franz (Darmstadt, 1963), p. 176. Cf. Peter Blickle, *Die Revolution von 1525* (Munich, 1981), pp. 25–26, 134–36.

28. This argument is made by the Strasbourg reformer, Caspar Hedio, *Von dem Zehenden zwu träffliche Predig/Beschehen in dem Münster zu Strassburg/auff den xx. tag novembris.* (n.p., 1525), OX-BOD T.L. 43.79, and by Andreas Keller, *Von dem Zehenden, Was darvon usz der Schrifft zu halten sey* (n.p., 1525), British Museum. Both emphasize the original criticism of tithes within the context of religious reform, that is, that they not be given to wanton, lazy, and unworthy clergy; ibid., pp. C 1 a–b.

29. Hedio, *Von den Zehenden*, pp. C 2 a–b.

30. "Der mit dir rechten will und deinen rock nehmen, so lass ihm auch den mantel. Dan hie mus die Christenliche gedult das unbillich und unrecht erleyden und doch nicht in die sunde des Wucherers bewilligen," *Das Wucher zu nemen und geben*, p. G 1 a. Resistance was pronounced to be utterly self-defeating. For the views of Luther and Melanchthon, see Benjamin N. Nelson, *The Idea of Usury: From Tribal Brotherhood to Universal Otherhood* (Princeton, 1949), pp. 41–49.

31. On Protestant glorification of the common man in pamphlets, see Kurt Uhrig, "Der Bauer in der Publizistik der Reformation bis zum Ausgang des Bauernkriegs," *Archiv für Reformationsgeschichte* 33 (1936): 70–125, 165–225; and Paul Böckmann, "Der gemeine Mann in den Flugschriften der Reformation," *Deutsche Vierteljahresschrift für Literaturwissenschaft und Geistesgeschichte* 22 (1944): 187–230.

32. Hans Sachs, "Es haist des geytz unter dez hütlein gespilt," *Eyn gesprech von den Scheinwercken der Gaistlichen/und yhren gelubde/damit sie zuverlesterung des bluts Christi vermaynen selig zu werden* (n.p., 1524), Yale, Beineke Library, pp. 2–4.

33. In *Brother Francis: An Anthology of Writings by and about St. Francis of Assisi*, ed. Lawrence Cunningham (New York, 1972), pp. 51–52.

34. "Ja yr spent ewer Vigilg/seelmessen und alle ewer gotsdienst miltigklich gnug auss/wie ich meyn Semel/und maister Hans seyne schuch/doch mit der undterschaidt/wer kaufft, der hat. Und brecht ainer ewerm Seckeldario. v. gulden fur ain opffer/und felet umb ain ort er nem dz gelt nit/keme mit yhm fur recht," *Eyn gesprech von den Scheinwercken*, p. 6.

35. "So muss ich mit meynen knechten den gantzen tag arbaitten/ubel essen/ unnd legen uns offt kaum umb metten zeit nider/da singen mir dann meyne kinder offt erst metten/ich hab vill ain herteren orden dan yhr," ibid., p. 7.

36. "Habt ain aigne ertichte gehorsam angenommen/daryn yhr frey seit von allem frönen/zehendten/rayssgelt/wachgelt/stewergelt/zynssgelt/lehengelt/zolgelt/ ungelt/und allen pürden/so wir alle brüderlich unter ainander tragen," ibid., p. 10.

37. Ibid., p. 11.

38. "Da würd yr erst rechte ware armut empfinden/und wurdt euch die unkeuschait vergenn/und erst recht gehorsam werden yederman," ibid., p. 12.

39. *Syben frumm aber trostloss pfaffen klagen ire not einer dem anderen und ist niemant der sie tröste, Gott erbarme sich jre* (Basel, 1521), in *Johann Eberlin von Günzburg. Sämtliche Schriften*, 3 vols., ed. Ludwig Enders (Halle, 1900), 2.60–63; henceforth Enders. The priest also reports that despite formal petitions for the right of clerical marriage in Switzerland (by Zwingli) and Saxony (by Karlstadt), both ecclesiastical and secular authorities firmly oppose it: "Bapst und keiser, Bischoff und Fürst, ertzpriester und schulteis halten zusamen, wöllen uns mit gewalt hinderen an Eelichen standt," ibid., 2.63.

40. Ibid. Like the other priests, he fears loss of his benefice and livelihood should he act as conscience directs him.

41. "Darzu ist kein grösser unglück, dann eigner gewissen täglichs nagen und unru, welches dem menschen alle freüd leidig macht, allen trost trawrig, alle süssigkeit bitter, und so man trostlich offt handelt wider eigen gewissen, wirt menschlich sinn doll und kumpff, das hertz wirt hart, natürlich erberkeit verhaltet, also das der menschen auch unburgerlich und unmenschlich wirt, daruff fallt offt spiritus compunctionis, ein soliche blindheit, das er auch hasset eigens heil und alle, weliche im guts günnen, und liebet sein eigen unglück. Psal. X," *Der siben trostlossen pfaffen klage* (1521), in Enders 2.81.

42. For a case study, see Robert W. Scribner, "Practice and Principles in the German Towns: Preachers and People," in *Reformation Principle and Practice: Essays in Honour of A. G. Dickens*, ed. Peter N. Brooks (London, 1980), pp. 95–118.

43. Enders 2. 65–66.

44. Ibid., 2.66–67.

45. "An keinem ort der heydenschafft ist mer geübt worden ein nerrscher gotsdienst, als wir christen uff diesen tag haben," ibid., 2.68.

46. A number of mostly Dominican and Franciscan sermon collections are mentioned either by title or by author; Enders 3.301–2. Among the examples of lay criticism, the priest cites the popularity among both laity and clergy of Eberlin's works! *Syben frumm . . . pfaffen*, Enders 2.70.

47. Ibid., 2.72.

48. Ibid., 2.73.

49. Ibid., 2.72–74.

50. Ibid., 2.75.

51. If directly confronted on the issue, however, a priest was advised to answer "wie jm der geist würt ingeben," which probably meant that he should not lie outright about being secretly married; *Der frummen pfaffen trost* Enders 2.83.

52. Ibid., 2.87.

53. Ibid., 2.88.

54. "Auch ist der schin irer verfolgung grösser dann der schad. Sie machen also ein spiegelfechten." Eberlin cites Christoph von Stadion, bishop of Augsburg (1517–43), Hugo von Hohenlandenberg, bishop of Constance (1496–1529), Christoph von Utenheim, bishop of Basel (1502–26), Adolf, prince of Anhalt, bishop of Merseburg (1514–26), and Georg III, bishop of Bamberg (1505–22); Enders 3.309–12.

55. Eberlin, *Der frummen pfaffen trost*, Enders 2.92–93.

56. Hans Sachs, *Ain Dialogus und Argument der Romanisten/wider das Christlich heüflein/den Geytz und ander offentlich laster betreffend* (Nuremberg, 1524), Yale, Beineke Library, p. C 2 b.

57. Ibid., p. C 1 b.

58. Ibid., pp. A 3 a–4 b.

59. Ibid., pp B 1 b–2 a.

60. Ibid., pp. A 3 b–4 a. Romanus denies that this is a serious problem; workers, he says, are easily enough broken by their physical needs and forced to do any employer's bidding.

61. Ibid., p. A 4 b. Romanus agrees that the irresponsible poor, in distinction from those impoverished by illness or accident beyond their control, deserve the harshness of the law; ibid., p. B 2 a.

62. Ibid., pp. B 3 a–b. In summary: "Die da kauffen/sollen thun als behielten sy es nit/Unnd die sich diser welt gebrauchen/als brauchten sy jr nitt/wa das hertz also frey ledig von den zeytlichen güttern gelassen steet seyn zuversicht in Gott und nit in die gütter setz/jm benügen lasst/nit geytzigklich darnach strebt/sonder berayt ist/sy zu lassen wenn Gott will/und sich seyn Christlichen braucht gen den armen."

63. "Ey man findt/Gott sey lob/vil Reycher/seytt das wort Gottes also klar gepredigt wirt/die hauss armen und andern miltigklich handraychung thun/leyhen und geben. . . . Sölt man yedem geben nach seynem beger/verliess sich manicher darauff/und lege auff der betlerey/und arbaytet nit/sy seynd nit all notdürfftig die bettlen/darumb ist man jn nit allen schuldig zu geben/wann wer nit arbaytt/der soll nit essen," ibid., pp. B 3 b–4 a. Romanus concurs in this basic judgment: the undeserving poor should not be permitted to disadvantage the deserving poor. Nevertheless, he warns against the tendency of many to reject all poor people as

undeserving whenever a few display the slightest means, for example, when they are seen drinking a glass of wine.

64. "So hör ich wol [from Reichenburger] man müss nur predigen Glaub/glaub/ Lieb/lieb und die hellisch grundtsup des geytzs/eebruch/unnd ander offentlich laster schweygen/die wider Gottes gesetzs täglich im schwanck geend/da wirdt sich die falsch vernunfft feyn auss wicklen/und jr sach gerecht glosieren," ibid., p. C 1 a.

65. Ibid., p. C 2 a.

66. Bernd Balzer, *Bürgerliche Reformationspropaganda. Die Flugschriften des Hans Sachs in den Jahren 1523–1525* (Stuttgart, 1973), esp. pp. 147, 151, 154–55. Böckmann had already in 1944 interpreted Sachs's first dialogue of 1524, the *Disputation zwischen ainem Chorherren und Schuchmacher*, as an example of the Reformation's confinement of its struggle to church doctrine, no longer addressing issues of social and political justice; "Der gemeine Mann," pp. 228–29.

### 5. Gaining a Big Stick: Ordinance and Catechism

1. These changes are documented by Hartweg Dieterich, *Das Protestantische Eherecht in Deutschland bis zur Mitte des 17. Jahrhunderts* (Munich, 1970); Walther Köhler, *Züricher Ehegericht und Genfer Konsistorium*, 2 vols. (Leipzig, 1932); François Wendel, *Le Mariage à Strasbourg à l'époque de la Reforme 1520–1692* (Strasbourg, 1928).

2. Karl Holl, "Luther und das landesherrliche Kirchenregiment," *Gesammelte Aufsätze zur Kirchengeschichte*, 1 (Tübingen, 1932), pp. 326–80.

3. *Usslegen und gründ der schlussreden*, in *Huldreich Zwinglis sämtliche Werke*, ed. E. Egli et al., 2 (Leipzig and Berlin, 1908), p. 343.

4. James M. Estes, *Christian Magistrate and State Church: The Reforming Career of Johannes Brenz* (Toronto, 1982), pp. 59–79.

5. Johannes Brenz, *Ain Christeliche Predig/von erhaltung gemaines frides/in sachen die Religion betreffend* (n.p., 1535), OX-BOD T.L. 83.26, p. B 1 b.

6. Philipp Melanchthon, *Das die Fürsten aus Gottes bevelh und gebot schuldig sind/ bey iren unterthanen abgötterey/unrechte Gottes dienst und falsche lehr abzuthun/und dagegen rechte Gottes dinst und rechte Christeliche lehr uff zu richten* (Wittenberg, 1540), trans. into German by Georg Major, British Museum 1568.4319, p. B 1 b.

7. Nicholas of Amsdorf, *Ein Christlich Gebet/darin der Churfürst von Sachsen etc. Seine unschuld/jetziges Kriegs/vor Gott und aller Welt bekendt/aus dem Siebenden Psalm genommen* (n.p., 1546), OX-BOD T.L. 119.17, p. A 2 a.

8. As reported from Weimar by Wolfgang Kisswetter, *Ein bevelhe des Churfurstenn von Sachssen und Hertzog Johann Fridrichs/Wie sich die priesterschafft in yrn F. G. Fursten-*

*thumb und landen halten solle/mit verkundung des heiligenn wort Gottis* ([Erfurt], 1525), OX-BOD T.L. 43.90, p. A 3 a.

9. "Nichts anders dann das Wort Gottes und haylig Evangelium/unvermengt menschlicher satzung predigen/und sollen damit das volck yn rechter lerr gesterckt und verfrydt werden," *Die xlj. artickel/so die gemain zu Frankfurtt aynem Radt hat für gehaldten/und jn auch ain ersamer Radt/bestett hat/und auch also auss gericht ist worden/ und man darauff geschworen hat* (n.p., 1525), OX-BOD Vet. Dle.112(9), art. 1.

10. *Ettlich artickel So der Cristlich und Wolgeporn Fürst Casimirus zu Brandenburg/seinen Prelatten auch ander clöstern/und auch ettlich Pfarrer/und prediger an der/darzu verordnent/ auff ettlich über schückt artickel/dan hayligen cristlichen glauben betreffent/so yetz in irrung gezogen werden/zwen radtschleg über Anttwurt seind* (Innoltzbach, 1524), OX-BOD T.L. 38.156, p. A 4 a–b. The recess of the Diet of Nuremberg (9 February 1523) had commanded all rulers loyal to the emperor to permit nothing to be preached or published within their lands "except the true, clear, and pure Gospel according to the doctrine and interpretation of Scripture as approved and accepted by the Christian Church." Cited by Harold Grimm, *Lazarus Spengler: A Lay Leader of the Reformation* (Columbus, Oh., 1978), p. 63. Rulers siding with the Reformation ignored the emperor's qualifying phrase ("as approved and accepted by the Christian church") and simply implemented the Scripture principle of the reformers. But even the diet's formulation of this solution can be viewed as a victory for the Lutherans, allowing them free preaching of the Gospel and effectively abrogating the Edict of Worms against Luther.

11. *Was der Durchleuchtig hochgeporn Fürst und Herr/Philips Landtgraffe zu Hessen/etc/ als eyn Christlicher Fürst mit den Closterpersonen/Pfarrherrn/und abgöttischen bildnussen/in syner gnaden Fürstenthümbe/auss Göttlicher geschrifft furgenummen hat* (n.p., 1528), British Museum 1226.a.79, p. A 2 b.

12. Ibid., p. B 1 2.

13. "Die Teuffels lere machen uns sonderliche sünde/da keine sünde ist/sonderliche heyligkeit/da keine heyligkeit ist," Johannes Bugenhagen, *Der erbarn Stadt Braunschwyg Christenliche Ordenung* (Nuremberg, 1531), Simmlerische Sammlung, CRR, p. G 7 a; *Die evangelischen Kirchenordnungen des 16. Jahrhunderts*, 1, ed. A. L. Richter (Leipzig, 1971), pp. 106–20; hereafter Richter.

14. Ibid., pp. F 6 b–G 1 b.

15. Johannes Brenz, *Kirchen Ordnung. In meiner genedigen Herrn der Margraven zu Brandenburg* (Nuremberg, 1533), Simmlerische Sammlung, CRR, pp. G 2 a, H 4 a–b; Richter 1.182, 195–97, 211.

16. "Allerlei missprüch/jrtung und verwändthe Gottes dienst/die sich on grund göttlicher warheit . . . in der kilchen Christi . . . ingerissen . . . nach anleitung seines heiligen worts/entweders gar abgethon/oder gebessert," *Bekanthnus unsers*

*heiligen Christlichen gloubens/wie es die Kilch zu Basel haltet* ([Basel], 1534), Simmlerische Sammlung, CRR, p. A 2 b.

17. *Ausschreiben an die Römisch Kaiserlich und Künigkliche maiestaten . . . von Burgermaister und Ratgeben des hailigen Reichstatt Augspurg/Abthuung der Päpstlichen Mess/unnd annderer ergerlichen Ceremonies und Missbreüch belangende* (Augsburg, 1537), Simmlerische Sammlung, CRR, p. B 3 a.

18. *Ains Erbern Rats/der Stat Augspurg/Zucht und Pollicey Ordnung* ([Augsburg], 1537), p. A 2 a.

19. Ibid., pp. A 3 a–b.

20. Elizabeth, duchess of Brunswick/Lüneburg, *Der durchleuthtigen/hochgebornen Fürstin und Frawen/Frawen Elizabeth geborne Marckgrävin zu Brandenburg etc. Hertzogin zu Braunszweig und Leunenburg beschlossen und verwilligtes Mandat in irem Fürstenthumb Gottes wort auffzurichten/und irrige/verfürte lerr ausszurotten belangent* (n.p., 1542), OX-BOD T.L. 70.10, pp. A 1 a–b.

21. "Götter werden sie geheissen darumb/das sie an Gotes stat/das Götliche wort/die rechte Gotes dienste fordern und handhaben/und eine gute erbarliche policey anrichten/und den fromen zu gut dem bösen aber zur straff/drob halten sollen," ibid., p. A 2 b.

22. *Ordnung/wie es soll mit dem gottesdienst/und desselben dienern in der Pfarrkirchen der Stat Elbogen/gehalten werden* (n.p., 1523), OX-BOD T.L. 31.174, pp. A 2 b–4 b.

23. *Ein kurtzer ausszug ein Reformation/wie es hynfürter die priester halten sollen/zu Regenspurgk* (n.p., 1524), OX-BOD T.L. 38.154.

24. *Die xlj. artickel/so die gemain zu Frankfurtt* (Frankfurt, 1525), arts. 1–7, 12.

25. *Gemayn Reformation: und verbesserung der bisshergebrachten verwendten Gotsdiensten/und Ceremonien/die neben dem wort Gottes/durch menschlich gutduncken nach und nach eingepflantzet/und durch des Bapstumbs hauffen tratzlich gehandthabet/aber diser zeyt auss gnaden Gottes/und bericht seins hailigen worts/durch Schulthayssen/klainen und grossen Radt/ der state Bern in üchtland [sic] auss gereütet seind und also dise Reformation in jren stetten/ landen und gebieten hinfür zu halten/angesehen und aussgesandt* (n.p., 1528), British Museum 2906.bb.88, arts. 1–13.

26. *Bekanthnus unsers heiligen Christlichen gloubens/wes [sic] es die Kilch zu Basel haltet* ([Basel], 1534), Simmlerische Sammlung, CRR, art. 11.

27. *Ausschreiben an die Römisch Kaiserlich . . . maiestaten*, pp. B 3 b–4 b, C 2 b–3 a.

28. *Warhaffte Verantwortung. An die Rö. Käy. und Kön. May. und andere ders hayligen Rö. Reichs Stende/von dem hochwurdigen fürsten und hern/hern Christoffen Bischoffen zu Augsburg/und seiner F. G. Thumb capitul. uff der Burgermaister und Ratgeben daselbst unerfindtlich Schmach gedicht/newelicher zeyt/jm druck aussgangen/gestellet* (n.p., 1537), Simmlerische Sammlung, CRR, p. B 1 a–b.

29. [Nürnberg] Catechismus oder Kinderpredig, in Emil Sehling, ed., Die evangelischen Kirchenordungen des XVI. Jahrhunderts, vol. 11.1: Bayern/Franken (Tübingen, 1961), p. 234. On the confessional age, see Wolfgang Reinhard, "Konfession und Konfessionalisierung in Europa," in Bekenntnis und Geschichte. Die Confessio Augustana, ed. Wolfgang Reinhard (1980), and idem, "Zwang zur Konfessionalisierung?" Zeitschrift für historische Forschung 10 (1983): 257–77.

30. Gerald Strauss, Luther's House of Learning: Indoctrination of the Young in the German Reformation (Baltimore, 1978), p. 306.

31. The Nuremberg Catechism also included a new, controversial article on "The Office of the Keys," which elucidated the pastor's claimed God-given power to bind and to loose in matters of sin—a revealing commentary on the aspirations of Protestant clergy to gain full disciplinary power over their congregations as the Reformation became settled.

32. Klaus Leder, Kirche und Jugend in Nürnberg und seinem Landgebiet 1400 bis 1800 (Neustadt an der Aisch, 1973), pp. 62–71.

33. "Feine geschickte leut, die andern leuten auch nutz sein und vil guts tun können," Catechismus, p. 207.

34. Ibid., pp. 209–10.

35. Ibid., pp. 212–13.

36. Ibid., p. 216.

37. Ibid., pp. 217, 220.

38. "Wir können ihn nimmer mer so vil guts tun das wir ihn möchten vergleichen und bezalen ihre guttat, die sie uns geton haben," ibid., p. 217.

39. Ibid., pp. 217–18, 220.

40. Ibid., p. 220. On the difficulty of regulating clandestine marriages, see Steven Ozment, When Fathers Ruled: Family Life in Reformation Europe (Cambridge, Mass., 1983), pp. 42–44, and Thomas Max Safley, Let No Man Put Asunder: The Control of Marriage in the German Southwest, 1550–1600 (1984).

41. Catechismus, p. 223.

42. Ibid., p. 260.

43. Ibid., p. 226. It is unclear who these libertines are.

44. "Man sol niemand unzüchtig anreden, niemand nichts unehelichs anmuten, nicht unzüchtige schandbare wort reden oder liedlein singen dardurch ander leut zur unkeuscheit und ehebruch mögen geraizt werden . . . [auch keine] hurerei . . . im herzen und gedanken," ibid.

45. "Sie das gelt, das zu schützen und schirmen gehört, verpanketiren, verspilen mit pracht, hoffart und sundlichen wollusten an werden. . . . Wann man das regiment und gericht nicht mit frommen, verstendigen leuten versorgt, die pfar-

und predigampt nicht mit gotsforchtigen, gelerten leuten versicht, schulen und andere nötige empter zergehn lest, nötige gemeine gepeu als kirchen, rathaus, statmaur, prucken, pronen, und dergleichen zerfallen lest, allain darumb das mans gelt spar, so wirt es den orten entzogen, dahin es gehört und dazu es geben ist," ibid., pp. 227–28.

46. Ibid., p. 228.

47. Ibid., pp. 228–29.

48. Ibid., p. 230.

49. Ibid., p. 232.

50. Ibid., p. 234.

51. Gerald Strauss, *Luther's House of Learning*, pp. 209–12. Lawrence Stone also allows modern values to becloud his historical judgment on this issue: *The Family, Sex, and Marriage in England, 1500–1800* (New York, 1977), pp. 116–17, 125–26.

52. *Catechismus*, p. 236.

53. Ibid., p. 213.

54. Apparently because, having alienated his parents, he is without an inheritance, or else too undisciplined to make a success of his life even with parental assistance.

55. Ibid., p. 220.

56. Ibid., p. 225.

57. Ibid., p. 236.

58. Ibid., p. 265.

59. Ibid., p. 215.

60. Ibid., pp. 249–50.

61. "Nichts ist so unglaublich, er kan es tun, wann er wil."

62. Ibid., p. 240.

63. Ibid., p. 256.

64. Ibid., p. 277.

65. Ibid., p. 210.

66. Ibid., p. 215.

67. Ibid., p. 228.

## 6. LUTHER'S POLITICAL LEGACY

The original version of this chapter appeared in *German-American Interrelations: Heritage and Challenge*, ed. James H. Harris (Tübingen, 1987), pp. 7–40.

1. Ernst Troeltsch, *The Social Teachings of the Christian Churches*, 2, trans. Olive Wyon (New York, 1960), pp. 494–96, 510, 529, 532.

2. Quentin Skinner, *The Foundations of Modern Political Thought* (Cambridge, 1978), 2.14–15, 18, 73–74.

3. Peter Blickle, *Deutsche Untertanen. Ein Widerspruch?* (Munich, 1981), pp. 29–36.

4. Ibid., pp. 15–20, 38, 41–43, 53–57. Robert L. Lutz has challenged Blickle's exceedingly general definition of the common man ("bestechend einfach"); he confines the term to heads of households with clear political rights and self-interests worth defending; *Wer war der Gemeine Mann?* (Munich, 1979), pp. 11–12, 103–4. For Blickle's rebuttal, see *The Revolution of 1525*, trans. Thomas A. Brady, Jr. and H. C. Erik Midelfort (Baltimore, 1982), p. 220 n. 43.

5. Blickle, *Deutsche Untertanen*, pp. 87, 92, 99, 105–6, 109. Blickle describes the Peasants' Revolt as "the last, most significant, and most threatening attempt to implement the communal principle as the organizational form of the state," ibid., p. 117.

6. Blickle, *The Revolution of 1525*, pp. 184–85; idem, *Reformation im Reich* (Stuttgart, 1982), pp. 47–158.

7. "Dem Gemeindeprinzip hat niemand eine treffendere ideologische Begründung geliefert als Luther"; Blickle, *Deutsche Untertanen*, pp. 125–26.

8. Ibid., p. 128.

9. Ibid., p. 129; idem, *Reformation im Reich*, pp. 46–47.

10. Blickle, *Reformation im Reich*, pp. 50, 52. The passage in question reads, "Darumb müssend christenliche fürsten gsatzt haben, die nit wider gott syind, oder aber man tritt inen uss dem strick, weliches darnach unruw gebirt": *Huldreich Zwinglis sämtliche Werke*, ed. E. Egli et al. (Berlin and Leipzig, 1905–), 2.324.

11. Blickle, *Reformation im Reich*, p. 53, and idem, *The Revolution of 1525*, p. 161. Heiko A. Oberman also regards the Peasants' Revolt as part of the religious revolution, "a true *Glaubensrevolte*"; Oberman, ed., *Deutscher Bauernkrieg 1525, Zeitschrift für Kirchengeschichte* 85 (1974): 157–72.

12. *An Open Letter to the Christian Nobility of the German Nation*, in *Martin Luther: Three Treatises* (Philadelphia, 1973), pp. 13, 16 ( = *Luthers Werke in Auswahl*, 5th ed., ed. Otto Clemen [Berlin, 1959], 1.366, 368).

13. *Dass eine christliche Versammlung oder Gemeine Recht und Macht habe, alle Lehre zu urteilen*, in *Luthers Werke in Auswahl* 2.395–96.

14. *On Temporal Authority: To What Extent It Should Be Obeyed*, in *Luther's Works* (hereafter *LW*), ed. Jaroslav Pelikan and Walter I. Brandt (Philadelphia, 1962), 45.83–84 ( = *Luthers Werke in Auswahl* 2.361–62). I have based my translations on existing ones when possible, but have freely modified portions according to the original where appropriate.

15. Gottfried G. Krodel, "State and Church in Brandenburg-Ansbach-Kulmbach: 1524–1526," *Studies in Medieval and Renaissance History* 5 (1968): 162–66.

16. *On Temporal Authority, LW* 45.105, 111–12 (= *Luthers Werke in Auswahl* 2.377, 381–82).

17. Ibid. 45.91 (= *Luthers Werke in Auswahl* 2.366).

18. Steven Ozment, *The Age of Reform: An Intellectual and Religious History of Late Medieval and Reformation History* (New Haven, 1980), pp. 341–42, and idem, *Mysticism and Dissent: Religious Ideology and Social Protest in the Sixteenth Century* (New Haven, 1978) chap. 3.

19. *On Temporal Authority, LW* 49.91 (= *Luthers Werke in Auswahl* 2.366).

20. *A Sincere Admonition by Martin Luther to All Christians to Guard Against Insurrection and Rebellion, LW* 45.57–74 (= *Luthers Werke in Auswahl* 2.299–310). See Luther's criticism of Ulrich von Hutten's militarism, *D. Martin Luthers Werke: Briefwechsel* (Weimar, 1930–48), 2.249 (16 January 1521).

21. *On Temporal Authority, LW* 45.90–91 (= *Luthers Werke in Auswahl* 2.366).

22. Ibid. 45.94–96 (= *Luthers Werke in Auswahl* 2.370).

23. Ibid. 45.95 (= *Luthers Werke in Auswahl* 2.370); *Whether Soldiers, Too, Can Be Saved*, in *Works of Martin Luther* [hereafter *WML*] (Philadelphia, 1931), 5.35–36 (= *Luthers Werke in Auswahl* 3.320).

24. *On Temporal Authority, LW* 45.100 (= *Luthers Werke in Auswahl* 2.373).

25. Ibid. 45.96 (= *Luthers Werke in Auswahl* 2.370).

26. *Against the Heavenly Prophets in the Matter of Images and Sacraments, LW* 40.89.

27. *Admonition to Peace: A Reply to the Twelve Articles of the Peasants in Swabia, WML* 4.234 (= *Luthers Werke in Auswahl* 2.59).

28. "Ihn unterthan sein und sich durch dasselbige richten, straffen, schaffen und meisten lassen," *Exposition of the 82nd Psalm, WML* 4.294–95 (= *D. Martin Luthers Werke: Kritische gesamtausgabe*, hereafter cited as *WA* [Weimar, 1883–], 31.1.195–96); Ozment, *Age of Reform*, pp. 269–72.

29. *Exposition of the 82nd Psalm, WML* 4.297 (= *WA* 31.1.197–98).

30. Johann Fundling (Findling), *Anzaigung zwayer falschen zungen des Luthers wie er mit der ainen die paurn verfüret/mit der andern sie verdammet hat* (1525), OX-BOD T.L. 44.98, p. A 4 a. See also Marc Lienhard, "Held oder Ungeheuer? Luthers Gestalt und Tat im Lichte der zeitgenössischen Flugschriftenliteratur," *Luther Jahrbuch* 45 (1978): 56–79.

31. Kurt Aland, "Martin Luther als Staatsbürger," in his *Kirchengeschichtliche Entwürfe* (Gütersloh, 1960), pp. 420–51; Hermann Kunst, *Evangelische Glaube und politische Verantwortung. Martin Luther als politischer Berater* (Stuttgart, 1976), pp. 399–402; Eike Wolgast, *Die Wittenberger Theologie und die Politik der evangelischen Stände. Studien zu Luthers Gutachten in politischen Fragen* (Gütersloh, 1977); Mark U. Edwards, Jr., *Luther's Last Battles: Politics and Polemics, 1531–1546* (Ithaca, N.Y., 1983), pp. 38–67.

32. *Admonition to Peace, WML* 4.242 (= *Luthers Werke in Auswahl* 3.66); *Exposition of the 82nd Psalm, WML* 4.292, 307–8 (= *WA* 31.1.193, 206–7).

33. In *Thomas Müntzer. Schriften und Briefe. Kritische Gesamtausgabe*, ed. Günther Franz and Paul Kirn (Gütersloh, 1968), p. 414. See my discussion in *Mysticism and Dissent*, pp. 76–78.

34. Irmgard Höss, "Georg Spalatins Bedeutung für die Reformation und die Organization der lutherischen Landeskirche," *Archiv für Reformationsgeschichte*, 42 (1951): 127, 129; hereafter *ARG*. Wittenberg's political structure was more so-phisticated than such modern caricature supposes. The city elected its magis-trates, and their relationship with the elector of Saxony, the city's overlord, was consultative and cooperative, not confrontational or coercive: Edith Eschenha-gen, "Beiträge zur Sozial- und Wirtschaftsgeschichte der Stadt Wittenberg in der Reformationszeit," *Luther Jahrbuch* 9 (1927): 2–3, 42–44, 52–55. On republi-can values in Lutheran cities, see Heinz Schilling, *Konfessions-konflikt und Staats-fildung* (Gütersloh, 1981).

35. Gerhard Müller, "Luthers Zwei-Reiche-Lehre in der deutschen Reforma-tion," in *Denkender Glaube. Festschrift Carl Heinz Ratschow*, ed. Otto Kaiser (Berlin, 1976), pp. 56–57.

36. Helmar Junghans, "Freiheit und Ordnung bei Luther während der Witten-berger Bewegung und der Visitationen," *Theologische Literaturzeitung* 97 (1972): 95–104, esp. 101.

37. In addition to Blickle, see also Müller, "Luthers Zwei-Reiche-Lehre," pp. 66–67.

38. *Luthers Werke in Auswahl* 2.397.6–34.

39. "Dz es unter den Christen gantz und gar ein and' ding ist/denn mit der welt. In d' wellt gepieten die herrn was sie woln/und die unterthanen nemens auff/Aber unter euch (spricht Christus) solls nicht also sein. Sondern unter den Christen ist ein iglicher des andern richter/und widderumb auch dem andern unterworffen," ibid. 2.398.10–15.

40. Ibid. 2.400.1–5.

41. Ibid. 2.397.6–8, 398.33–39, 400.31–35, 401.5–9, 402.1.

42. Höss, "Georg Spalatins Bedeutung für die Reformation," pp. 119, 127.

43. Karl Holl, "Luther und das landesherrliche Kirchenregiment," in *Gesammelte Aufsätze zur Kirchengeschichte* (Tübingen, 1923), 1.364–69, 372; Irmgard Höss, "The Lutheran Church of the Reformation: Problems of Its Formation and Organization in the Middle and North German Territories," in *The Social History of the Reformation*, ed. L. P. Buck and J. W. Zophy (Columbus, Oh., 1972), p. 322.

44. Holl, "Luther und das landesherrliche Kirchenregiment," pp. 361–62.

45. *Eyn Schrifft Philippi Melanchthon widder die artikel der Bawrschaft* (1525), OX-BOD T.L. 41.43, pp. C 1 a–b.

46. *Von göttlicher und menschlicher Grechtigkeit, wie die zemen sehind und standind*, in *Zwingli: Hauptschriften*, ed. Fritz Blanke et al. (Zurich, 1942), vol. 7, esp. 52, 70–71; see also Steven Ozment, *The Reformation in the Cities: The Appeal of Protestantism to Sixteenth-Century Germany and Switzerland* (New Haven, 1975), pp. 133–34.

47. *Usslegen und gründ der schlussreden oder articklen*, in *Huldreich Zwinglis sämtliche Werke* 2.343.7–21.

48. Ibid. 2.244.17; 345.3; 345.17–346.10. In discussing the first option, Zwingli warned against resorting to "assassination, war, or revolt." If a communal vote had placed a ruler in office, then such a vote should also remove him; if he were in office by the action of a small group of princes, then they should remove him in an orderly fashion—all in accordance with procedures established by law. Regarding a providentially inspired revolt (one "mit got"), Zwingli drew an analogy to Old Testament examples of hardened tyrants deposed by their subjects (the example is the tyrant Manasseh, 2 Kings 21).

49. Letter to Ambrosius Blarer (4 May 1529), in *Huldreich Zwinglis sämtliche Werke* 9.454.15–21, 458.17–18.

50. Ibid. 9.456.30–35, 458.22–23.

51. Ibid. 9.460.13–461.3. Some recent scholarship has found in this letter a perfect summary of the differences between Zwingli and Luther (and Reformed Protestantism and Lutheranism), the former allegedly restricting the Gospel to the inner man, the latter determined to extend it to the whole of human life, body and soul, society and church; see Hans Rudolf Lavater, "Regnum Christi etiam externum—Huldrych Zwinglis Briefe vom 4. May 1528 an Ambrosius Blarer in Konstanz," *Zwingliana* 15 (1981): 338–81. Drawing on Lavater, Heiko A. Oberman proclaims this letter to be "the clearest expression of the alternative within Protestantism between 'Wittenberg' and 'Zurich' "; *Masters of the Reformation*, trans. Dennis Martin (Cambridge, 1981), p. 260 n. 3. Zwingli's own testimony indicates that the letter may more accurately be portrayed as a clear expression of the alternatives within Protestantism between Wittenberg and Zurich on the one hand, and sectarian Protestantism (along with certain Lutherans who have failed to understand Luther) on the other.

52. Ozment, *Age of Reform*, p. 299.

53. *Sincere Admonition*, LW 45.63 (= *Luthers Werke in Auswahl* 2.302–4).

54. *Whether Soldiers, Too, Can Be Saved*, WML 5.44–45, 50 (= *Luthers Werke in Auswahl* 3.327, 331).

55. *Exposition of the 82nd Psalm*, WML 4.296 (= *WA* 31.1.197). In this light, the

term *schrecklich* has a special meaning in the title of Luther's denunciation of Thomas Müntzer: *Eine schreckliche Geschichte und ein Gericht Gottes über Thomas Müntzer, WA* 18.371.

56. *Whether Soldiers, Too, Can Be Saved, WML* 5.55 (= *Luthers Werke in Auswahl* 3.335).

57. Cited by Hubert Kirchner, "Der deutsche Bauernkrieg im Urteil frühen reformatorischen Geschichtsschreibung," in *Deutscher Bauernkrieg*, ed. Oberman, p. 100.

58. "Eyn freier herr/uber alle ding/und niemandt unterthan . . . eyn dienstpar knecht aller ding und jderman unterthan"; *Von der Freiheit eines Christenmenschen*, in *Luthers Werke in Auswahl* 2.11.

59. Only "fully entitled members of a community," namely, the land- or property-owning *Hausväter*, were politically enfranchised in the villages and small towns, according to Blickle, *Deutsche Untertanen*, pp. 56–57. On peasant hierarchies, with wealthy and middling peasants lording it over lowly cottagers and small peasants, see Blickle, *The Revolution of 1525*, p. 52. On conflict in villages between the tenant farmers and disenfranchised day laborers, see David Sabean, "Family and Land Tenure: A Case Study of Conflict in the German Peasant War of 1525," *Peasant Studies Newsletter* 3 (1974): 1–15.

60. On their disunity and "particularism" (a truism always being rediscovered), see Willy Andreas, "Die Kulturbedeutung der deutschen Reichsstadt zu Ausgang des Mittelalters," *Deutsche Vierteljahrschrift für Literaturwissenschaft und Geistesgeschichte* 6 (1928): 62–113, esp. 65–66, 71–72, 75–76; Karlheinz Blaschke, *Sachsen im Zeitalter der Reformation* (Gütersloh, 1970), esp. pp. 34–35, 52–54, 76–77; and Thomas A. Brady, Jr., *Ruling Class, Regime and Reformation at Strasbourg, 1520–1555* (Leiden, 1978), which takes Bernd Moeller to task for romanticizing the late medieval city.

61. Walter Köhler, *Zürcher ehegericht und Genfer konsistorium*, vol. 1: *Das Zürcher ehegericht und seine Auswirkung in der Deutschen Schweiz zur Zeit Zwinglis* (Leipzig, 1932), pp. 154, 156, 202–3.

62. Only by such government and citizenship, it was argued, could contemporaries cope with "the formidable volume of social and economic problems and with the fears of chaos"; Miriam Eliav-Feldon, *Realistic Utopias: The Ideal Imaginary Societies of the Renaissance 1516–1630* (Oxford, 1982), pp. 109, 119, 121–33.

63. Steven Ozment, *When Fathers Ruled: Family Life in Reformation Europe* (Cambridge, Mass., 1983), chaps. 2, 4.

64. Kirchner, "Der deutsche Bauernkrieg," pp. 113, 116.

65. Otto Brunfels, *Von dem Evangelischen Anstoss. Wie/unnd in was gestalt das wort Gottes uffrur mach* (1523), OX-BOD T.L. 31.169, pp. D 2 b–3 a.

66. Hieronymus von Endorff, *Ain wunderbar schön, notdürfftig Prophetisch schaydung/*

*ganz unpartheysch/zwischen allenthalben auffrüriger Bawrschafft/und jrer herren* (1525), OX-BOD T.L. 44.97, p. B 1 a–2 a. Like Luther, imperial counselor von Endorff viewed the Peasants' Revolt as divine punishment on the lords for their failure to rule in a just and responsible manner; and in the aftermath, he appealed to both sides to recognize the corporate, interdependent nature of society: as the eye needs the hand and the head the foot, and vice-versa, so rulers need their subjects and subjects their rulers.

67. *Ain nutzlicher Dialogus oder gesprechbüchlein zwischen ainem Münzerischen Schwermer und ainen Evangelischen frümen Bauern/Die straff der auffrürischen Schwermer zu Frankenhausen geschlagen/belangende* (1525), OX-BOD T.L. 44.95, p. A 4 a. The same criticism is made by Johannes Brenz, who complained that once "Herr Omnes" (the mob, the masses) hears that Christians are free in Christ, he believes "er dörff auch schwere bürde/schmach oder schatzung nit meer leiden," *Von Gehorsam der Underthon/gegen jrer Oberkait* (1525), OX-BOD T.L. 43.85, p. A 3 b.

68. "Es wer nötten/eyn solch wild ungezogen volk/als teutschen sind/noch weniger freyheyt hette/dann es hat. . . . Es ist ein solch ungezogen muttwillig/blutgirig volck/teutschen/da billich vil herter harten solt/denn . . . Eccle. 33, Eym esel gehort/futer/geyssel/und bürde/also eim knecht narung/straff und arbeyt," *Eyn schrifft . . . widder die artickel der Bawrschafft*, pp. C 3 b–4 a.

69. Jacob Schenck, *S. Paulus Spruch/zu den Ephesern am V. Cap. Suffet euch nicht vol Weins/Daraus ein unordig wesen folget* (Wittenberg, 1540), OX-BOD T.L. 67.7, pp. A 4 b, F 2 a.

70. Sebastian Franck, *Vonn dem grewlichen laster der trunckenheit* (1528), OX-BOD T.L. 57.23.

71. *Vormanung/aus unsers gnedigsten herrn des Chürfursten zu Sachssen befehl/gestellt/durch die prediger zuvorlesen/widder Gotslesterung und füllerey* (Wittenberg, 1531), OX-BOD T.L. 106.7, pp. B 1 b, C 4 a, E 2 a.

72. Melchior Ambach, *Von Tantzen/Urteil/Auss heiliger Schrifft/und den alten Christlichen Lerern gestelt* (Frankfurt, 1544), British Library 3307.bb.10(3), pp. B 2 a, B 3 a. Leonhard Culman also recommended ordered indulgence befitting a Christian and a human being: "Christen mögen auch fröhlich sein Zymlich essen/und trincken wein Dantzen/singen/sprengen zur Zeyt Wie jn dann Gott darzu mut geyt," *Ein Christenlich Teütsch Spil/wie ein Sünder zur Buss bekärt wird/Von der sünd Gsetz und Evangelion* (Nuremberg, 1539), British Library, 11747.a.41, p. A 4 a. The Cologne city councillor and wine merchant Hermann Weinsberg devoted ten and a half pages in the modern edition of his family chronicle to a description of the use and abuse of wine, citing advantages when used in moderation (drives away pain, consoles, helps one sleep, brings the timid to speech), but comparing hard drinkers to various breeds of animals: *Das Buch Weinsberg*, ed. Josef Stein (Bonn, 1926), 5.260–65.

73. *Ein kurtze Christlich Ermanung/Wie man inn diesen geferlichen zeitten sich zu Gott keren/und dem Türken obsigen möge* (1542), OX-BOD T.L. 117.6, pp. B 1 a–2 a; John W. Bohnstedt, *The Infidel Scourge of God: The Turkish Menace as Seen by German Pamphleteers of the Reformation Era* (Philadelphia, 1968).

74. "Und summa/kainer will nach dem andern/sondern ain jegklicher will vor dem andern sein. . . . Niemandts mehr bei seinem Ampt/berüff und stand/darein jn Gott gesetzt/bleiben will/das er seines segens warte/und sich davon erneere/ sondern ain jeglicher will on arbait mit handlen . . . [und] reich werden"; Michael Höfer, *Wes man sich in diesen gefährlichen Zeyten halten/und wie man dem zorn Gottes/ so über die Welt entzündet ist zuvor kommen soll/Auch was die ursach solches zorns sey* (1546), OX-BOD T.L. 75.26, pp. C 1 b–2 a.

75. Blickle blames such hesitation on the betrayal of the common man's cause by initially supportive "reformers and bourgeoisie"; he views the comparatively restrained violence of the common man—which one might as well explain in terms of his military incompetence—as a commentary on his moral superiority over his conquerors: *The Revolution of 1525*, p. 136.

76. Cf. Ozment, *When Fathers Ruled*, pp. 172–77.

77. Paul Althaus, *The Ethics of Martin Luther*, trans. R. C. Schultz (Philadelphia, 1972), pp. 51–54, 114; Wilhelm Maurer, "Die Entstehung des Landeskirchentums in der Reformation," in *Staat und Kirche im Wandel der Jahrhunderte*, ed. W. P. Fuchs (Stuttgart, 1966), p. 77; Karl Holl, "Die Kulturbedeutung der Reformation," in *Gesammelte Aufsätze zur Kirchengeschichte*, vol. 1: *Luther* (Tübingen, 1948), pp. 468–543.

78. "Because there is no hope of getting another government in the Roman Empire . . . it is not advisable to change it. Rather let him who is able darn and patch it up as long as we live; let him punish the abuse and put bandages and ointment on the smallpox," *Exposition of Psalm 101, LW* 13.217 (= *WA* 51.258).

79. As Blickle himself points out: *The Revolution of 1525*, pp. 168, 182.

80. *Abschidt des Reichstags zu Speyer Anno. M.D. XXVI gehalten* (1526), OX-BOD T.L. 47.44, p. A 4 a.

## 7. LUTHER ON FAMILY LIFE

Chapter 7 grew out of research for my book *When Fathers Ruled: Family Life in Reformation Europe* (Cambridge, Mass., 1983) and first appeared in *Harvard Library Bulletin* 32 (1984): 36–55.

1. Heiko A. Oberman, *Luther: Mensch zwischen Gott und Teufel* (Berlin, 1981).

2. *The Estate of Marriage*, in *Luther's Works* (hereafter *LW*), ed. Jaroslav Pelikan and Walter I. Brandt (Philadelphia, 1962, 45.36 (*Von dem Eelichen Leben. D. M. Luther durch ine gepredigt* (1522), Harvard, Houghton Library, GC5 L9774.522vk, p. C 1

r). For examples of the misogyny Luther had in mind, see *Womanhood in Radical Protestantism 1525–1675*, ed. Joyce L. Irwin (New York, 1979), p. 67, and Waldemar Kawerau, *Die Reformation und die Ehe* (Halle, 1892), pp. 41–63.

3. Leonhard Culman, *Jungen gesellen/Jungkfrauen and Witwen/so Ehelich wollen werden/zu nutz ein unterrichtung/wie sie in ehelichen stand richten sollen* (Augsburg, 1568; first pub., 1534), British Library, 8416.aa.34, pp. A 3 r, D 6 v.

4. See especially *Jean Gerson: Oeuvres complètes*, ed. Palémon Glorieux (Paris, 1966), 7.416–21.

5. *Luthers Werke in Auswahl*, vol. 8: *Tischreden*, ed. Otto Clemen (Berlin, 1950), p. 4, no. 55 (1531).

6. Ian Maclean, *The Renaissance Notion of Woman: A Study in the Fortunes of Scholasticism and Medical Science in European Intellectual Life* (Cambridge, 1980), pp. 9–10, 18; Vern Bullough, "Medieval Medical and Scientific Views of Women," *Viator* 4 (1973): 485–501.

7. "Nihil digne de coniugio scripserunt," *Luthers Werke in Auswahl* 8.209, no. 3983 (1538).

8. Saint Augustine, *The City of God*, trans. Marcus Dods (Grand Rapids, Mich., 1956).

9. *Ain püchlein von der erkanntnuss der sünd* (Augsburg, 1494), p. C 4 b, in Ozment, *When Fathers Ruled*, p. 12.

10. Cited by David Herlihy, *Medieval Households* (1985), p. 22.

11. Johannes Bugenhagen, *Von dem ehelichen stande* (Wittenberg, 1525), pp. D 1 a–3 b; Erasmus Alberus, *Ein Predigt vom Ehestand* (Wittenberg, 1536), p. C 3 b.

12. Dagmar Lorenz, "Von Kloster zum Küche: Die Frau vor und nach der Reformation Dr. M. Luthers," in *Die Frau von der Reformation zur Romantik*, ed. Barbara Becker-Cantarino (Bonn, 1980), pp. 25–26; Lyndal Roper, *The Holy Household: Religion, Morals, and Order in Reformation Europe* (Oxford, 1989). Fairer and more sensible is Merry Wiesner, *Working Women in Renaissance Germany* (New Brunswick, N.J., 1986).

13. "[Every father] is duty bound to get his child a good mate who will be just right for him or her, or who seems to be just right": *That Parents Should Neither Compel nor Hinder the Marriage of Their Children and That Children Should Not Become Engaged Without Their Parents' Consent* (1524), in *LW* 45.392 (*Das Eltern die kinder zu der Ehe nicht zwingen noch hindern/und die kinder on der elltern willen sich nicht verloben sollen* [1524], Harvard, Houghton Library, GC5.L9774dd, p. A 4 v).

14. Martin Luther, *Ursach. Und anttwort. das iungkfrawen kloster gottlich v[er]lassen* (Wittenberg, 1523), Harvard, Houghton Library, GC5.L9774.523ua, pp. A 3 v–4 v.

15. Florentina of Ober Weimar, *Eynn geschicht wye Got eyner Erbarn kloster Jung-*

*frawen aussgeholffen hat. Mit eynem Sendebrieff D. Mar. Luthers. An dye Graffen tzu Manssfelt* (Wittenberg, 1524), Harvard, Houghton Library, GC5.L9774.524fg, pp. B 1 r–3 v.

16. Luther discusses these impediments in *The Babylonian Captivity of the Church*, in *Martin Luther: Three Treatises* (Philadelphia, 1973), pp. 226–32; *The Estate of Marriage*, in *LW* 45.22–30. See also François Wendel, *Le Mariage à l époque de la Réforme 1520–1692* (Strasbourg, 1928), pp. 125–43.

17. Jacob Strauss, *Ein Sermon in dem deutlich angezeigt und gelert ist die Pfaffen Ee/ yn Evangelischer leer nitt zu der freiheyt des fleischs/und zu bekrefftygen den allten Adam/ wie ettliche fleischlich Pfaffen das Elich wesen mit aller pomp/hoffart und ander teuffels werck anheben gefundiert* (Erfurt, 1523), in *Flugschriften des frühen 16. Jahrhunderts. Microfiche Serie 1978*, ed. Hans-Joachim Köhler (Zug, 1978–), henceforth Tü fiche, 290/838, p. B 3 r.

18. Hartweg Dieterich, *Das Protestantische Eherecht in Deutschland bis zur Mitte des 17. Jahrhunderts* (Munich, 1970); Wendel, *Le Mariage*; and Walther Köhler, *Zürcher Ehegericht und Genfer Konsistorium*, 2 vols. (Leipzig, 1932–42).

19. *LW* 45.388–89 (*Das Eltern die kinder*, pp. A 3 r–v).

20. Ibid., p. 392.

21. *Luthers Werke in Auswahl* 8.28, no. 185 (1532).

22. *The Babylonian Captivity of the Church*, in *Three Treatises*, p. 226.

23. *The Estate of Marriage*, in *LW* 45.24 (*Von dem Eelichen Leben*, p. B 1 v).

24. Barbara Beuys, *Familienleben in Deutschland. Neue Bilder aus der deutschen Vergangenheit* (Reinbeck bei Hamburg, 1980), p. 231.

25. "In conjugio non potest esse unkeuscheit"; discussed by Manfred Fleischer, "The Garden of Laurentius Scholz: A Cultural Landmark of Late-Sixteenth-Century Lutheranism," *Journal of Medieval and Renaissance Studies* 9 (1979): 43–44; see also Oberman, *Luther*, pp. 287–88. "Sine peccato non potest carere uxore," *Luthers Werke in Auswahl* 8.32, no. 244 (1532).

26. Ibid. 8.1, no. 7 (1531).

27. Ibid. 8.304, no. 5458 (1542).

28. Ibid. 8.100, no. 3528 (1537).

29. "Ut delectent viros, ut misereantur," ibid. 8.1, no. 12 (1531).

30. Ibid. 8.223, no. 4081 (1538).

31. Ibid. 8.244, no. 4910 (1540); 8.275, no. 5189 (1540).

32. Ibid. 8.140–41, no. 3692 (1538); 8.36, no. 255 (1532).

33. Ibid. 8.260, no. 5041 (1540).

34. Beuys, *Familienleben in Deutschland*, pp. 224–25.

35. *Luthers Werke in Auswahl* 8.35, no. 250 (1532).

36. Ibid. 8.100–101, no. 3530 (1536).

37. Ibid. 8.318–19, no. 5524 (1542–43).

38. Ibid. 8.28, no. 185 (1532).

39. The accusation is made by Joachim von der Heyden, secretary to Duke George of Saxony, *Ein Sendtbrieff Kethen von Bhore Luthers vormeynthem eheweybe sampt eynem geschenck freuntlicher meynung tzuvorfertigt* (Leipzig, 1528), Tü fiche, 64/165, p. A v. On the gossip about Luther and von Bora, ridiculed by Melanchthon, see Richard Friedenthal, *Luther*, trans. John Nowell (London, 1970), pp. 431–33.

40. Steven Ozment, *The Age of Reform, 1250–1550: An Intellectual and Religious History of Late Medieval and Reformation Europe* (New Haven, 1981), p. 388.

41. *The Babylonian Captivity of the Church*, in *Three Treatises*, p. 236.

42. *The Judgement of Martin Bucer Touching Divorce. Taken Out of the Second Book Entitled, Of the Kingdom of Christ*, trans. John Milton, in *The Complete Prose Works of John Milton* (New Haven, 1959), 2.471–74.

43. *The Babylonian Captivity of the Church*, in *Three Treatises*, pp. 233–34.

44. *Luthers Werke in Auswahl* 8.241, no. 6934.

45. *The Estate of Marriage*, in *LW* 45.45 (*Von dem Eelichen Leben*, p. D 3 r).

46. *Luthers Werke in Auswahl* 8.122–23, no. 3613 (1537).

47. The most outspoken is Lawrence Stone, *The Family, Sex and Marriage in England 1500–1800*, abridged ed. (New York, 1979), esp. p. 125.

48. Cited by H. Buchwald, *D. Martin Luther. Ein Lebensbild für das deutsche Haus* (Leipzig, 1902), p. 354. Luther believed that up to seven years of age a child had no fear of death; the appearance of the fear of dying was a sign of a child's maturation into adulthood: *Luthers Werke in Auswahl* 8.113, no. 3576 (1537).

49. *Luthers Werke in Auswahl* 8.2, no. 18 (1531).

50. Ibid. 8.208, no. 3964 (1538).

51. Klaus Petzold, *Die Grundlagen der Erziehungslehre im Spätmittelalter und bei Luther* (Heidelberg, 1969), pp. 84–90.

52. Gerald Strauss, *Luther's House of Learning: Indoctrination of the Young in the German Reformation* (Baltimore, 1978), pp. 100–102.

53. *Eine Predigt, dass man Kinder zur Schulen halten solle* (1529), in *D. Martin Luthers Werke: Kritische Gesamtausgabe* 30.2 (Weimar, 1909), p. 532.

54. *Luthers Werke in Auswahl* 8.140, no. 3690 (1538). See also H. G. Haile, *Luther: An Experiment in Biography* (New York, 1980), pp. 87, 285–87.

55. Buchwald, *D. Martin Luther*, p. 356.

56. *Luthers Werke in Auswahl* 8.111, no. 3566A (1537).

57. Buchwald, *D. Martin Luther*, p. 356.

58. *LW* 50.248. 50.248.

59. Ibid. 50.19.

60. Ibid. 50.248.

61. *Luthers Werke in Auswahl* 8.313, no. 5500 (1542).

62. *LW* 50.246.

63. This very popular statement by Luther is elaborated by Kaspar Güthel, Lutheran pastor in Eisleben: *Ueber das Evangelion Johannis/da Christus seine Junger/ wären auff die Hochtzeyt geladen/Wass mit worten und wercken daselbst gehandelt, Eyn Sermon dem Ehlichen standt fast freudsam und nützlich* (1534), OX-BOD T.L. 39, 178, pp. B 4 r–v.

## 8. TURNING PROTESTANT: THE REVOLUTION WITHIN

A sizable portion of this chapter was originally published in German translation: "Die Reformation als intellektuelle Revolution," in *Zwingli und Europa*, ed. Peter Blickle (Zurich, 1985), pp. 27–45.

1. Philipp Melanchthon, *Die fürnemisten unterschaid/zwischen rainer Christlichen Lere des Evangelii/und der Abgöttischen Papistischen Lere* (Augsburg [1539]), OX-BOD T.L. 66.6, arts. 1–16.

2. Such resistance has become the focal point of numerous studies of the Reformation and popular culture. In addition to Gerald Strauss, *Luther's House of Learning: Indoctrination of the Young in the German Reformation* (Baltimore, 1978), see also David Sabean, *Power in the Blood: Popular Culture and Village Discourse in Early Modern Germany* (Cambridge, 1985); Susan Karant-Nunn, *Zwickau in Transition: The Reformation as an Agent of Change* (Columbus, Oh., 1987). On the daily religious lives of Protestant laity, see especially Bernhard Vogler, *Vie religieuse en pays rhénan dans la seconde moitié XVIe siècle*, 3 vols. (Lille, 1974), and Peter Zschunke, *Konfession und Alltag in Oppenheim: Beiträge zur Geschichte von Bevölkerung und Gesellschaft einer gemischtkonfessionellen Kleinstadt in der frühen Neuzeit* (Wiesbaden, 1984).

3. Robert W. Scribner, "Ritual and Popular Religion in Catholic Germany at the Time of the Reformation," *Journal of Ecclesiastical History* 35 (1984): 47–77; Bossy, *Christendom in the West, 1400–1700* (New York: 1985).

4. Carlo Ginzburg, *The Cheese and the Worms: The Cosmos of a Sixteenth-Century Miller*, trans. John Tedeschi and Anne Tedeschi (Baltimore, 1980); Natalie Zemon Davis, *The Return of Martin Guerre* (Cambridge, Mass., 1983). Compare also the remarkable works of historical anthropologist William Christian, Jr., among them, *Local Religion in Sixteenth Century Spain* (Princeton, 1989).

5. Two illustrative collections are Marianne Beyer-Fröhlich, *Deutsche Selbstzeug-*

*nisse*, vol. 4: *Aus dem Zeitalter des Humanismus und der Reformation* (Leipzig, 1931), vol. 5: *Aus dem Zeitalter der Reformation und der Gegenreformation* (Leipzig, 1932; repr. 1964); and Horst Wenzel, *Die Autobiographie des späten Mittelalters und der frühen Neuzeit*, 2 vols. (Munich, 1980). See also Ernst Walter Zeeden, *Deutsche Kultur in der frühen Neuzeit* (Berlin, 1968), pp. 479–81, and Kaspar von Greyerz, "Religion in the Life of German and Swiss Autobiographers (Sixteenth and Early Seventeenth Centuries)," in his *Religion and Society in Early Modern Europe, 1500–1800* (London, 1984), pp. 223–41.

6. Compare Ronnie Po-Chia Hsia, *Society and Religion in Münster, 1535–1618* (New Haven, 1985), and Marc R. Forster, *The Counter Reformation in the Bishopric of Speyer* (Ithaca, N.Y., 1991), who document this circumstance in post-Reformation Catholic regimes.

7. Philip Greven, *The Protestant Temperament: Patterns of Child-Rearing, Religious Experience, and the Self in Early America* (New York, 1977).

8. Thomas Platter, *Lebensbeschreibung*, ed. Alfred Hartmann (Basel, 1944), pp. 24–26, 28–33, 35. I follow the editors in dating Thomas's birth in 1507 rather than 1499: ibid., pp. 153–54.

9. Ibid., pp. 62–63.

10. Ibid., pp. 63–64.

11. Ibid., pp. 66–70.

12. Ibid., pp. 76–77.

13. Ibid., pp. 80–81.

14. Ibid., pp. 86–87.

15. Ibid., pp. 87, 90–91.

16. Ibid., p. 94.

17. Ibid., pp. 113–15.

18. Ibid., pp. 131–35.

19. Compare Donald R. Kelley's discussion of the break with familial and public authority among Calvinists: *The Beginning of Ideology: Consciousness and Society in the French Reformation* (Cambridge, 1981).

20. Thomas Platter, *Lebensbeschreibung*, pp. 23–33, 70–71, 92.

21. Ibid., pp. 142–43.

22. The 1569 episcopal visitation in the archdiocese of Cologne discovered 40 of the 118 parishes visited to be "more or less strongly influenced by anti-church, Anabaptist or Protestant, Lutheran or Calvinist, ideas." Only four of the parishes were Lutheran to the point of being deemed heretical. On such matters as lay reception of the Eucharist and clerical marriage, much of the sentiment was Erasmian or reform-Catholic and stopped well short of Protestantism, despite

strong criticism of abuses: August Franzen, "Die Visitation im Zeitalter der Gegenreformation im Erzstift Köln," in *Die Visitation im Dienst der kirchlichen Reform*, ed. Ernst W. Zeeden and Hansgeorg Molitor (Münster, 1967), pp. 16–17. On reform movements in and around Cologne in the sixteenth century, see Joseph Klersch, *Volkstum und Volksleben in Köln*, vol. 3 (Cologne, 1968), and Paul Holt, "Beitrag zur Kirchengeschichte Kurkölns im 16. Jahrhundert," *Jahrbuch des kölnischen Geschichtsvereins E.V.* 18 (1936): 111–43.

23. On Weinsberg's life, see Josef Stein, "Hermann Weinsberg als Mensch und Historiker," *Jahrbuch des kölnischen Geschichtsvereins* 4 (1917): 109–69; Steven Ozment, *When Fathers Ruled: Family Life in Reformation Europe* (Cambridge, Mass., 1983), passim; and Robert Jütte, "Household and Family Life in Late Sixteenth Century Cologne: The Weinsberg Family," forthcoming in *The Sixteenth Century Journal*.

24. Hermann says the injury also made him shy toward women, as he believed it hindered his ability to have children ("quia metuebam, ne forte partim generationi obesset"): *Das Buch Weinsberg. Kölner Denkwürdigkeiten aus dem 16. Jahrhundert*, vol. 1, ed. Konstantin Höhlbaum (Leipzig, 1886), p. 50. See also *Das Buch Weinsberg*, vol. 5, ed. Josef Stein (Bonn, 1926), p. xiii.

25. *Das Buch Weinsberg*, vol. 3, ed. Friedrich Lau (Bonn, 1897), p. 21.

26. Ibid., p. 24.

27. Ibid., p. 25.

28. Ibid., p. 29.

29. Smarting over an argument in which his more well-to-do opponents wished him "more learned and well-read" than they believed him to be, Hermann defended himself privately in his chronicle as one who was "neither too learned nor too unlearned," but who knew enough Latin and German, law and history, for the "middling burgher" he was. He went on to declare himself *mittelmeissich* in other respects as well: "neither the richest nor the poorest in land, not the greatest or the least in the government," and made clear his pride and pleasure in being "in the middle": *Das Buch Weinsberg* 5.270–71.

30. *Das Buch Weinsberg* 1.49–50, 59.

31. *Das Buch Weinsberg* 5.2–3.

32. *Das Buch Weinsberg*, vol. 2, ed. Konstantin Höhlbaum (Leipzig, 1887), pp. 277–79; ibid. 5.23.

33. *Das Buch Weinsberg* 5.46–48.

34. *Das Buch Weinsberg* 1.231.

35. Ibid. 1.40–41.

36. *Das Buch Weinsberg* 2.269–71.

37. Ibid., p. 67.

38. Ibid., p. 297.

39. *Das Buch Weinsberg* 5.129.

40. Ibid., pp. 150–51, 153–54.

41. Ibid., pp. 356–57.

42. *Das Buch Weinsberg* 3.10–11.

43. *Das Buch Weinsberg* 5.302–3.

44. Ibid., pp. 147–48. On Hermann's opposition to the witch craze and search for natural explanations of the phenomena associated with witches, see Stein, "Hermann Weinsberg als Mensch und Historiker."

45. *Das Buch Weinsberg* 5.197–98.

46. *Das Buch Weinsberg* 1.111, 2.193, 5.430.

47. *Das Buch Weinsberg* 2.162. On Jesuits and the Counterreformation in Cologne, see Brigette Garbe, "Reformmassnahmen und Formen der katholischen Erneuerung in der Erzdiözese Köln (1555–1648)," *Jahrbuch des kölnischen Geschichtsvereins* 47 (1976): 136–37, 145–46.

48. *Das Buch Weinsberg* 5.143.

49. *Das Buch Weinsberg* 3.232. Hermann associated his own birthday (January 1518) with the beginning of Luther's reform: "Do hat sich Martinus Lutherus widder diss papst [Leo X, whom Hermann cites as pope at his birth] eirst gelagt und disputiert," *Das Buch Weinsberg* 5.420.

50. *Das Buch Weinsberg* 1.21, 76; 2.50.

### 9. THE RELIGIOUS BELIEFS OF TEENAGERS

1. Richard van Dülmen, *Kultur und Alltag in der frühen Neuzeit*, vol. 1: *Das Haus und seine Menschen 16.–18. Jahrhundert* (Munich, 1990), pp. 124–28.

2. To contemporaries they were *Jünglinge*, youth who were no longer children, but also not yet fully adults by the standards of the age. On the work and culture of apprenticed German youth in our period, see Kurt Wesoly, *Lehrlinge und Handwerksgesellen am Mittelrhein. Ihre soziale Lage und ihre Organization von 14. bis ins 17. Jahrhundert* (Frankfurt am Main, 1985); in broader perspective, see the important new work of Mathias Beer, *Eltern und Kinder des späten Mittelalters in ihren Briefen. Familienleben in der Stadt des Spätmittelalters und der frühen Neuzeit mit besonderer Berücksichtigung Nürnbergs (1400–1550)* (Nuremberg, 1990).

3. Three of the four boys—Michael, Friederich, and Stephan Carl—are featured in my edition of their letters: *Three Behaim Boys: Growing up in Early Modern Germany: A Chronicle of Their Lives* (New Haven, 1990).

4. Rudolf Endres, "Zur Einwohnerzahl und Bevölkerungsstruktur Nürnbergs in 15./16. Jahrhundert," *MVGN* 57 (1970): 260–61.

5. Friederich VII Behaim, Briefe, 1524–1533, Historisches Archiv, Germanisches National Museum (henceforth FB VII), 14 July 1532. Michael's letters are written to his cousin and guardian, Friederich VII Behaim, who received and preserved them. The Roman numeral "VII" accompanying his name indicates that he is the seventh member of the Behaim family to bear the name Friederich. English: *Three Behaim Boys*, no. 18 (22 March 1529), p. 52; no. 32 (14 July 1532), p. 70.

6. "So soll es doch gross ungewitter und meuterei under den fürsten bedeuten," Friederich VIII Behaim, Briefe, 1578–1582, Historisches Archiv, Germanisches National Museum (henceforth FB VIII), 14 January 1580; *Three Behaim Boys*, no. 63 (14 January 1580), p. 136.

7. Altdorf was twenty-six kilometers southeast of Nuremberg, a couple of hours' journey by cart.

8. Stephan Carl Behaim, Briefe, 1622–1639, Historisches Archiv, Germanisches National Museum (henceforth SCB), 10 October 1635; *Three Behaim Boys*, no. 54 (10 October 1635), p. 259.

9. SCB, 17 April 1634; *Three Behaim Boys*, no. 47 (17 April 1634), p. 239.

10. SCB, 21 August 1635; *Three Behaim Boys*, no. 53 (21 August 1635), p. 254.

11. "Da vlobet Ich mich zu einer walfurt dy heyst man Sancta Maria da Loreta inn Welscher sprach unnd ist 25 Welsch meyl wegs dass ist 5 meyl teutscher von Roma da unnd mein her hin handelt unnd ich glaub unnd hab alle meine hoffnung dass mich von ersten got und darnach dieselbig Sancta Maria da Loreta hat beschutzt und beschirm[t] vonn solchenn ubel und kranckheit wie wol unnd mir ein Junckfrau marya uberal ist," FB VII, 14 March 1525; *Three Behaim Boys*, no. 3 (14 March 1525), p. 19.

12. FB VII, 6 January 1528; *Three Behaim Boys*, no. 7 (6 January 1528), p. 26. Stephan Carl's schoolboy friend, Georg Wilhelm Pömer, employed a most Protestant salutation in his letters to Stephan Carl: "Greetings from the fount of salvation [Christ, who comes] with favors and without deceit (*S.P. fonte salutis cum officiolis sine offuciis*)," SCB, 17 March 1630; *Three Behaim Boys*, no. 24 (17 March 1630), p. 199. The salutation both affirms Christ as sole savior and insinuates Catholic distraction from Christ's exclusive role as mediator.

13. "Ich hette selbs nicht gemaynt das mir got hette also gnedigklich helffen solle," FB VII, 21 May 1532; *Three Behaim Boys*, no. 30 (21 May 1532), p. 68.

14. 13 December 1534. "Aus Paulus Behaim I. Briefwechsel," ed. J. Kamann, *MVGN* 3 (1881): 134. In early modern literature for girls, religion was deemed the surest way to preserve chastity and escape the many deleterious effects of premarital sex: see Cornelia N. Moore, *The Maiden's Mirror: Reading Material for German Girls in the Sixteenth and Seventeenth Centuries* (Wiesbaden, 1987).

15. "So ist alssdann nicht zuzweifeln wann du dich also nach den geboten Gotes

verhelst, es werde derselbe auch zu allen deinen thun und vorhaben gluck und heil geben und verleihen," SCB, 28 December 1630; *Three Behaim Boys*, no. 33 (28 December 1630), p. 218.

16. Friederich reports her request in a letter no longer extant; see below, n. 24.

17. *Nürnberger Reformation* (1479), title 12, law 2, in *Quellen zur neueren Privatrechtsgeschichte Deutschlands*, ed. W. Kunkel et al. (Weimar, 1936), p. 7.

18. "Das sie mir unnd ich Ir ersehenn unnd also von got zusammen gefügt seindt weyl ers dann der gestalt nach seinem gotlichen willen verordnet. So sag ich Im [Gott] dannck, das er mich mit einer frümmen erbarnn Junckfraw, der sich meiner freundt kheiner schemmen darff begabt unnd nit mit zuchtenn zu redenn etwo mit einer lösen hürn die schon vil gelts unnd alsdan mennigklich davon zu redenn het gestrafft hat," FB VII, 25 July 1533; *Three Behaim Boys*, no. 39 (25 July 1533), p. 79; see also ibid., no. 36 (22 May 1533), pp. 75–76.

19. *Three Behaim Boys*, no. 9 (31 August 1528), p. 29; no. 10 (1 November 1528), p. 34; no. 24 (2 September 1530), p. 60.

20. "Hatt in summa gott der allmechtig mich bisher in Welschlandt an leib und gutt angriffen und gestrafft, damitt ich seinen zorn, den er wider die sündt tregt, sehe und mich von denselben forthin abthete, dagegen aber er mir grösser gnadt erzeigt, indem er in mir dazienige, so meiner seelen seligkeitt betrifft, als nemblich sein göttlich wortt, welchs in diesen landen also misgebraucht wirdt, gantz und unversehrtt erhelt, lob und danck im gesagt," 3 January 1577, in "Deutsches Studentenleben in Padua 1575 bis 1578," ed. Wilhelm Loose, *Beilage zur Schul- und Universitätsgeschichte* (Meissen, 1879), p. 25.

21. ". . . soll der stadt Patron sein, soll viel wunderzeichen gethan haben sampt viel andern lügen, die man von im erdicht hatt das arme volck zu betriegen," ibid., 8 June 1576, p. 42 n. 94.

22. "Den es allhie so mans sonderlich nicht iederman zeigett, kein noth nicht hatt," P.S. 4 January 1576, ibid., p. 22.

23. Steven Ozment, *Magdalena and Balthasar: An Intimate Portrait of Life in 16th Century Europe* (New Haven, 1989), pp. 187–88 n. 142.

24. FB VIII, 29 November 1581; *Three Behaim Boys*, no. 98 (29 November 1581), pp. 156–57.

25. SCB, March 1629; *Three Behaim Boys*, no. 5 (March 1629), p. 168.

26. "Er einem solchen herrn angehangt werdet, welcher ihn mit hunger und straichen also castige damit er der füllerey und mussiggangs darbey vergesse," SCB, 2 March 1630; *Three Behaim Boys*, no. 19 (2 March 1630), p. 91.

27. SCB, 25 May 1629; *Three Behaim Boys*, no. 8 (25 May 1629), pp. 172–73.

28. SCB, 23 June 1629; *Three Behaim Boys*, no. 13 (23 June 1629), p. 179.

29. "Bestia illa tetra . . . digna et haec mulier mala herba," SCB, 9 July 1629; *Three Behaim Boys*, no. 16 (9 July 1629), p. 183.

30. SCB, 6 July 1629; *Three Behaim Boys*, no. 14 (6 July 1629), p. 180.

31. "Dann gleich wie ein grosser übelthater u. Sünder bessers nichts thun kahn als so er sich in ein Closter begibt, da er alles böses mit gütten werckhen ersetzen, allen weldlichen begierden u. begienen abstehen u. Gott allein dienen kahn: also begieb ich mich ja auch in das besste Closter der Gottseeligkeit, da aller weltlichen üppigkeit vergessen, u. wegen besster erkandnuss der grösten noth niemand mehr als Gott gedienet wird/ich auch kein besser mittel erdenckhen kahn, alles vorgangene besser zuersetzen, als auff dieser Seefahrt," SCB, 21 August 1635; *Three Behaim Boys*, no. 53 (21 August 1635), p. 255.

32. "Aus Paulus Behaims I. Briefwechsel," pp. 110–11.

33. SCB, 16 November 1629; *Three Behaim Boys*, no. 19 (16 November 1629), p. 189.

34. "Mir solches [Ausgeben] zum höchsten zuwider, u. wider alle meine gedanckhen u. müglichkeit geschehen sey. Dann wo solche unzehlbare uncosten gern mit freuden und vorsetzlich von mir sollten gemacht worden sein, würde ich nit allein kein Christ noch ehrliche Ader in meinen Leib haben, sondern auch wegen unausprechlicher betrübnus, der Frau Mutter deswegen gemacht, von Gott an Seel u. Leib hie zeitlich nit allein, sondern vielmehr dort ewig gestrafft werden, davor mich u. alle Menschen Gott [gnadenlich] behütten wolle," SCB, 18/28 November 1635; *Three Behaim Boys*, no. 55 (18/28 November 1635), p. 260.

35. SCB, 1630. On dating this letter, see *Three Behaim Boys*, no. 5 [March 1629], p. 168.

36. "Es kan doch nichts anderest sein, du must verzeyhen (ob es dich . . . saurer ankombt) wiltu anderst, das dir Gott auch verzeyhe," SCB, 8 July 1629; *Three Behaim Boys*, no. 15 (8 July 1629), p. 181. The parallels with Lutheran catechetical instruction are remarkable; see above, Chapter 5.

37. "Derhalben ich dir nach gott, der mir dich beschert hatt, nicht gnugsam dancken kahn, der ich itzundt allerest sihe and erfahre, was ich vor ein mutter hab, daz ich auch selbst in mir erschreck und bewein, so ich dran gedenck, wie mancherlei ich dich drausen in 6 wochen beleidigett und erzurnt hab, wie mancherlei mich der leidige teuffel wider dich gehetzt hatt, daz ich auch nicht werd bin gewesen, das du mich vor ein sohn erkent hast. Derhalben ich gentzlich der zuversicht zu dir bin, du solches meiner sundt und missethat nimmer gegen mir gedencken werdest und mir solches als einem unverstendigen, der ich gar zu hoch hatt hinauss gewolt, verzeihen und vergeben, mitt gewisser zusagung mich forthin gegen dir zu halten und dich zu ehren, als einem sohn gegen seiner mutter geburt und zusteht": Loose, "Deutsches Studentenleben in Padua 1575 bis 1578," p. 17.

APPENDIX. A DIGEST OF THEORIES ABOUT THE REFORMATION

1. Robert M. Kingdon, "Was the Protestant Reformation a Revolution? The Case of Geneva," in *Transition and Revolution: Problems and Issues of European Renaissance and Reformation*, ed. Robert M. Kingdon (Minneapolis, 1973), pp. 73–74.

2. Donald R. Kelley, *The Beginning of Ideology: Consciousness and Society in the French Reformation* (Cambridge, 1981); Michael Walzer, *The Revolution of the Saints: A Study in the Origins of Radical Politics* (New York, 1970).

3. The cultural consequences of the Reformation were largely "unforeseen and even unwished-for": *The Protestant Ethic and the Spirit of Capitalism*, trans. Talcott Parsons (New York, 1958), p. 90. On the modern debate over the origins of capitalism and its affinity with the Protestant ethic, see *Protestantism, Capitalism, and Social Science: The Weber Thesis Controversy*, ed. Robert W. Green (Lexington, Mass., 1973).

4. Miriam U. Chrisman, *Lay Culture, Learned Culture: Books and Social Change in Strasbourg, 1480–1599* (New Haven, 1982), pp. xx–xxi, 121, 140–41, 209, 221.

5. Keith Thomas, *Religion and the Decline of Magic: Studies in Popular Beliefs in Sixteenth- and Seventeenth-century England* (London, 1971), pp. 52, 57, 76, esp. 495–97, 561; more generally, A. D. J. MacFarlane, *Witchcraft in Tudor and Stuart England* (London, 1970). The Reformation's contributions to witch beliefs are discussed by Nikolaus Paulus, *Hexenwahn und Hexenprozess vornehmlich im 16. Jahrhundert* (Freiburg im Breisgau, 1910), pp. 23–58, and by E. W. Monter, who alleges Luther to be "a great primitive" in these matters: "Law, Medicine, and the Acceptance of Witchcraft, 1560–1580," in his *European Witchcraft* (New York, 1969), pp. 58–59. The larger issues are framed by Brian Levack, *The Witch Hunt in Early Modern Europe* (London, 1986).

6. Carlo Ginzburg, *The Cheese and the Worms: The Cosmos of a Sixteenth-Century Miller*, trans. John Tedeschi and Anne Tedeschi (Baltimore, 1980), p. 21.

7. Thomas A. Brady, Jr., *Ruling Class, Regime and Reformation at Strasbourg, 1520–1555* (Leiden, 1978); Dieter Demandt and Hans-Christoph Rublack, *Stadt und Kirche in Kitzingen* (Stuttgart, 1978); Kaspar von Greyerz, *The Late City Reformation in Germany: The Case of Colmar, 1522–1628* (Wiesbaden, 1980). Christina Larner argued a similar thesis for the Scottish Reformation in *Enemies of God: The Witch-Hunt in Scotland* (Baltimore, 1981), pp. 51, 53. More appreciative of the ability of church and religion to manage the political currents of the age is Heinz Schilling, *Konfessionskonflikt und Staatsbildung* (Gütersloh, 1981).

8. Jean Delumeau, *Catholicism Between Luther and Voltaire: A New View of the Counter Reformation* (London, 1977).

9. Gerald Strauss, *Luther's House of Learning: Indoctrination of the Young in the*

*German Reformation* (Baltimore, 1978), pp. 2–3, 9, 136–38, 142, 299, 307. Cf. James M. Kittelson's sharp critique: "Successes and Failure in the German Reformation: The Report from Strasbourg," *Archiv für Reformationsgeschichte* 73 (1982): 153–74.

10. For Keith Thomas, the religion that survived the decline of magic and the rise of modern science was not that of the Reformation, but Deism: *Religion and the Decline of Magic*, pp. 639–40. Brian Easlea portrays both Catholicism and Protestantism as one-horse shays, neither compatible with a cosmology that banishes supernatural forces from the world and makes people masters of their own fate: *Witch-Hunting, Magic, and the New Philosophy* (Brighton, Sussex, 1980), pp. 43, 78–79. A more positive interpretation of the relationship of Protestantism and science are H. A. Oberman, "Reformation and Revolution: Copernicus' Discovery in an Era of Change," in *The Nature of Scientific Discovery*, ed. Owen Gingerich (Washington, D.C., 1975), pp. 134–69, and Brian Gerrish, *The Old Protestantism and the New* (Chicago, 1982), pp. 163–78.

# Index